> "America's leading source of self-help legal information." ★★★★
> —YAHOO!

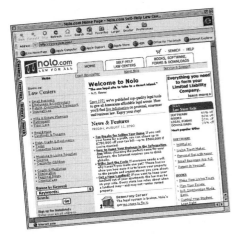

LEGAL INFORMATION ONLINE ANYTIME

24 hours a day

www.nolo.com

AT THE NOLO.COM SELF-HELP LAW CENTER, YOU'LL FIND

- **Nolo's comprehensive Legal Encyclopedia filled with plain-English information on a variety of legal topics**
- **Nolo's Law Dictionary—legal terms <u>without</u> the legalese**
- **Auntie Nolo—if you've got questions, Auntie's got answers**
- **The Law Store—over 250 self-help legal products including: Downloadable Software, Books, Form Kits and eGuides**
- **Legal and product updates**
- **Frequently Asked Questions**
- **NoloBriefs, our free monthly email newsletter**
- **Legal Research Center, for access to state and federal statutes**
- **Our ever-popular lawyer jokes**

Quality LAW BOOKS & SOFTWARE FOR EVERYONE

Nolo's user-friendly products are consistently first-rate. Here's why:

- A dozen in-house legal editors, working with highly skilled authors, ensure that our products are accurate, up-to-date and easy to use
- We continually update every book and software program to keep up with changes in the law
- Our commitment to a more democratic legal system informs all of our work
- We appreciate & listen to your feedback. Please fill out and return the card at the back of this book.

An Important Message to Our Readers

This product provides information and general advice about the law. But laws and procedures change frequently, and they can be interpreted differently by different people. For specific advice geared to your specific situation, consult an expert. No book, software or other published material is a substitute for personalized advice from a knowledgeable lawyer licensed to practice law in your state.

3rd edition

Marketing Without Advertising

by Michael Phillips & Salli Rasberry
edited by Peri Pakroo

Keeping Up-to-Date

To keep its books up-to-date, Nolo issues new printings and new editions periodically. New printings reflect minor legal changes and technical corrections. New editions contain major legal changes, major text additions or major reorganizations. To find out if a later printing or edition of any Nolo book is available, call Nolo at 510-549-1976 or check our website at http://www.nolo.com.

To stay current, follow the "Update" service at our website at http://www.nolo.com/update. In another effort to help you use Nolo's latest materials, we offer a 35% discount off the purchase of the new edition of your Nolo book when you turn in the cover of an earlier edition. (See the "Special Upgrade Offer" in the back of the book.)

This book was last revised in: **April 2001.**

THIRD Edition	APRIL 2001
Editor	PERI PAKROO
Cover Design	TONI IHARA
Book Design	TERRI HEARSH
Production	SARAH HINMAN
Proofreading	SHERYL ROSE
Index	NANCY MULVANY
Printing	BERTELSMANN SERVICES, INC.

Phillips, Michael, 1938-
    Marketing without advertising / by Michael Phillips & Salli Rasberry.--3rd ed.
        p.   cm.
    Includes index.
    ISBN 0-87337-608-0
        1. Marketing. 2. Small business--Management. I. Rasberry, Salli. II. Title.

HF5415 .P484 2000
658.8--dc21

                                                                    00-056863

Acknowledgments

With special thanks to Soni Richardson and Michael Eschenbach, Daniel Phillips, Tom Hargadon and Mary Reid.

Full Disclosure Note

All the businesses and business owners mentioned in the book are real. The great majority operate under their own names in the cities indicated. However, because some of our examples are less than flattering, and for other reasons, including privacy, we have changed the names and/or locations of businesses in a few cases.

In some cases, the businesses used as examples in the book do advertise—their marketing ideas are so good we included them anyway. In most cases, if a business used as an example does advertise, it is a small part of their marketing mix.

Table of Contents

Introduction

By the Publisher

*T*ake a look around your community and make a list of truly superior small businesses—ones you trust so thoroughly you would recommend them to your friends, your boss and even your in-laws. Whether your mind turns to restaurants, plumbers, plant nurseries or veterinarians, chances are good your list is fairly short.

Now think about all the ads for local businesses that fill your newspaper, clutter your doorstep, spew out of your radio, cover the back of your grocery receipts or reach you in dozens of other ways. How many of these businesses are on your list? More than likely, not many. In fact, I'll bet the most heavily advertised local businesses are among the businesses you never plan to patronize—or patronize again—no matter how many 50%-off specials you are offered.

If, like me, you have learned the hard way that many businesses that loudly trumpet their virtues are barely average, how do you find a top-quality business when you need something? Almost surely, whether you need a roof for your house, an accountant for your business, a math tutor for your child or a restaurant for a Saturday night out, you ask for a recommendation from someone you consider knowledgeable and trustworthy.

Once you grasp the simple fact that what counts is not what a business says about itself, but rather what others say about it, you should quickly understand and embrace the message of this brilliant book. Simply put: The best way to succeed in business is to run such a wonderful operation that your loyal and satisfied customers will brag about your goods and services far and wide. Instead of spending a small fortune on advertising, it's far better to spend the same money improving your business and caring for customers.

It's the honest power of this honest message that made me excited to publish *Marketing Without Advertising* ten years ago. Uniquely among small business writers, Phillips and Rasberry were saying the same things I had learned as a co-founder of Nolo—that the key to operating a profitable business is to respect what you do and how you do it. This means not only producing top-quality services and products, but demonstrating your respect for your co-workers and customers.

After many years of success, it's a double pleasure for Nolo to publish another new edition of *Marketing Without Advertising*. Yes, lots of things about small business marketing have changed in the interim. To mention just a few, today many of us routinely use fax machines and e-mail to keep close to our customers, and some of us have learned to use the Internet as an essential marketing tool. But some things haven't changed. A trustworthy, well-run business is a pleasure to market, and the personal recommendations of satisfied customers are still the best foundation of a successful and personally rewarding business.

Marketing Without Advertising has been updated to provide a new generation of entrepreneurs with the essential philosophical underpinnings for the development of a successful, low-cost marketing plan not based on advertising. But this isn't just a book about business philosophy. It is full of specific suggestions about how to put together a highly effective marketing plan, including guidance concerning business appearance, pricing, employee and supplier relations, accessibility, open business practices, customer recourse and many other topics.

Consumers are increasingly savvy, and information about a business's quality or lack thereof circulates faster than ever before. The only approach worth taking is to put your planning, hard work and money into creating a wonderful business, and to let your customers do your advertising for you.

Ralph Warner
Berkeley, California

Chapter 1

Advertising: The Last Choice in Marketing

"Really high spending on advertising sales is an admission of failure. I'd much prefer to see investments in loyalty leading to better repeat purchases than millions spent for a Super Bowl ad."

**—Ward Hanson,
author of *Principles of Internet Marketing*.
From *The Industry Standard*, 4/10/2000.**

*M*arketing means running a first-rate business and letting people know about it. Every action your company takes sends a marketing message. Building a business image is not something invented by a P.R. firm; it's a reflection of what you do and how you do it.

A clever ad is what pops into most people's minds when they think about getting the word out about their business. The fact is, most of us know little about advertising and a whole lot about marketing. We are really *the* marketing experts for our business because we know it better than anyone else.

It may surprise you to know how many established small businesses have discovered that they do not need to advertise to prosper. A large majority—more than two-thirds in the U.S., certainly—of profitable small businesses operate successfully without advertising.

 In this book we make a distinction between "advertising," which is broadcasting your message to many uninterested members of the public, and "listing," which is directing your message to specific people interested in the product or service, such as in the Yellow Pages.

Here's where the figure about small business and advertising comes from: There are about 20 million non-farm businesses in the United States. Of these, about two million are involved in construction; another five million deal in wholesaling, manufacturing, trucking or mining. A small minority (30% of the total) generate customers by advertising. The rest rely on personally knowing their customers, on their reputations and sometimes on salespeople or commissioned representatives. Of the remaining 13 million businesses, 70% are run by one person. It's very rare for the self-employed to find advertising useful; the single-person business, whether that of a lawyer, doctor or computer consultant, relies almost exclusively on personal recommendations. That leaves the percentage of businesses who might even consider advertising useful at less than 19%. We think most of them don't need it either.

There are four main reasons why advertising is inappropriate for most businesses:

- Advertising is simply not cost-effective. Claims that it produces even marginal financial returns are usually fallacious.
- Customers lured by ads tend to be disloyal. In other words, advertising

does not provide a solid customer base for future business.

- Dependence on advertising makes a business more vulnerable to changes in volatile consumer taste and thus more likely to fail.
- Because a significant percentage of advertising is deceptive, advertisers are increasingly seen by the public (both consciously and unconsciously) as dishonest and manipulative. Businesses that advertise heavily are often suspected of offering poor quality goods and services.

Let's now look at these reasons in more detail.

A. The Myth of Advertising's Effectiveness

The argument made by the proponents of advertising is almost pathetically simple-minded: If you can measure the benefits of advertising on your business, advertising works; if you can't measure the beneficial effects, then your measurements aren't good enough. Or you need more ads. Or you need a different type of ad. It's much the same type of rationalization put forth by the proponents of making yourself rich by visualizing yourself as being prosperous. If you get rich immediately, you owe it all to the system (and presumably should give your visualization guru at least a 10% commission). If you're still poor after six months, something is wrong with your picture. It reminds us of the man in Chicago who had marble statues of lions in front of his house to keep away elephants: "It works," he said. "Ain't no elephants in this neighborhood."

James B. Twitchell, the author of *Adcult*, notes, "Although elaborate proofs of advertising's impotence are available, the simple fact is that you cannot put a meter on the relationship between increased advertising and increased sales. If you could, agencies would charge clients by how much they have increased sales, not by how much media space they have purchased."

Paradoxically, even though some small business owners are beginning to realize that advertising doesn't work, many still advertise. Why? For a number of reasons: because they have been conditioned to believe that advertising works, because there are no other models to follow and because bankers expect to see "advertising costs" as part of a business proposal.

It's important to realize that your judgment regarding advertising is likely to be severely skewed. You have been surrounded by ads all your life and you've heard countless times that advertising works. To look at advertising objectively may require you to re-examine some deeply held beliefs.

According to *E* magazine, advertising budgets have doubled every decade since 1976 and grown by 50% in the last ten years. "Companies now spend about $162 billion each year to bombard us with print and broadcast ads; that works out to about $623 for every man, woman and child in the United States" ("Marketing Madness," May/June 1996). Information Resources studied the effect of advertising and concluded, "There is no simple correspondence between advertising and higher sales.... The relationship between high copy scores and increased sales is tenuous at best."

To illustrate how pervasive the "advertising works" belief system is, consider that if the sales of a particular product fall off dramatically, most people look for all sorts of explanations without ever considering that the fall-off may be a result of counterproductive advertising.

Skeptics may claim that you simply can't sell certain consumer products, beer, for example, without an endless array of mindless TV ads. We refer these skeptics to the Anchor Steam Brewing Company of San Francisco, which very profitably sold 103,000 barrels of excellent beer in 1995 without any ad campaign. They believe in slow and steady growth and maintain a loyal and satisfied client base. (See Chapter 12 for details on how.)

And consider this: The fabulously sucessful discount warehouse, Costco, had profits of 25% in 1999 thanks largely to their cost-cutting business approach— which includes absolutely no advertising.

Even apparent successes may not be what they seem. The California Raisin Advisory Board ran an ad campaign that produced the most recognized ad in the history of advertising. In the mid-1980s its advertising agency, Foote Cone and Belding, used the first popular national clay animation campaign. (Claymation is a trademark of the Will Vinton studios.) The annual budget was over $40 million. The dancing raisins and their song "I Heard It on the Grapevine" created such a popular image that sales from dolls, other toys, mugs and secondary products generated nearly $200 million in revenue and resulted in a Saturday children's television program using the raisin characters. Raisin sales went up for the first two years of the campaign, largely because cold breakfast cereal marketers were so impressed with the popularity of the ad campaign that they increased the raisin content of their raisin cereals and joined in the advertising.

After four years, the dancing raisin campaign was discontinued. Sales were lower than before the ads started (*Forbes*, June 17, 1996). By the early 1990s, the California Raisin Advisory Board had been abolished.

The Internet and World Wide Web have introduced a new test of advertising effectiveness. Billions of dollars had been spent on advertising before the advent of the Web, yet no major offline advertiser was able to create an online presence of any significance. Even Toys 'R' Us, the major American toy retailer, ranked far behind eToys in brand awareness online, despite the fact that Toys 'R' Us is a 25-year-old company and eToys lasted barely two years. For Toys 'R' Us, decades of advertising simply had no staying power (March 20, 2000, *The Industry Standard*). One of the biggest successes on the Internet, eBay, used no advertising at all.

One magazine with a significant audience on the Internet is *Consumer Reports,* a magazine that carries no advertising. By eliminating advertising from its business model, *Consumer Reports* is able to maintain a high degree of integrity and cultivate trust among its readers, who value the magazine's objective information.

"Unlike many others who dispense online advice, *Consumer Reports* does not accept advertisements, does not earn a referral fee for directing customers to specific merchants and does not repackage and sell its data as market research to the companies whose products are reviewed" (*The New York Times,* 3/22/2000).

One giant aircraft manufacturing company, to look at the effectiveness of heavily advertising an in-house computer service through one of its subsidiaries, conducted a survey to find out how its 100 newest customers had found out about it. The results: 13% of these new customers came because of the advertising campaign, 23% because of sales calls, 56% signed up because of recommendations of other satisfied customers and professionals in the field and 8% weren't sure why they had chosen that computer service.

This is actually a fairly common survey result. Yet, as we can see from their bloated advertising budgets, very few companies act on the information. If they did, they would obviously budget funds for promoting personal recommendations. Indeed, some businesses are apparently so unwilling to believe what market research tells them—that personal recommendations work and advertising doesn't—that they run ads like the one on the following page.

It's not only large national corporations that are disappointed in the results of advertising. Local retail stores that run redeemable discount coupons to measure the effectiveness of their advertising usually find that the business generated isn't even enough to offset the cost of the ad.

Despite this, supporters of advertising continue to convince small business owners that:

- The ad could be improved; keep trying (forever).
- All the people who saw the ad but didn't clip the coupon were reminded of your business and may use it in the future. Keep advertising (forever).
- The effects of advertising are cumulative. Definitely keep advertising (forever).

But what about the favorable long-term effects of continuous advertising? Isn't there something to the notion of continually reminding the public you exist? Dr. Julian L. Simon, of the University of Illinois, says no: "[attributing] threshold effects and increasing returns to repetition of ads constitutes a monstrous myth, I believe, but a myth so well-entrenched that it is almost impossible to shake."

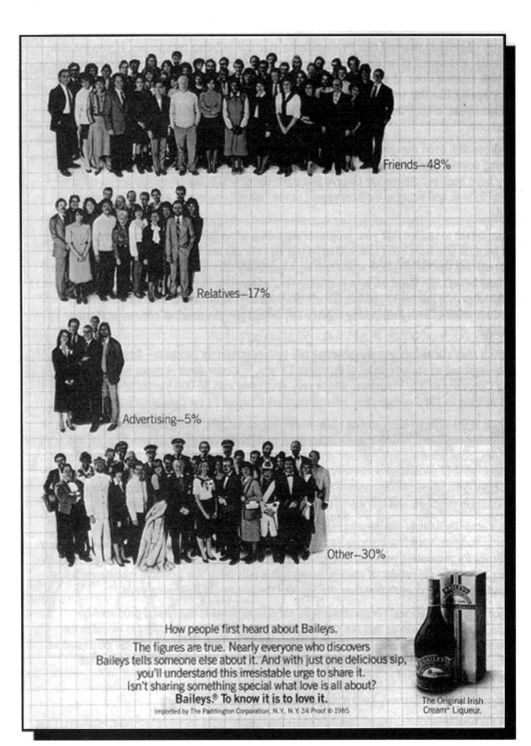

Using advertising to make your business a household word can often backfire; a business with a well-advertised name is extremely vulnerable to bad publicity.

Take the Coors brewery as an example. Thirty years ago, after it had vastly expanded its original territory and become a household word throughout much of the country with heavy advertising ($100 million per year in the 1980s), the Teamsters' Union waged a very effective consumer boycott against it. In Seattle, a strong union town, less than 5% of the market in the 1990s was drinking Coors. The Coors of the 1960s, known primarily to its loyal customers in the Rocky Mountain states, where it had a third of the beer-drinking market, was far less vulnerable to such a boycott.

Or how about the stockbroker E.F. Hutton, which spent many millions creating a false advertising image: "When E.F. Hutton talks, people listen." The image backfired spectacularly when Hutton was caught engaging in large-scale illegal currency transactions. The many jokes about who really listens when E.F. Hutton talks contributed to the dramatic decline of the firm, which was ultimately taken over by another broker at fire sale prices. Similarly, the huge but little-known agricultural processing company Archer Daniels Midland, headquartered in rural Illinois, made itself a household name by underwriting public

television programs. The public was well acquainted with "ADM, Supermarket to the World," by the time it became embroiled in a price-fixing scandal and had to pay $100 million in fines. The moral of this little story is simple. If these companies had relied less on advertising, their problems would have been much less of a public spectacle.

Sadly, many small businesses make sacrifices to pay for expensive ads, never being certain they are effective. Sometimes this means the quality of the business's product or service is cut. Other times, business owners or employees sacrifice their own needs to pay for advertising. We think it's far better to use the money to sponsor a neighborhood picnic, take the family on a short vacation or put the money into a useful capital improvement to the business. As John Wanamaker, turn-of-the-century merchant and philanthropist, put it, "Half the money I spend on

REPRINTED BY PERMISSION: TRIBUNE MEDIA SERVICES

advertising is wasted, and the trouble is, I don't know which half."

B. Why Customers Lured by Ads Are Often Not Loyal

Perhaps the worst aspect of traditional advertising, one apparent to anyone who runs a retail store, is that customers who respond primarily to media ads don't usually return. The same truth has been discovered by magazines and publishing companies that rely heavily on junk mail solicitations to sell their wares. The fact is that customers recruited through scatter-gun advertising techniques such as TV spots, newspaper ads, direct mail, contests, unsolicited telephone sales and Internet freebies rarely come back. Unscrupulous Internet businesses such as DoubleClick have used the Internet to invade your privacy and sell your e-mail address to other businesses who beseige you with so-called "targeted" marketing based on sites you have visited and purchases you have made.

An example of this phenomenon familiar to most owners of small service-type businesses comes from the experience of Laura Peck. She wrote to us that she used to advertise her assertiveness workshops, but due to financial problems discontinued the ads. Instead, she started cultivating her own community of friends and acquaintances for clients. Two years later, her business was thriving, and she noted:

"When I advertised, I seemed to attract people who came because of the discount I offered. These clients often did not return, would cancel sessions and generally were not repeaters. The people who were most enthusiastic, most loyal, and continued with their sessions were almost always clients who had been personally referred. Had it not been for the economics involved, I would probably not have learned this important lesson: Personal recommendation is the best advertising there is."

C. Why Dependence on Advertising Is Harmful

To an extent, advertising is an addiction: once you're hooked, it's very difficult to stop. You become accustomed to putting a fixed advertising cost into your budget, and you are afraid to stop because of a baseless fear that, if you do, your flow of new customers will dry up and your previous investments in advertising will have been wasted.

While of course there are rare occasions when a particular ad can produce lots of business, it's as rare in the small business world as catching a 30-pound lake trout off a recreational fishing boat or winning a $100,000 jackpot at a gambling casino. The story of the great advertising success (the "pet rock" fad of years ago is an extreme example) becomes widely known in the particular community and is picked up by trade journals and sometimes even the general media. As a result, many inexperienced business people are coaxed into spending money on ads. Overlooked in all the hoopla is the rarity of this sort of success; also overlooked is what often happens to the person whose ad produced the quick profits. Flash-in-the-pan advertising success may bring an initial influx of customers that your business isn't prepared for. This usually has two unfortunate consequences: many loyal long-term customers are turned off when service declines as the expanding business stretches itself too thin, and most of the new customers will not be repeaters.

Mary Palmer, a photographer in San Jose, California, started her business with a simplistic but traditional marketing strategy, advertising on her local newspaper's "weddings" page. Palmer was one of the first photographers in her area to insert an ad for wedding photos. She very happily took in $12,000 during the prime April-to-August wedding season. The next year she advertised again, but this time her ad was one of many. Not only did the ad fail to generate much business, she got few referrals from the many customers she had worked for the previous year. Concerned, Palmer called us for emergency business advice.

Visiting her, we found her business to be badly organized and generally chaotic. The overall impression it gave was poor. It was easy to see why so few of Palmer's customers referred their friends, or themselves patronized her business for other occasions. Palmer was a victim of her own flash-in-the-pan advertising success. Believing that "advertising works" had lulled her into the false belief that she didn't really have to learn how to run a high-quality business. There wasn't much we could really tell her except to start over, using the solid business techniques and personal recommendation approaches discussed in this book.

Palmer's business is in direct contrast to Gail Woodridge's, who also specializes in wedding photography. Woodridge doesn't do any advertising in the conventional sense, although she does list her services widely in places likely to produce referrals, as discussed later in this chapter and in Chapter 9. Her clients are primarily referred to her by wedding planners, bridal gown and flower stores, friends and former clients—people who know her and trust her to do a good job. Since this approach has meant that her business has grown fairly slowly, she has had the time, and the good sense, to make sure that the many details of her business are in order, including her office work and finances, as well as her camera equipment, darkroom supplies and filing system.

D. Advertisers: Poor Company to Keep

It is estimated that each American is exposed to well over 2,500 advertising messages per day, and that children see over

50,000 TV commercials a year. In our view, as many as one-quarter of all these ads are deliberately deceptive. Increasingly, the family of businesses that advertise is not one you should be proud to be associated with.

What a Marketing Expert Says About Advertising

"Increasingly, people are skeptical of what they read or see in advertisements. I often tell clients that advertising has a built-in 'discount factor.' People are deluged with promotional information, and they are beginning to distrust it. People are more likely to make decisions based on what they hear directly from other people: friends, experts, or even salespeople. These days, more decisions are made at the sales counter than in the living-room armchair. Advertising, therefore, should be one of the last parts of a marketing strategy, not the first."

—Regis McKenna, *The Regis Touch* (Addison-Wesley, 1985)

Do you doubt our claim that a significant portion of advertising is dishonest? Do a little test for yourself. Look through your local newspaper as we did one recent morning. Here are a few of the ads we found:

- An ad for a weight reduction center that promises its clients will lose five,

ten or 20 pounds a week. True, some people just might shed some of those unwanted pounds, but how many will keep them off for more than three months? According to Joan Price, in her book *The Honest Truth About Losing Weight and Keeping It Off,* 90% of dieters regain their lost weight within one year. She explains, "Sorry, folks, there's no miracle way to block, burn, rub, jiggle, vacuum, melt or wrap fat off our bodies. There's no magic pill, injection, cream or potion. If there were, don't you think it would make the front page of all the newspapers and medical journals instead of being buried in an ad?" Nowhere in the ad is there a mention of permanent weight loss, because, of course, whatever the method it won't work over the long term. If the ad told the truth, no one would use the service.

- Our friends bought their son a highly advertised remote control car for Christmas. It had just hit the market, and our friends joined the long line at the checkout stand picturing the delight on their child's face Christmas morning. It was not clear to our friends from the ads that the car needed a special rechargeable battery unit and when they returned to the store a week before the big day they were informed that the batteries were sold out and wouldn't be available until after Christmas. They went back week after week until finally, two months after Christmas, the batteries arrived. To add insult to injury, the charger unit for the $50 car cost an extra $20.

- An ad that offers home security at a bargain price in big letters sounds like just the ticket to protect your family, until you read the fine print. In very tiny letters the ad explains that the $99 price covers only the standard installation and that an additional 36-month monitoring agreement is also required. In addition, a telephone connection fee may also be required.

We won't belabor the point with the many other examples we could cite from just one newspaper. Obviously, whether you look in a newspaper, magazine or the electronic media, it is not difficult to find many less-than-honest ads. Even if you advertise in a scrupulously honest way, your ads keep bad company. The public, which has long since become cynical about the general level of honesty in advertising, will not take what you say at face value. For example, suppose you own a restaurant, and instead of extolling the wonders of your menu in exaggerated prose you simply state that you serve "excellent food at a reasonable price." Many people, cynical after a lifetime of being duped by puffed-up claims, are likely to conclude that your food couldn't be too good if that's all you can say about it.

One type of dishonest advertising is especially irritating because it's a bit more subtle and involves magazines and newspapers that you might have respected before you discovered their policy. It works like this: The publication touts the products and services of its advertisers in its news stories. For example, some computer magazines have been known to favorably review the products of their heavy advertisers, and small newspapers often fawn over the products and services of businesses that can be counted on to buy space. Once you discover this sort of policy, everything the publication reviews, even businesses that are truly excellent, is thrown into question.

Devious advertising is rampant in our culture; from "enhanced underwriting" of public broadcast shows, featuring announcements that look identical to commercial television ads, to paid product placement (inserting brand-name goods into movies and TV). And we have come a long way from the dairy industry giving free milk to children at recess. School districts across the country sell exclusive ad space to the highest bidder on school buses, hallways, vending machines and athletic uniforms. Channel One, which gives participating schools video equipment in exchange for piping ads into the classroom, is the tip of the iceberg. Corporations have begun writing the very lesson plans themselves.

Thirty years ago, a study done for the Harvard Business School made clear how the American public felt about traditional advertising: "43% of Americans think that most advertising insults the intelligence of the average consumer. 53% of Americans disagree that most advertisements present a true picture of the product advertised." The chief reasons for hostility to advertising are that it is intrusive and patronizing (73%), morally objectionable (50%), and false and misleading (36%). That the judgment of the general public about honesty in advertising has not improved is demonstrated by this quote from the October 1983 issue of *Advertising Age:*

"Industry studies repeatedly show the image of advertising very close to the bottom of the ladder in comparison to other professions. A study presented at a recent industry conference shows advertising professionals next to last, just above used car salesmen."

Let's take a minute to look at the advertising slogans of some of America's most prominent corporations. While the advertising business considers the following slogans "good" advertising and not dishonest hype, ask yourself, is this good company for your business to keep?

- Bayer works wonders
- Come to where the flavor is (Marlboro)
- With a name like Smucker's it has to be good
- You can be sure if it's Westinghouse
- We build excitement (Pontiac)
- Quality is Job 1 (Ford)
- You asked for it, you got it (Toyota)

- Just do it (Nike)
- It's a Maalox moment
- Winston tastes good like a cigarette should
- Not your father's Oldsmobile
- Travelers Insurance TV ad showing a child with the caption: "This is not a 4-year-old; this is $3.4 million in lifetime income."

We've all heard these slogans or ones like them for so many years, and they're so familiar, that we have to concentrate to even hear them and really pay attention to understand if they are hype or simply not true. And more of them bombard us every day. You can undoubtedly think of many more with no trouble at all.

People are apparently so sick of traditional advertising hype that occasionally even counter-advertising is successful. Bernie Hannaford, who runs a diner named "The Worst Food in Oregon," was quoted in *USA Today* as saying: "I'm a lousy cook, and my father always told me to tell the truth, no matter what." Signs outside invite diners to "Come in and sit with the flies!" and warn, "Food is terrible—service is worse."

E. Honest Ads

Lest you become completely discouraged about the possibility of a better standard of honesty in advertising, there is hope. At least two nations, Japan and Sweden, encourage honesty in their advertising. In

STICK·O·RAMA!

Are you tired of ads in your face? Well put some in theirs! This page of graphics is for you to look at with wonder, but under no circumstances should you ever...

- Take this page to a copy shop
- Ask that it be photocopied onto commercial self-adhesive paper, like Mactac
- Clip, peel, and adhere to appropriate surfaces

HEY! If you don't like these ideas, then come up with your *own*! Whaddya think, we're gonna do ALL the work?

BIG NOISE is a supplement of **ADBUSTERS** Magazine published by the Media Foundation 1243 West 7th Ave. Vancouver, B.C. V6H 1B7 Tel. (604) 736-9401

neither country do ads have "fine print" that contradicts the main message, nor do they permit the sorts of puffery and hype we are used to and which all too often amounts to little more than lying.

Japan's tradition of honest advertising is a long one. In the first century A.D., Chinese visitors were so impressed with the honesty of Japanese businesses that they recorded it as a main attribute of their culture. This 2,000-year-old history of honesty is today reflected in many details: Restaurants display samples of their food in the window and quote prices in round numbers, including sales tax and tip. If you see an 800-yen price advertised for an item, it is the total price you pay. Nolo.com's Stephanie Harolde, who lived and worked in Japan, adds that Japanese businesses never put down their competitors or used comparisons that intimated their product was better than the competitors'.

In Sweden, whose culture is closer to our own, there has been a more deliberate political decision to foster truthful advertising. In that country, it has been against the law since the early 1970s to be deceptive in advertising. To accomplish this, the government not only extended its criminal code to proscribe deceptive advertising, but also formed an administrative agency to enforce the law. As a result, the Swedish people now strongly defend the integrity of their advertising. Perhaps someday we, too, will be proud of ours.

Deceptive advertising is technically illegal in the United States, but enforcement is minimal. The legal standards for advertising are discussed in *The Legal Guide for Starting and Running a Small Business,* by Fred Steingold (Nolo.com).

We mention the Japanese and Swedish use of advertising to urge that, should you ever decide to advertise, you be sure your advertisements are scrupulously honest and that they are as distinct as possible in style, content and location from the general run of other ads. For example, if you limit an offering in a print ad in any way, do so in print as large as the offer itself. If you advertise a service, don't overstate the likely beneficial result of using it, and include a warning as to any risk.

F. Branding

"Branding" has been a catch phrase in advertising for the past decade and brand managers can now be found in the marketing departments of large companies. Branding is an ingenious response to the fact that traditional advertising doesn't work. The idea is to make a product or service so well known that its consumer recognition magically places it in the category of widely recognized and respected brands. The concept of branding is that a minor brand, Electronic Product X, can become as well known as a major brand such as Sony Electronics if Electronic Product X simply spends enough in advertising to "establish" its brand name.

The problem with this concept is that true brand identity is created when a company produces quality products or services and stands by them with solid warranties, product recalls and other methods to ensure customer satisfaction. Running a business this way—not spending a fortune on advertising—is what creates trust and goodwill. In recent decades, several brand names were devastated when they did a lousy job of handling problems with their products. Perrier, Gerber baby products, Sears Auto Centers and Firestone each mismanaged product recalls and took years to recover. Gerber was ultimately sold to new management, and Sears even damaged its reputation with its non-auto business. On the other hand, Tylenol handled a recall beautifully and made its brand even stronger.

For a branding strategy to be effective, a company must be vigilant about its product and service quality—and be prepared for emergencies. Without addressing these issues, a company's reputation is a sitting target, waiting to be ruined. No amount of advertising will be able to develop a good repuation for a company unless there's solid product integrity behind it.

G. Listings: "Advertising" That Works

"Hey, wait a minute," you may be saying. "Traditional media advertising may not be as worthwhile as it's cracked up to be, but many types of advertising do work for small businesses."

The types of "ads" that often work for small businesses include the telephone Yellow Pages, business directory listings, flyers posted in laundromats, good Internet Web pages and "notification" type ads placed in all sorts of appropriate locations, from free "penny saver" newspapers to, in the case of a restaurant with late evening hours, the program of the local symphony.

We make a major distinction between these types of ads directed at interested prospects and traditional print, broadcast and electronic advertising. In fact, we prefer to call these sorts of notices, whether paid for or not, "listings." One good rule to distinguish the two is that a listing is found where people are looking for it. A traditional ad, on the other hand, like a billboard in front of some lovely scenery or a deodorant commercial in the middle of an engrossing TV show, is usually intrusive and often annoying.

Another aspect of traditional advertising, but not of listings, is that advertising agencies get what amounts to a kickback for selling an advertisement: They make most of their money from the discount the media offers only to them. For example, an ad agency might sell you an ad for $100,000 and then buy media time for $85,000. If you list your business in the Yellow Pages, even using a large ad, you and the ad agency are charged the same rate. Putting up a successful website can draw hundreds of thousands of viewers, even if you create it yourself. In other words, listings almost never have an ad agency discount policy.

We strongly encourage the use of listings, and, for most businesses, insist on the importance of having a website. Indeed, for most businesses, listings are essential, particularly Yellow Pages ads for businesses that people use primarily in an emergency: a drain cleaning service, a plumber or a locksmith, for example. Listings in the phone book Yellow Pages— and, where appropriate, the Silver Pages for seniors and ethnic Yellow Pages—are invaluable.

In a few instances, the concepts of listing and advertising have all but merged. For example, in many areas of the country, Wednesday is traditionally the day grocery stores put items on sale. Thrifty shoppers therefore check the full-page lists (ads) of items for the best bargains. In our view, this sort of advertising qualifies as a listing as long as it is placed where consumers normally check.

Similarly, in the computer software business, a great deal of software is sold at discount prices by companies that regularly advertise their wares in computer magazines. The ads feature, in very small print, long lists of available software. Sophisticated customers know to check these listings first whenever they need software, because the prices offered are usually lower than in retail stores.

The Chamber of Commerce, employment and rental agencies, professional newsletters, magazines and journals, and special interest books, such as those geared to the writer or photographer, are commonly accepted places to list goods or services. And in some instances, newspapers have developed such strong special-interest sections that it also makes sense to list one's services there. For example, a travel agency specializing in charter flights to Asia might place a list of prices in the Sunday travel section. Similarly, small community newspapers exist primarily thanks to local advertising, which usually consists of listings of goods and services. Many merchants find that this type of listing does produce good results. Local schools and theater groups also depend on the support of the business community. We consider those kinds of ads as listings of the best sort.

In this vein, we have long been associated with the Common Ground directory, a very successful cooperative enterprise that publishes information in newspaper form about businesses involved in personal transformation. Interested people subscribe or pick up a copy at coffee shops, health spas or wherever the businesses listing in Common Ground feel it is appropriate to leave a stack of papers. Since distribution is taken care of by the people who list in the directory, the paper has an uncanny ability to be located exactly where people who are interested in the services listed are likely to find it.

Nonprofits face the same challenge that for-profit businesses do: They need to tell as many people as possible about the service or product they provide. The Palo Alto, California, Information & Referral Service has come up with a clever way to disseminate a lot of information in a convenient package. It puts out an easy-to-use directory that lists some 200 local agencies and organizations and gives the Service's number for further information.

It's important also to realize that listing can take lots of forms other than paid space in publications. For example, in many areas, if your cat or dog runs away from home, you list this fact as poignantly as possible on the corner telephone pole or fence post. This sort of listing is so common that if someone in your neighborhood finds a pet, she is very likely to check out that same pole or fence. In rural areas all kinds of information is posted in this way. When Salli was out on a walk along her country road recently she noticed a cardboard sign nailed to a pole: "Warning! Don't buy! Carl Chase [not his real name] delivers wet wood and won't return deposit. Ex-buyer." There is nothing new about this. The Romans used to paint information about upcoming gladiator

---

The Arts

A is for Acting

with
RUTH ZAPORAH

Take a risk! Meet the characters inside yourself. This eight week class combines improvisation and scripted theatre in an easy, fun, and non-threatening way. I work on the principles of support, trust, cooperation, and building, strengthening your choices and helping you to find new levels of believability.

Whether you are conquering stage fright, renewing rusty performance skills, making presentations, developing artistic skills, or looking for the high that only comes from performing, this class can help you. Join us!

The experience is useful for actors, authors, salespeople, teachers, advertisers, novices, and anyone who wants to stretch creatively.

Instructor Lynn Goodwin has taught theatre and directed, mostly in schools and colleges, for the last twenty years. Call (510) 838-9057 for information or to be on mailing list.

Action Theater is a unique training process that integrates movement and acting as expression of presence. The student practices, within an improvisational mode, skills of moment to moment awareness and attention, freedom of movement, voice, and imagination.

The training is appropriate for all those interested in enlivening personal expression, from day to day transactions to theatrical performance.

Ruth Zaporah leads workshops in Berkeley and San Francisco, some meeting once or twice a week, others intense daily month long sessions. She also works privately with individuals focusing specifically on their needs.

For further information, call (510) 841-9140.

Adventures In Quantum Creativity.™

What is Quantum Creativity? When specific symbols are consciously manipulated and integrated into everyday environments — we are able to move energy at subatomic levels, and dramatically recreate our reality. We may then magnetize to ourselves anything we desire. This is Quantum Creativity.™

Within this electromagnetic movement or transformation of energy, healing may occur.

Practical issues related to health, relationships, money, and career may be objectified and resolved through the consistent practice of electromagnetic restructuring and through the conscious manipulation of symbols. © 1994 All Rights Reserved.

These practices are easily learned with the assistance of the Imaginal therapies.

Life-Masking In The Ancient Tradition, Wish-Mapping, Voice Dialogue, Synergistic Writing, Dream Interpretation, And Dream Re-Entry engage us in altered states of consciousness that facilitate restructuring. We can learn to access these altered states of consciousness safely, and at will.

Our Open Studio/ Retreat is open to individuals and groups weekdays and weekends, by appointment. In a beautiful, relaxing environment we will encourage you to Create Your Perfect Day. Bask on our sunroof, alone or in company. Expand your Creative Life-Force as you gaze at nature's design in a forested canyon below Mt. Tamalpais. Go hiking and dialogue with the Artist in an accessible Paradise.

Experience Mask-Making, Collage, Assemblage, and other creative adventures. Indulge yourself completely in a dream-like setting where nature and creativity will nurture and free you.

Deep tissue and Shiatsu bodywork and/ or healthful meals may be provided by prior arrangement.

About The Artist:

Sharry Rose, M.A., M.F.A., has degrees in Fine Art, Transpersonal Psychology, and Counseling Psychology. She is an artist and a published poet. Sharry's twenty-five years working both as an artist and as a facilitator in the Imaginal therapies have created in her a special sensitivity toward the needs of artists, writers, musicians, and all women and men who desire to live a more creative and fulfilling life.

Please call Sharry Rose at (415) 389-9012 for a brochure and more information. The Retreat is located near transportation in Mill Valley, just 20 minutes from San Francisco.

A PAGE FROM *COMMON GROUND*, A DIRECTORY OF BUSINESSES INVOLVED IN PERSONAL TRANSFORMATION

fights on the walls of buildings, and the Greeks posted important notices on rotating columns at busy locations.

For home service businesses such as chimney sweeping, babysitting and house sitting, the laundromat bulletin board is where many people look for help. Colleges and universities are a good source for language schools, tutors, dance instructors, typists and roommate referral services. In rural areas, being listed on the Farm Trails Map (a guide for visitors interested in buying agricultural products) is one of the most important marketing tools for people selling fruit, nuts, vegetables, livestock and Christmas trees. And artists who live in a certain area will print a map along with a short description of their work and host "open studio" weekends. Motels and bed and breakfast inns are good places for many small businesses to be listed as part of the establishment's recommended services.

Having a Web page is automatically a "listing." Helping people find your website is a unique and specific marketing issue that we cover in every chapter and in detail in Chapter 11. No matter what your business, there are sure to be many excellent places to list its availability at low cost. ■

Chapter 2

Personal Recommendations: The First Choice in Marketing

"It is the thing you look for, ache for."
—Charles Glenn, Orion Pictures

We hope we have succeeded in getting you to think about the dubious value of advertising for your business, if you hadn't already independently arrived at this conclusion. Now it's time to talk about a marketing strategy that does work: personal recommendations. In our view, promoting personal recommendations is a superior, yet often overlooked, strategy to attract and keep customers.

The idea of people making recommendations to other people is so familiar to us that it often takes a big stretch of the imagination to understand what a significant factor it can be in improving the profitability of your business. Most business owners have no idea just how powerful this tool is because they don't know how to use it efficiently. Yet ask yourself how many of the interesting people you have met, places you have visited, and more to the point, high quality small businesses with whom you have had positive relationships, have come to you from friends who cared enough to tell you about them.

A. Cost-Effectiveness

The overriding reason why personal recommendations are a better source of new customers than advertising is that they are more cost-effective. Monetary success in business obviously comes from selling a product or service at a price that substantially exceeds your cost to provide it. The three main costs involved in doing this in any business are:

- Providing the product or service the customer wants,
- Getting new customers, and
- Getting repeat business.

Notice that two out of three of these categories have to do with attracting customers. If you can accomplish both of them at a reasonable cost, your business should prosper.

Clearly, the customer who is referred comes to you at a lower cost than the one who sees an advertisement. In addition, as we will discuss in more detail below, a customer who is referred to you is both more likely to return and more apt to tell a friend about your business than is the person who responds to an advertisement. To better illustrate this point, let's look at some businesspeople who have prospered using a personal recommendation marketing strategy.

Sam DuVall, who conceives of eating places as theater, has owned very successful restaurants: The Ritz Cafe in Los Angeles and the Elite Cafe in San Francisco. The Elite Cafe was one of the first places in Northern California to serve New Orleans cuisine. Money was invested in good food, good service and in creating a unique ambiance worth talking about, not in advertising. DuVall neither advertises nor does any paid promotion in the conventional sense, yet the Elite Cafe has been packed every night for years. When asked about his success, DuVall said, "Nothing works as well as word of mouth. People believe in it."

The equally famous and exclusive Los Angeles restaurant, Ma Maison, takes an anti-advertising stand still further, refusing even to list its phone number in the Yellow Pages and totally depending on personal recommendations to produce customers. And should you doubt this sort of marketing approach can be successful except for the most exclusive of restaurants, there is TGIFriday's, an estimated $500-million-grossing restaurant chain that is part of the Carlson Group (started in 1965 in New York) that caters to singles. According to a July 1985 piece in *Inc.* magazine, Friday's "has marketed itself successfully without spending a dime on advertising. And that is not likely to change. . . . [According to the founding president, Dan Scoggin], 'if you're performing by a standard of excellence, you don't have to advertise. People know and they'll tell their friends. If you're a restaurant that is advertising, you must be mediocre.'"

The most highly recommended restaurant in the United States, the French Laundry in Yountville, California, has never advertised.

eBay, as noted in Chapter One, doesn't advertise but encourages their users to spread the good word by hosting a feedback forum. To help assure new users that the auction really works, eBay created a "gripe and praise" forum where people share their experiences, which have been overwhelmingly positive.

Substituting personal recommendations for advertising doesn't mean that you do nothing but hope that your customers will tell others about your business. In fact, for most businesses, encouraging positive word of mouth is an active and ongoing endeavor involving the creation of a marketing plan that goes to the heart of the business. For example, the Caravan Traveling Theatre Company of Armstrong, British Columbia, relies heavily on personal recommendations to promote its shows. As they travel from town to town in covered wagons pulled by Clydesdale horses, this naturally colorful group attracts a lot of attention and creates good publicity in an honest, fun way.

The Caravan Company doesn't, however, just rely on this sort of attention. At the end of each performance, the cast asks members of the audience to encourage their friends in the next town (they schedule shows in towns reasonably close together) to attend. Often, audience members get so excited about the show that they not only call their friends but arrange to join them at the next stop to enjoy the show with them.

The movie industry is one of those most obviously affected by personal recommendations. Even though well over a billion dollars is spent every year on promoting new movies, people talking to people is what really counts. According to Marvin

Antonowsky, head of marketing for Universal Pictures, "word of mouth is like wildfire." This point is well illustrated by the number of low-budget movies that have succeeded with little or no advertising—and by the number of big-budget flops.

Like the movies, book publishing is another industry where lots of money is traditionally spent on advertising but can't begin to compete with the power of friends telling friends about their discoveries. A few years ago, *The Road Less Traveled,* by psychiatrist M. Scott Peck, was just another psychology/relationship book languishing on bookstore shelves. Then a few people read it, told their friends, and started a chain reaction that's still going on. Today there are well over two million copies in print.

The two people most responsible for spreading word of the book were one of the publisher's sales representatives, who was so impressed that he insisted that book buyers at stores read the book, and a teacher in Buffalo, New York, who gave copies to teachers and ministers she knew. As a result, two churches invited the author to speak, the local bookstore began selling hundreds of copies, and the publisher (Simon & Schuster) took another look at the book. A promotional tour boosted sales, which have kept rising. The author has since published a teaching guide to the original book and a new book expanding on the ideas in *The Road Less Travelled.*

B. Overcoming Established Buying Habits

Personal recommendations are also one of the best ways to overcome a big hurdle for a business that wants more customers: the tendency of people to patronize the same businesses over and over. The average number of significant monetary transactions (not counting newspapers, carfare, etc.) for a family in the United States is about 65 per month. This means that if you are typical, someone in your family opens a wallet, writes a check or hands over a plastic card 65 times each month to pay for something. For most of us, the great majority of these transactions are conducted with people we have done business with before. Consider your own habits. You probably tend to repeatedly patronize the same dry cleaner, hardware store, dentist, plant nursery and exercise facility. If you're like most people, it takes a substantial nudge to get you to change one of these business relationships.

Given the fact that most people are fairly stable in their daily business patterns, how do you encourage a significant number to give your business a chance? Or, put more concretely, how do you get people to try your stress reduction class, law firm, laundromat or the new computer you are selling out at the shopping center? Personal recommendations are the answer.

Overcoming buying habits is difficult. However, once you realize that the majority of people locate a new product or service based on personal recommendations, not advertising, you have at least half the battle won. To win the other half, you must make your loyal customers, employees, suppliers and friends an integral part of your marketing plan so that your business will be recommended enthusiastically and often.

C. Basing Your Marketing Plan on Personal Recommendations

Once you have decided to base your marketing plan on personal recommendations, your next job is to understand why people go out of their way to recommend certain goods and services and not others. What gets them motivated to sing the praises of a business they think highly of? Have you told a friend about a particular business—perhaps a seamstress, gardener, dentist or cheese store—in the last six months? What were the things about each of these businesses that caused you to recommend them?

Most of this book is devoted to analyzing these kinds of questions. But the answers can be summed up as follows: If your business is truly worthy of being recommended, you will be able to answer all or most of the following questions in the affirmative:

- Is your business running smoothly on a day-to-day basis?
- Are your financial records in order and up-to-date?
- Are your employees knowledgeable about your product or service and enthusiastic about working for you?
- Do you offer top-quality goods or services?
- Do your customers have confidence that if something goes wrong with the products or services you sell, you stand behind them?
- Is your website being kept up-to-date?

Just the simple exercise of asking and answering these few questions may prompt you to make changes in your business. The rest of this book should help you implement changes that will really allow you to take advantage of personal recommendations.

Before we deal with the many practical techniques you can use to encourage customers to recommend your goods and services, it's important to understand the elements that go into a positive recommendation. To succeed in the long run, a marketing campaign based on personal recommendation must be in tune with all of them.

1. Trust

Before you accept a recommendation from someone, you must trust his or her judgment and integrity. Dr. Sidney Levy, chairman of the marketing department at

Northwestern University, explains it this way: "More personal than advertising and smacking of 'inside' information, word of mouth can be a uniquely powerful marketing tool. If somebody you trust suggests something is meaningful, that is more important to you than information presented in an impersonal way."

A good example is when a friend goes out of his way to introduce you to someone. Such introductions are explicit or implied personal recommendations, and most people are careful about making them. When you are on the receiving end of one, you evaluate the person making the introduction as carefully as you do the person being introduced. For instance, think of three people you work with and then imagine that each recommends a different pilot (none of whom you know) to take you up in a small plane. Whom would you be more likely to go with? Would you go with any of them? How much would your choice be influenced by the person doing the recommending?

2. Backing Up a Good Recommendation With Information

We must also consider whether or not our friends know what they are talking about when they make a recommendation about a business. One friend, Walter, once ordered bouillabaisse, tasted it, made a face and quietly sent it back, complaining it "tasted fishy." Did he confuse bouillabaisse with borscht? Would you take seriously his recommendation of a seafood restaurant or fish market?

Another friend, Linda Richardson, spent three months traveling around the U.S. and Asia studying coffee roasting methods in preparation for starting her own coffee shop. Linda knows more about coffee than anyone else we know, so when we took a trip to San Diego recently, we tried out her favorite shop. The espresso was great, as we knew it would be. The difference between Walter's and Linda's ability to make reliable recommendations is obvious. Linda knew her coffee. Walter did not know his fish.

Finally, think for a minute about how many people you know who almost always steer you accurately, and others who sound off on every subject whether they know anything about it or not.

Word of mouth works incredibly fast on the Internet. Even a seemingly innocuous e-mail sent to a good-sized mailing list with an instruction to "pass this e-mail on" can easily spread like wildfire. Some people like to keep everyone on their mail lists informed about things they deem important—which can sometimes be virtually anything and everything. Our advice is to carefully consider and check out information before passing it on. A friend or business associate might understand one "save a starving child, click on this website" scheme, but will quickly learn to mistrust your judgment if you do it over and over.

3. Responsibility

Because of the nature of friendship, personal recommendations carry with them a degree of responsibility for the outcome. If your friend introduces someone to you who turns out to be untrustworthy, it can deeply strain the friendship, and your friend must make a sincere attempt to make the situation right or risk eroding your friendship.

Obviously, carelessly recommending a business can also strain a friendship. Imagine your feelings if a friend recommended a carpenter who tried to jack up the price in the middle of the job, or a computer consultant who screwed up your payroll system and then disappeared two days before payday.

And if a product or service you recommend to someone doesn't work out, it's not always clear what you can do to deal with your friend's hurt feelings. For example, if your favorite hairdresser gives your mother-in-law a frizzy permanent, you will probably hear about it for years, whether you buy her a filet mignon dinner or not.

Given the responsibility that goes with making a recommendation, people will not recommend your business unless they feel confident in it. As a direct consequence, your business policies and practices concerning errors, mistakes and problems are of great concern to your customers who make recommendations. They will recommend your business only if they can really trust you to stand behind your product or service should something go wrong.

D. When Not to Rely on Word of Mouth for Marketing

We come now to an important warning about the power of word of mouth. There is an extremely good reason why many American businesses may not want to adopt a marketing plan based on the sorts of things we discuss in this book. This reason is simple. Word of mouth is just as effective in getting out the bad news about a business as it is to spread good tidings. In fact, the Ford Motor Company estimates that a dissatisfied car owner tells 22 people, while a satisfied car owner tells eight.

These figures may be going up; with the Internet, it is easy for knowledgeable people to complain to tens of thousands of other people—and they do.

A good example is the former website, DrKoop.com. Dr. C. Everett Koop was a well-respected Surgeon General in two Republican administrations. He started a website that used his name to dispense medical information and advice. His site spent $147 million to solicit business on other websites and was one of the most visited health sites on the Web. Why did it fail? Negative word of mouth. Nurses in America had complained for years about rashes caused by rubber gloves and been told by Koop when he was the Surgeon General that it was an imaginary problem. When DrKoop.com was founded, word got out that Dr. Koop had been on retainer to a rubber glove company at the time he dismissed the nurses' complaints. Moreover, "the site came under attack...for failing to notify visitors that a group of hospitals had paid to be included in a section on community resources, and that Koop himself was receiving a commission for products sold on the site." (*Industry Standard,* April 17, 2000.)

Certainly, if your product or service is no better than average, you should put down this book and avoid like the plague a marketing plan based on word of mouth. Businesses with average or negative attributes succeed only if they rely on such things as extensive advertising and high-rent locations. Such is often the case with businesses that cater to (or prey upon) tourists. For example, in Boston's wharf area, there are numerous restaurants that Bostonians sneer at but unsuspecting tourists are eager to patronize. Many visitors don't know any Bostonians and don't have the benefit of the natives' negative word of mouth. They don't know that when they trustingly order local lobster, far from getting a freshly caught crustacean, they are being served lobster fresh from the freezer.

Even a media blitz won't save an inferior product from bad word of mouth in the long run. Two products come to mind when we think of expensive national TV advertising campaigns that initially touted

poor quality merchandise successfully to gullible viewers but were eventually destroyed by word of mouth. One was a miniature fire extinguisher, about six inches long, designed to be placed near the kitchen stove, and the other, an aerosol can of air used to inflate flat tires. Neither product worked in an emergency, as promised in the ads. In each instance it took about six months for enough people to buy them, rely on them in an emergency, and tell their friends what rotten products they were. The advertising continued, but word of mouth was so powerful that both companies were soon out of business.

We've also found, after years of giving marketing advice to small businesses, that it's bad practice to help a business devise a marketing plan to encourage personal recommendations unless it can handle more customers. Even if your business is in decent shape, it may still not be run well enough to handle the expansion that a marketing plan based on personal recommendations will bring and still maintain its quality. When a business is not ready for expansion, a large influx of new customers can easily produce a waking nightmare complete with dissatisfied customers, low employee morale and general frustration at not being able to provide good service. Naturally, when this happens, customers will tell their friends, and a downward business spiral begins.

For example, a well-known shoe manufacturer sent out a mailer advertising a sale. Rasberry was excited as she has a very narrow foot and they advertised her size in styles she liked. When she went to the store, she was very disappointed as not one of the styles was available in her size. She was told by a frazzled saleswoman that they only stocked one of each style in each size! Still, since she was promised the shoes she wanted were available from the warehouse, Rasberry decided to order two pairs. A week later, she received a phone call saying one pair was actually no longer being made. A week after that came a rather poignant note from the salesgirl and her manager saying the other pair was also unavailable. They did enclose a 20% off coupon for her next visit. Needless to say there won't be a next time.

Another, dramatic example of this phenomenon occurred when *The Last Whole Earth Catalog* (Random House), a publication that reviewed thousands of high-quality products designed for simple living, sold over a million copies and produced a huge upsurge of orders for some of the products reviewed. When a year later the catalogue was updated, the names of dozens of businesses that had failed in the interim had to be omitted. In a significant number of instances, the reason for failure was that the business didn't know how to cope with the large volume of new orders.

It's not only small businesses that are vulnerable to this phenomenon. One of the largest HMOs in the country continually spends large sums of money advertising for new clients while leaving their current clients standing in long lines at the pharmacy and unable to get appointments with their doctors. When they finally are able to schedule an appointment, they are allotted such a short time as to leave both patient and doctor frustrated. The results: an exodus of doctors who can no longer tolerate the situation and dissatisfied customers who are not shy to tell anyone who will listen. One of the authors listened to the complaints of an elderly woman propped up on her cane as she waited in line for her medicine while another patient went ranting down the hallway shouting, "Stop spending money for commercials and get me a doctor!"

Marketing Without Advertising Checklist

☐ 1. My product or service is up-to-date and is the best it can be.

☐ 2. I have an open, visible, understandable and very generous recourse policy, which is clearly posted on my website.

☐ 3. I can clearly describe my business and so can most of my clients, suppliers, friends and employees.

☐ 4. My pricing is clear and complete and tells customers what they need to know about my level of expertise and my target clientele. The price allows them to tailor elements to their needs.

☐ 5. My business is open in its financial information, management policies, physical layout and its operating functions.

☐ 6. My clients know as much as they want to know about my product or service, including the ways it is outstanding and unique. Referrals and evaluations from other respected people in the field as well as from customers are easily available and posted on the website.

☐ 7. Old clients and others who have lost track of the business can easily find it in countless listings, reference materials, Internet search engines, Web directories, and through neighbors and business associates.

☐ 8. I have a complete list with mailing addresses and phone numbers of my current and former clients as well as my suppliers, friends and interested parties. When relevant, referral sources are noted.

☐ 9. I have a current calendar of marketing events and regularly schedule activities of interest to which I invite my customers and other appropriate associates. Everyone who attends feels a part of my community when they leave.

☐10. I know how big I want my business to be and am prepared to handle growth created by my marketing. I am prepared and alert to cutting it off whenever a new customer gets better treatment than an old client.

Chapter 3

The Physical Appearance of Your Business

*M*ost of us give the physical appearance of our business a great deal of thought—at least at the beginning. Signs, packaging, window displays and office layout are all given great attention. Unfortunately, as the months turn into years, we tend to develop sloppy habits. Window displays that were once cleaned weekly and redone monthly now stay up a couple of weeks longer and are rarely cleaned in the interim. Employees who were once required to look fresh and clean now sometimes work in T-shirts and raggedy jeans, and no one has gotten around to fixing the dent in the delivery truck or thought to run it through a car wash.

While the graphic presentation (especially packaging, promotional material and listings) of most businesses improves with time, carelessness almost always creeps into other areas. Sloppy storage areas and restrooms, messy bookshelves in offices, boxes of files piled in inappropriate places and half-dead plants in the corner of the office are all things that a business owner may hardly see, but are sure to turn off customers. If this is what it looks like in the visible parts, customers wonder, what might lurk in the file cabinets and drawers hidden from view? And more important, who can have confidence in the skill of management?

Whether you are about to open a business or have been in operation for some time, review all of the key elements of the appearance of your business. Pretend to be a customer and ask yourself whether the appearance of the business would inspire your trust. If you feel you are just too close to your business to really see it with fresh eyes, elicit the help of a friend, or offer to check out another business in exchange for getting an assessment of your own.

Keep in mind five goals for your business's appearance:

- It should conform to, or exceed, the norms of the business you are in.
- It should be squeaky clean.
- It should have an appropriate smell.
- It should be uncluttered.
- Your website should be updated as often as is possible and appropriate.

A. Conforming to Industry Norms

When your business's appearance isn't what your customers expect, you risk making them uncomfortable—even when the divergence improves the look of your business. Customers have a fairly clear image of what most businesses "should" look like. If they don't know it from their own observation, they rely on movies, television or magazines for models.

When they encounter a business that doesn't conform to these ideas, they feel dissonance, the sense that something is out of whack, out of balance. It's an uncomfortable feeling that many people won't be able to verbalize; they just know something is wrong.

The point is simple. If you give your customers something that they don't expect, it is essential that you examine how they will react to this divergence. In retailing, for example, a large amount of densely packed stock is generally associated with low prices, while widely spaced stock conjures up images of high price tags. A clothing store such as Ross's Dress for Less, displaying racks packed with clothes, is presumably cheaper than a store such as Comme des Garcons, of San Francisco, Tokyo, Paris or New York, where each display features a very limited number of items. By tinkering with these customer expectations, you risk creating confusion. A customer shopping in a jewelry store that offers a few items, widely spaced, would very likely find low prices disconcerting and might wonder if the pricing were wrong, the goods were fakes, or worse yet, stolen. Disconcerting customers a little is by no means always bad. The store selling bargain jewelry in an uncluttered atmosphere might well prosper, assuming other marketing techniques were used to reassure the customer.

Carefully planned deviations from the norm can be effective. For instance, an inexpensive restaurant can emphasize widely spaced tables and a quiet atmosphere if this deviation from the expected is clearly understood, as might be the case if it used a name such as "Beggar's Banquet." Similarly, an uncluttered discount

appliance store which displays a relatively small amount of merchandise works fine if it clearly communicates to customers that the appliances displayed are samples and orders are filled from a nearby warehouse. Consumer Distributing, a discount retail hard goods chain, uses this model.

Many types of businesses traditionally have miserable surroundings. Auto scrap yards are an extreme example; many laundromats are another. This is almost certainly one of the reasons why many small yards have failed in the last few years. Customers will no longer put up with greasy, dangerous surroundings. If the appearance of typical businesses like yours is generally considered to be poor, rising above the industry norm is an essential part of building customer trust. An example of a business that exceeds the industry norm is an optometrist who has a clear, meaningful display in the window instead of the usual pile of empty eyeglass frames and faded photos of models wearing last year's sunglasses. Another is a plumber with a clever and educational window display featuring different types of pipes and fittings instead of a couple of pink toilets. Similarly, auto repair shops with clean offices, waiting areas and spotless restrooms are a welcome improvement over the usual dirty, battered-looking garage waiting areas we have all come to dread.

Professional office waiting areas provide another example where standards are commonly low. A doctor, dentist, architect or lawyer who has a well-designed office with comfortable furniture, often-changed educational displays and materials about the particular area of practice, as well as a broad selection of magazines less than six months old, is still a welcome exception to the norm. Many Nordstrom's department stores make their atmosphere more pleasant than most retail stores by inviting local piano teachers to play a grand piano in their high fashion departments. It's good for the teachers, too, who can give out their cards.

Going beyond industry norms and communicating the improvements to your customers should be a goal in any good marketing plan. The upholsterer across the street from our office, who currently displays two beautifully restored art deco chairs in his window instead of the more typical pile of fabric (which tells us nothing about the quality of his workmanship or his specialties), is a good illustration. And then there is a travel agent we know who decided that the usual run of travel posters was simply a bore and instead displays (and changes monthly) period costumes of the country he is featuring. In this regard, one of our favorite store windows is Campus Shoe Repair in Westwood, California, near UCLA. It displays a mechanized cobbler resoling a shoe, along with miniature replicas of a football, baseball glove, boots and other items the proprietor can fix.

In the course of our work, we have been asked to go into a lot of business settings and suggest changes. Indeed, we have done this so often that it has become almost second nature to walk into a business and mentally redesign it. Perhaps you, too, have been tempted to do this. If not, why not begin? Think about how you would improve the appearance of the next ten businesses you visit, keeping in mind that your redesign plan should work with, not against, industry norms. Once you get adept at this, apply the lessons you have learned to your own business.

British Airways wanted to keep customers happy, so asked regular customers on the transatlantic run what they most wanted. The answer was an overwhelming "Leave us alone and let us sleep!" Passengers wanted their own comfy universe, and they got it. British Airways first-class passengers currently dine on a five-course meal with fine linen and candlelight in the waiting lounge before they board the aircraft, and then it's to sleep right after take-off.

The seat reclines almost to horizontal— as close to a bed as you can get. The airline lends you a two-piece running suit that is like a nice pair of pajamas and provides you with a comforter and face mask. If you don't want to sleep, you have your choice of movies at your own seat and an in-flight banquet.

B. Fantasy: A Growing Part of Retail Marketing

For many centuries there has been a trend to mix fantasy and product sales. Today, the trend has grown to such an extent that all businesses need to think about fantasy—especially when considering a business's appearance.

Medieval trade fairs in Europe and West Africa had clowns, dancers, musicians, puppets and storytellers to create a festive atmosphere. The fantasy that these entertainers were trying to create was "paradise." Today, businesses create fantasies that stimulate demand for their products.

We have fantasies in the form of physical locations; Disneyland is a good example. Disneyland has a fantasy turn-of-the-century Main Street, jungles and underwater worlds. At Tinseltown Studios near Disneyland in Anaheim, California, you can totally indulge your desire to be a star at a fantasy Academy Awards ceremony. Customers at Tinseltown are not treated as guests but as screen idols. Once you enter through the door you are barraged by autograph seekers, the paparazzi, reporters and TV crews. As you walk down the long red carpet, all eyes are on you. Tinseltown lives up to its slogan of "taking unknown people and turning them into screen legends."

Many retail stores go directly for a Disneyland-like reproduction. Victoria's Secret lingerie stores, for example, have a racy boudoir ambiance. Store windows are usually fantasy-land creations on a miniature scale. Many retail business interiors are sketches of a fantasy, with images and artifacts on the walls and in the aisles.

Restaurants often invoke a fantasy atmosphere, whether is it is Olde England with leather benches, wooden beams and imitation pewter mugs or a Polynesian island with bamboo, fish nets and tropical paintings.

Many direct-mail catalogues are 100% fantasy creations. They show people in landscapes and exotic settings with distinctive clothing and accoutrements for sale. In many cases the descriptions of the items read like an exotic travel brochure.

The growth of direct-mail catalogues in the past two decades has played a role in accelerating the active use of fantasy in business. There are many cases of catalogues that paved the way for retail stores in keeping with the catalogue's fantasy theme, from Smith & Hawken and Crabtree & Evelyn to Victoria's Secret and The Sharper Image.

In traditional businesses, it is hard to know how much fantasy to invest in. A law office that has a modest investment in shelves filled with law books (rarely used anymore, in the electronic age) and high-back leather chairs is better off than a similar office resembling a sterile dental waiting room. But putting a large investment into maple burl paneling, a fireplace with a real fire and a courtroom railing might not be justified.

Gone are the days when a vacation hotel is sought for its uniformity. Today's pleasure traveler who can afford it seeks the thrill of a unique experience. She wants to escape the familiar and try on a new identity—if only for a weekend. Bill Kimpton operates several such fantasy-oriented boutique hotels; the one we personally enjoy is the Triton near San Francisco's Chinatown. The Triton is a showcase for local artists. A dreamy, flowing mural of pastel hues covers the wall and ceiling of the lobby. Handcrafted tables and lamps and rock and roll music create a mad-hatter tea party type atmosphere. Like most of Kimpton's boutique hotels, the occupancy rate is around 80%.

A new business based entirely on fantasy, such as a multimedia production company, needs to put a significant investment into the fantasy appearance of the workspace. Fantasy is the industry norm in this emerging field.

No existing business is exempt from thinking about the fantasy aspect of business. Whole new businesses are being created out of the consumer's immense appetite for new fantasies.

We can expect to see marketing in the near future where the customer who fantasizes being an academic can order an entire cozy, academic reading room with a complete wall of books, bookshelves, framed prints for the wall, a leather chair, reading lamps, Persian carpets, suitable clothes, pens, eyeglasses and videotapes with information and suggested conversations for the would-be academic.

Our favorite recent example of a business that fully comprehends the notion of fantasy is in Tokyo (always the leading edge in marketing) near Roppongi Corner. This retail store was named after an imaginary island with an imaginary culture. In the store is everything one could buy on a trip to this island: clothes, sandals, jewelry, fabrics, art pieces for the wall, furniture and incense. The design of everything was perfect to the last detail and was a synthesis of elements from Southeast Asia. All the pieces for sale are custom-made for the store.

Whatever your business, it is worth thinking about the fantasies concerning your product or service that would support additional sales. Think boldly, because we are in an era of bold immersive fantasies. Doctors, lawyers, chimney sweeps and taxi drivers are not immune to this emerging marketing trend. We have already seen doctor's offices that feel like a science lab and sell books, videos and magazine subscriptions about their specialties, including toy medical equipment and hospital uniforms—all done with style and professional dignity. We already know of taxi drivers who drive outrageous classic cars, sell models of their vehicle and offer photos of the passenger sitting in the driver's seat, properly attired.

One client, Terry Miller, a women's clothing designer and manufacturer whose business is based in San Francisco (the

Terry McHugh store), had been selling to major department stores for many years. Finally, she grew tired of having to produce a high volume of top quality goods under tight time pressure on a slim profit margin and then wait months to be paid. Sensibly, Miller decided to cut back on department store sales at the same time she opened the doors of her manufacturing studio to customers and developed a direct sales business. Unfortunately, her direct sales business took off with all the pizzazz of a cold turtle.

Convinced that her direct sales concept was a good one despite the poor results, Miller called in one of the authors for a consultation. When Michael visited her manufacturing studio, he realized immediately that the physical setup was not what most people would expect from a top-of-the-line design studio. Too many details conflicted with the romantic popular image of what such a business should look like that people see in movies and on TV. For example, the women sewing the garments had unattractive piles of cloth and racks of hangers next to their stations, the design table was cluttered with books, papers and the occasional abandoned coffee cup. Worst of all, the finished clothing hanging on the racks in the work space displayed price tags.

Michael recommended that Miller redesign her studio to conform more to her customers' image as seen on TV and in the movies. Miller agreed to give it a try. She brought in several mannequins, which she draped with a design the women were currently sewing. She also displayed elegant sketches and pattern swatches on the walls near the design table, cleaned up the table itself and created a little sitting area complete with the new editions of high-fashion magazines such as Vogue and Elle. Most important, she removed price tags from the garments in the work room; only the clothing in a separate sales room was tagged. Miller also kept the boxes used to ship clothing to stores such as Bloomingdale's and Saks stacked prominently in the workroom. Direct sales doubled in two months and doubled again in four.

Later she moved to a retail store that has a design and manufacturing section that could have come from anyone's fantasy of what such a set-up should look like. Her business is booming, and she's looking to expand.

1. Cleanliness

Cleanliness is crucially important in all businesses, and is perceived by the public as a measure of management competence. Despite this, most businesses, whether retail, wholesale, restaurant, consulting or professional, are not clean. If you doubt it, think about how many businesses you know that are spotless. Not very many, we bet. And those that do meet this high standard are almost surely very successful.

Years ago, when gasoline stations were trying to attract customers, many displayed signs extolling how sanitary their restrooms were. These signs often stated that the restrooms were for the convenience of customers and if everything wasn't perfect to let the management know. Some large oil companies even had strict national inspection programs to support their claims. Then along came the gasoline shortage, and many gas station operators became so arrogant they forgot about time-tested good business principles, including clean restrooms and friendly service. While there are, of course, a number of complicated economic reasons why so many gas stations have failed in the last few years, certainly one is that most are so poorly run that customers have absolutely no reason to be loyal to them. Restrooms remain a good barometer as to how well a business is run.

By contrast, part of the phenomenal growth of several national franchises, including McDonald's, Supercuts and Midas Mufflers, is directly connected to their reputation for cleanliness. Before these companies changed industry norms, many hamburger stands, barber shops and brake shops were notoriously dirty. In each of these instances, the commitment to be extremely clean was powerful enough to transform an industry.

2. Smell

Smell is such an important, but often overlooked, aspect of a good marketing plan that it's worth focusing on in detail. Good smells can be an incredibly powerful part of the image of many businesses—and inappropriate ones can ruin it.

The smell of disinfectant can be a positive attribute in a medical environment and a definite negative in a bakery. Certainly the location of bathrooms and the resulting smells in a retail store, coffee shop or medical clinic can influence clients very strongly. For example, the authors visited a well-known luncheon restaurant that boasted great sandwiches accompanied by a fashion show, but left after five minutes because they were seated close to the restroom, which reeked of cleansers.

Peet's Coffee stores in the San Francisco Bay area are a famous instance of a business that owes a large part of its success to a magnificent smell. Over 30 years ago, Mr. Peet opened a tiny neighborhood shop to sell the coffee beans he imported and roasted on the premises. Coffee drinkers could not resist the aroma of fresh-roasted coffee that permeated the immediate neighborhood. When they ventured inside, they were met with a pleasant surprise—a little coffee bar where they could enjoy a superior cup of coffee for a reasonable price. These and other techniques contributed to Peet's becoming the first extremely successful coffee store in an area of Berkeley, California, that has since become famous as the first true gourmet ghetto in modern America. The original Peet's was the model for Seattle's Starbucks in its early days. The many coffee stores in our neighborhoods are there at least in part because Mr. Peet opened the windows next to his roaster, and the customers flooded in.

Fine Design, which sells furnishings, antiques and sweaters in New York City, uses pine boughs to fill the store with a pleasant aroma around the holidays. Although this technique may sound obvious, we encounter very few businesses that use smell positively. Unfortunately, smells more commonly detract from the atmosphere. Ice cream stores—because sugar and oil don't smell good—top the list.

Good smells aren't an effective marketing technique only for retailers. A real estate broker friend in Dallas, Scott Park, is very successful in the residential market. One of his approaches is to fill the houses he is showing with fragrant fresh flowers and to bake an apple pie in the oven at a very low temperature for the four to six hours that a house is typically shown.

Similarly, in the Urasenke Tea School in New York, which teaches students the traditional art of the Japanese tea ceremony, the teachers wipe with a moist rag the tatami mats the students walk on, to bring out the delicate bamboo-like fragrance of fresh tatami.

3. Clutter

Small neighborhood grocery stores traditionally have a problem with clutter, not only because they are inefficiently designed to handle the high volume of incoming products but also because they are often short of storage space. This is one factor that led to the success of 7-11 or Quick-Stop type convenience stores, which feature an open, uncluttered look that is much more appealing to many customers.

Cleanliness and lack of clutter aren't only important to retail stores, of course. For example, one of our editors recently reported stopping by the office of the company that delivered diapers for his baby. The dirty, sloppy office looked like it belonged to a poorly run machine shop. Recordkeeping was so disorganized that it took five minutes to find the correct account card. In addition, the counter was dirty, the windows hadn't been washed recently and there was no display material, publications or anything else to create a feeling that anyone cared about babies. Indeed, the whole atmosphere was so disheartening that he cancelled the diaper service, even though the diapers delivered to his house had always seemed clean enough.

Or how about a picture framing shop that, of all businesses, ought to be aesthetically pleasing. The one down the street sports streaky windows behind which are piles of dusty frames and dull racks of unassembled frames instead of framed artwork that would capture the attention of passers-by.

Nearby there is another marketing disaster: a store large enough to run ads on television that has for months had seven sloppy handwritten signs stuck to its glass door with yellowing scotch tape. The signs aren't even of the temporary "closed for vacation" variety; they appear to be permanent. To make matters worse, the store sells eyeglasses!

In the late 1950s, Lawrence Ferlinghetti, well aware of the industry norms for small independent bookstores, was determined to let his staff and customers know that their store wasn't going to have the typical dingy cave-like atmosphere. He built his idea into the name of his now-famous City Lights Bookstore, which was truly a pleasant, bright and uncluttered store. His customers appreciated this innovation. Today, this idea has been copied by bookstores nationwide, including many of the national chains. Interestingly, it has most enthusiastically been adopted by a very profitable three-store California business named A Clean Well-Lighted Place for Books, which through its name elevates its inviting atmosphere to the position of the centerpiece of its marketing strategy.

On the Internet, one of the best examples of an uncluttered website is Google, one of the first online businesses to understand the allure of keeping a site simple and straightforward. Many people may not remember the days when search engine sites typically were cluttered with banner ads and blinking messages almost to the point of obscuring the search results themselves. Since the intuitive measure of search engine competence is the ability to deliver a focused group of results, Google communicated the correct message: a clean uncluttered page with nearly 98% of white space. Google rose to be one of the top three search engines and established the cleanliness norms for the industry.

When Salli brought her new-to-her car in for its first tune-up at the C&W Ford repair shop in Sebastopol, California, she was surprised and impressed with how uncluttered and clean the shop was. The place she had been taking her car to did a good enough job but always left her with a slightly queasy feeling. The carpet in the waiting room was stained and full of lint, and the entire office was grungy. She couldn't quite see through the grimy window where they worked on her car. The contrast was amazing. At the Ford company, every tool was in its place, the shop was open, airy and clean and the office sparkled.

Now it's time for you to do some work. Look at your business as an outsider might, using the checklist below to evaluate whether your business conforms to or exceeds industry norms, is truly clean, smells appropriate and is free of clutter.

C. Evaluating Your Business's Physical Appearance

Step 1. In the "Your Business" column, list the key aspects of the physical appearance of your business. We can't do this for you because there are thousands of types of businesses. To give you ideas, we've included at the top of the worksheet a list of elements that commonly apply to retail and wholesale businesses, organized by category: outside elements such as signage and architecture; inside aspects such as cleanliness, lighting, etc.

Step 2. Rate your business on each of the elements you have listed as "poor," "adequate" or "excellent." Use the "Comments" column to describe specific details.

Step 3. Also in the "Comments" column, make a note of any particular elements in your business that differ significantly from industry norms, and ask yourself if the positive reasons for this difference are clearly communicated to your customers.

Physical Appearance That Develops Trust

Outside	Inside	Sales Staff	Sales Materials	Product	Mail Order/Online
signage	cleanliness	clothes	neatness	protected	answers key questions
display	clutter	breath	clutter	well marked	clear meaning
architecture	lighting	teeth	understandable	return address	exciting
cleanliness	smell	car clean	standard sizing	design	consistent style
neighborhood	spacing, general	identifiable	completeness	dated	convincing
	spacing, merchandise	prompt		labels	
	amount of stock				
	decor				

Your Business   **Comments**   POOR ADEQUATE EXCELLENT

_____   _____   ☐   ☐   ☐

_____   _____   ☐   ☐   ☐

_____   _____   ☐   ☐   ☐

_____   _____   ☐   ☐   ☐

_____   _____   ☐   ☐   ☐

_____   _____   ☐   ☐   ☐

_____   _____   ☐   ☐   ☐

_____   _____   ☐   ☐   ☐

_____   _____   ☐   ☐   ☐

_____   _____   ☐   ☐   ☐

_____   _____   ☐   ☐   ☐

_____   _____   ☐   ☐   ☐

_____   _____   ☐   ☐   ☐

_____   _____   ☐   ☐   ☐

_____   _____   ☐   ☐   ☐

_____   _____   ☐   ☐   ☐

_____   _____   ☐   ☐   ☐

_____   _____   ☐   ☐   ☐

_____   _____   ☐   ☐   ☐

_____   _____   ☐   ☐   ☐

Chapter 4

Pricing

A crucial element in any good marketing plan based on building customer trust is a sound pricing policy. Pricing is a key factor in determining your customers' expectations. To use a somewhat exaggerated example, a classy saloon that has cognac on its menu for $3.99 and serves it in a plastic glass will never be considered trustworthy. Similarly, a lawyer or architect who charges $37.75 an hour will have a very difficult time convincing potential clients that she does high quality work.

Some pricing tips:

- Make your prices straightforward and easy to understand.
- Pricing should be complete, including everything a customer expects.
- In setting your prices, give the customer reasonable control over the purchase transaction.
- On the Internet, you may need to break prices down to the lowest useable unit.

Let's look at each of these elements individually.

A. Straightforward and Easy-to-Understand Prices

It's important to make sure your pricing policy does not confuse or mislead your customers. The price you state should reflect the total cost of the transaction. It should also be an honest one considering all the circumstances of the transaction. For example, if you specialize in selling bulk goods, your price per unit should go down as volume increases, at a regular and reasonable rate. A produce market that offers grapefruit at "25 cents each or four for a dollar" is sure to drive away customers. A customer may not do the arithmetic the first time he visits the store, but eventually he will note that the retailer is misusing a standard marketing device by charging the same amount for volume purchases rather than offering customers a small discount to encourage such purchases.

Similarly, the parking garage that advertises in big letters "75 cents for the first hour" and then charges 75 cents for each additional ten minutes is attempting to mislead its customers. You may park in such a place once, when you are late for an appointment and don't have time to read the fine print on the sign carefully, but you are almost certain to go someplace else next time, even if it means parking a few blocks farther from your destination.

Confusing and misleading incremental prices aren't the only way a business can abuse its customers' trust, of course. There are many ways to list prices in a misleading way. For example, how do you feel about a rug cleaner who offers to clean "five rooms for $89," and then, in small print, defines a room as being 6' by 8'? Although this might appear to border on the dishonest, it is actually a typical practice in the rug cleaning business. Rug cleaners who avoid this type of pricing, however, are appreciated by their customers. For example, a friend recently told us about a service that prided itself on cleaning any rug, regardless of size, for a fixed price, and doing up to three throw rugs free as part of every job. We plan to try that business next time we clean our rugs, and if it is as good as claimed, will surely tell others.

To be clear, a price should also be easily discernible by all potential customers. This is particularly important for service businesses, which don't have a tangible product to which a price can easily be attached. Many potential customers shy away from some businesses simply because they don't know what the service costs and for one reason or another feel shy about asking. So, whether you run a typing service, a commercial fishing boat or are a child care provider, tell customers clearly how much your service costs before they have to ask. For example, a typist might do this with a fact sheet listing prices of $3 per page or $30 per hour, with a 20% surcharge for rush work that must be done after 5 p.m., a 50% surcharge for rush jobs typed after midnight, and $1 extra per page for statistics and address lists.

If you doubt that communicating prices can be a big part of any marketing plan, think about how many times you have shied away from patronizing a particular business or service because you didn't know how much it charged and feared the worst. Enough said, we hope.

Don't be afraid to be redundant. No one gets angry at a lawyer who finds three ways to tell you her hourly (and incremental) rates for consultation, research and court time, but everyone dislikes getting an unexpectedly large bill after services are rendered. For instance, many people in the home contracting business don't inform their clients of their overhead and profit billing. A naive client assumes the contractor works as a salaried person instead of growing a business as in other fields. Naturally the customer goes ballistic when they see 20% or more "tacked" onto their bill.

Chapter 10 discusses in detail the issues of customer recourse and warranties (also part of any description of price). People often want to know if they will get their money back if they are not satisfied, and under what conditions deposits, partial payments and full payments are refundable.

B. Complete Prices

The completeness of a price is determined both by the norms of a particular business and by general honest business principles. Ideally, your price for a particular good or service should include everything that a typical person expects to pay for, and a little bit more.

Examples of incompleteness in pricing that annoy customers are:

- Computers priced without keyboards or software.
- Hotel room prices for rooms without private baths.
- Legal fees for incorporating a business that don't include state registration fees.
  - "Price-fixed" meals that don't include coffee.
- Expensive flowers that don't include greens.
- A high-priced suit that doesn't come with free alterations.

Surely you can think of similar examples in your field. Also, pay particular attention to the fact that customary pricing practices in some businesses do not give customers a very good deal. In this situation, a business can quickly build customer trust by offering a little extra. For example, in most communities, it is customary for a used car dealer to sell cars "as is," with the expectation that they are probably in such rotten condition that they will expire ten minutes after a purchaser takes title. By contrast, a used car dealer that offers a real 90-day warranty violates this custom in a positive, business-building way.

Similarly, the norm in American hotels and motels is a bathroom supplied with soap, towels, washcloth, shampoo, conditioner, shower cap, water glass and toilet paper. To this, many establishments have added fax services, modem plugs for portable computers, body lotion, bathrobes, slippers, shoe cleaning supplies, disposable toothbrushes, free newspapers, coffee and orange juice as part of the room price. Speaking of hotels and pricing, there is nothing more annoying than a confusing phone policy. You have probably stayed (most likely only once) at an establishment that charged an exorbitant rate for calls and as you were checking out were presented with an extra $10 or $15 charge for those few calls you made back home.

If you are a regular traveler, chances are you will return to establishments that offer extra amenities. In one little neighborhood restaurant in Kyoto, Japan, customers who sit down alone are given the latest edition of the daily newspaper after the food order is taken. The restaurant rarely has an empty seat.

To take an example of how something extra can make a big difference, consider how the Japanese auto companies successfully captured a large part of the U.S. auto market. They established a reputation for good value, at least partially because they priced cars to include most of the optional features that purchasers of American cars customarily paid extra for, such as a radio or outside rear view mirror. By contrast, pricing in the U.S. auto industry is so confusing that *Consumer Reports* magazine, which rates products, has had to develop an almost impossibly complicated formula to compare prices, and even sells computer printouts to help readers determine what they are paying for.

In some industries, no service at all is the norm—and nowhere is this more evident than in the Internet service provider

(ISP) business. Almost everyone has horror stories of the constant busy signal, being put on endless hold, or only being able to access the provider through e-mail whose system always seems to be down. Rasberry has found an ISP, Monitor.net, that not only has a friendly human that answers your phone calls if your computer crashes, but immediately answers questions that are e-mailed to its technical support staff. You can be sure that Monitor.net benefits from the customer loyalty engendered by these business practices.

A friend rented a car at a New Jersey airport for a few weeks, and when he went to pay his bill there was a large additional charge for a dirty, bottom-of-the-line child's safety seat that could have been purchased retail for half that amount. Nothing had been said about this extra cost when the car, with baby seat, was reserved. Contrast this unpleasant and expensive example with the young couple who moved to Hawaii and had to rent a car for a few weeks before theirs was shipped over. Not only was the car seat free, but when the couple's own car arrived and they returned the rented car, the rental company offered to rent them a baby seat for a few dollars until they could buy their own.

If in your business, bidding on a job is the norm, as it is in house painting, consulting or carpentry, the issue of "completeness" in pricing is a fairly common and often sticky problem. If it is not addressed forthrightly, it can develop into a nightmare of misunderstanding between business and customer and result in the worst kind of word of mouth about the business. Trustworthy businesses in these fields must go out of their way to identify all items included and not included in their price and be sure this information is accurately communicated to customers. And when a customer makes changes to the original bid, a trustworthy business writes them down accurately along with the extra charge and has the client read and sign the "change orders" so there won't be any surprises.

This is especially important when dealing with inexperienced clients who may not be familiar with industry norms. You should go out of your way to clarify items that are excluded from a bid, even if such exclusions are standard in your particular business.

For example, a website designer, when quoting a price to build a client's site, should make it clear from the beginning exactly what the customer is expected to provide, such as graphics, text or any other features that will be available at the site. In addition, it should be clear to the customer that the price does not include maintaining the site. Similarly, if a house painter customarily charges separate fees for paint and labor, or a building maintenance company expects the building owner to supply cleaning equipment and supplies, the business should say so from the beginning.

Carefully consider whether everything you do on a job is included in the price you quote. If you identify extras that you charge for separately, ask yourself if there is really a good reason for the additional charge. How much would you lose if you included some or all of the extras in your base price? Next, ask yourself whether charges for extras are really fair. Finally, check whether you adequately communicate your pricing policy to your customers by asking yourself how many of them have ever been confused as to what was and wasn't included in your price. If even a small number have been, you obviously need to make some changes.

A store that solved an unusual price-completeness problem was Filene's, a fancy French store in San Francisco known for its expensive, beautiful handbags. A large portion of Filene's business involved sales to Japanese tourists and businesspeople.

For the first six months Filene's was open, many Japanese customers were annoyed by the addition of a sales tax to the price of their purchases. In Japan, all quoted prices are in round numbers, with the sales tax included. Filene's solved the problem by using the Japanese method of prefiguring tax into the final price rather than adding it on, and only had to explain to its non-Japanese customers that the price includes sales tax. These customers were delighted, because the total price was less than they thought. Interesting problem. Interesting solution.

C. Giving Customers Reasonable Control Over the Price

If a customer has to buy too much, too often or in inconvenient units to get a good price, your pricing policies simply do not engender trust. Customers should have as much choice as you can give them over the final price or the amount of goods or services they want to buy.

Good examples of businesses that provide customers with a high level of control over pricing include:

- A car repair garage that phones the customer before installing an unexpectedly high-priced replacement part.
- A hardware store that sells nails by weight as well as by the bag.
- A laundromat that has washers and dryers in several different sizes so that a customer with a small load doesn't have to pay for a large one.
- A printer who tells the customer that preparing a page layout that can be put on a larger press will mean a lower unit cost.
- A bike repair shop that takes the time to show customers how to make their own routine repairs.
- A natural foods store that gives customers credit for recycling peanut-butter tubs.
- A lawyer who encourages people with a self-help bent to do a portion

of their own work on routine matters and discounts the fee accordingly.

- A picture framing shop that has a facility for customers to do their own framing at a reduced rate.

Your pricing goal should be to give your customers maximum choice of sizes, amounts, hours of time purchased and so on—consistent, of course, with the sensible operation of your business. For example, if someone asks for plain ice cream rather than the "Strawberry Delight" you have on the menu, you may make a loyal customer if you not only serve the ice cream without the fruit sauce, but also subtract an appropriate amount from the bill.

A good example of a business that offers flexible pricing is Sonoma Compost in Petaluma, California, which provides premium quality compost and mulches made from recycled organics. It has a very clear written pricing policy and offers a wide variety of mulch. The customer has complete control over the pricing and can order as little as 1 to 2,000 yards, with generous discounts for the larger amounts. Sonoma Compost is located at the county landfill and "recycle town." As a bonus to its customers, if you bring your trash or recyclables in you get a 50% discount on up to five yards of screened organic compost on that day. This "bring a load . . . take a load" offer is very popular.

Bad examples of pricing situations in which the customer is treated with little respect include:

- Lunchmeat packaged only in large amounts.
- Undertakers who promote super-fancy, overpriced caskets and keep the reasonably priced ones out of sight, and when asked for the "plain pine box" wrinkle up their noses and attempt to make customers feel cheap and uncaring.
- Service businesses and professionals who bill a half-hour for a five-minute phone call without making this incremental billing policy clear to clients before the fact.

SONOMA COMPOST PRICE LIST

SONOMA MULCH		SONOMA COMPOST	
QUANTITY	SCREENED MULCH	QUANTITY	SCREENED COMPOST
1-12 Yds.	$8.00 Cubic Yard	1-12 Yds.	$12.00 Cubic Yard
13-24 Yds.	$7.00 Cubic Yard	13-24 Yds.	$10.50 Cubic Yard
25-100 Yds.	$6.00 Cubic Yard	25-100 Yds.	$ 9.00 Cubic Yard
101-500 Yds.	$5.00 Cubic Yard	101-500 Yds.	$ 7.50 Cubic Yard
500 - 2000 Yds.*	$4.00 Cubic Yard	500 - 2000 Yds.*	$ 6.00 Cubic Yard
SONOMA EARLY MULCH		SONOMA PATH MULCH	
QUANTITY	YOUNG COMPOST	QUANTITY	RECYCLED WOOD CHIPS
1-12 Yds.	$5.00 Cubic Yard	1-12 Yds.	$11.00 Cubic Yard
13-24 Yds.	$4.50 Cubic Yard	13-24 Yds.	$10.50 Cubic Yard
25-100 Yds.	$4.00 Cubic Yard	25-100 Yds.	$10.00 Cubic Yard
101-500 Yds.	$3.50 Cubic Yard	101-500 Yds.	$ 9.50 Cubic Yard
500 - 2000 Yds.*	$3.00 Cubic Yard	500 - 2000 Yds.*	$ 9.00 Cubic Yard

- Appliance repair businesses that charge an arm and a leg to come and check out a problem, even though you have already accurately diagnosed it.

- A car rental company that, instead of prorating by the hour, charges for an extra day when you keep a car an hour or two too long.

A Different Pricing Mechanism: Online Auctions

The Internet has provided the opportunity for individuals to be sellers in a large market, particularly with the growth of online auctions. In the last few years, auction sites have become enormously popular as garage sales and flea markets have migrated online. Besides allowing sellers and buyers to bargain over prices, selling items by auction also offers entertainment value. Case in point is eBay, a lively online auction that has succeeded in large part because it has figured out how to form an online community.

For small businesses, auctions can be an opportunity to obtain publicity for their products and services. By auctioning off a few examples of their product or service online, the business can not only generate sales but gain exposure. This strategy is not new; it has been common since the mid 1970s for businesses to donate products and services to be auctioned at charitable events. Such price-entertainment activity can be useful publicity.

One caution is worth considering. In the 1990s the term "commodity" came into use with a specific meaning: a product or service that is so standardized in quality and performance that it can be industrially produced and replicated. The word has a negative connotation because it means that the lowest cost producer will be the most successful in a business dealing with a commodity. You can unintentionally make your product or service appear to be a "commodity" by offering too many samples in auctions. If your product or service does become perceived as a commodity, you will be faced with other entrants in the market who will aim for the lowest cost of production.

D. Internet Pricing

If you're in the business of selling information, particularly over the Internet, your pricing strategy needs an additional consideration. Perhaps the biggest impact of the electronic revolution on media businesses is the fact that information can now be efficiently packaged and delivered to customers in entirely new ways. One of the most popular developments has been to deliver smaller packages of information, such as individual articles from *The New York Times* or single tracks from popular CDs. Besides developing a system for distributing small information packages (many ingenious systems continue to be introduced by pioneering online businesses), you'll need to figure out how much to charge for them, and how to collect payments efficiently.

One example of an information package tailored to the Internet infrastructure is found at Nolo.com's website. Nolo offers downloadable WebForms which address a particular need such as buying a car or executing a promissory note. For example, one form allows the user to appoint a temporary guardian for their minor child who's traveling abroad with someone other than the parent. The customer provides the information online, and the document is instantly generated and available to download, all for a price much lower than buying a whole book. Nolo also sells downloadable eGuides which contain focused information about specific legal problems for users who simply want to answer a particular question, rather than to buy a whole book. Like Nolo's WebForms, the eGuides are considerably less expensive than books.

One piece of the puzzle that's still being worked out is how to efficiently collect micro-payments online. Due to credit card transaction fees, it's generally not profitable to conduct individual transactions for anything less than $5 or so. Several companies have been working on payment systems to overcome this problem; at the moment, the most successful appears to be PayPal (www.paypal.com), in which users set up a PayPal account connected to an online bank. As payment methods on the Internet improve, people will become more comfortable paying twenty-five cents for just one article, photo or graphic; fifty cents for a favorite song or $2.00 per month for a service that reminds them of birthdays, events and personalized news. As online customers increasingly expect to be able to purchase just what they want and nothing more, it's important for online media purveyors to remember to break down your product or service into smaller packages and price them accordingly.

Evaluating Your Pricing Policy

YES NO

☐ ☐   Some customers complain about prices.

☐ ☐   Some of the trivial but necessary things I offer with my basic product or service (for example, keys, base stands, containers, refills, etc.) are priced at an amount that is more than people expect.

☐ ☐   My product or service is offered in enough different measures that by and large my customers can buy what they need.

☐ ☐   My product(s) can be bought in more than one unit of measure (bunches, pounds, bags, lugs, liters, cartons, gross, boxes).

☐ ☐   My services can be bought in time increments convenient to my customers (days, half-days, hours, minutes, etc.).

☐ ☐   My pricing practices are written down on: (flyer, price sheet, website, the wall).

☐ ☐   Any exceptions from my standard pricing practices are well explained (for example, senior citizen discounts are stated on a sign with large type).

I estimate that approximately _____% of my customers pay for more of my product or service than they really need or want, because:

_____

_____

I estimate that approximately _____% don't buy all of my product or service that they really need because:

_____

_____

My volume discounts are:

_____

_____

My volume discounts are available to:

_____

_____

Chapter 5

The Treatment of People Around You

*T*he way you treat employees, suppliers and friends is an important element in gaining and keeping the trust of your customers. In fact, it is not an exaggeration to say that positive relations with all of them is one of the invisible foundations of any successful business. Why? Because how you relate to these people is routinely communicated to your customers and potential customers.

A. Tracking Reputations via the Grapevine

Assume you live in Kansas City, Missouri, and a friend tells you about Joe Green, a skilled bootmaker, who specializes in just the type of custom-made boots you want. Aside from Joe's name and occupation, you know nothing about him. A few days later, when you decide to call Joe, you find you can't get his number from your friend because she's left on an extended vacation.

You consider giving up the hunt, but then, looking at your old battered boots, you wonder if you can find Joe yourself. But no Joe Green is listed in the phone book. You decide to persevere and ask friends and acquaintances if they know Joe. No luck. Your next step is to ask them to check with their friends who might know him. Believe it or not, at this point there is an excellent statistical chance that you will locate Joe. One of your friends is

quite likely to have a friend who either knows Joe or knows someone who does.

Think of it this way. If you have 400 friends and acquaintances (although this sounds like a lot, if you include old school chums, business associates and casual social acquaintances, you probably know lots more than that), and each of them also has 400, you have an immediate friendship network of 160,000 people. (There will probably be some overlap between your friends and your friends' friends, but just the same, the numbers are impressive.) These 160,000 friends of your friends are linked in the same way to 64 million people, or about one-third of the adult population in the United States.

You can try a similar experiment yourself. Randomly pick the name of any businessperson in the Yellow Pages of another city. Next, ask any friends who live or do business in that city if they know anyone in that or a related business. If they do, call that person and ask about the person whose name you picked. Chances are that if they don't know the person you are looking for, they can refer you to someone who can. If there is either very good or very bad news about this person's business, you're even more likely to find him.

The point of these exercises is not to teach you to run your own detective agency, but to illustrate that even in our large and complex society, we are still amazingly connected to each other, especially when we run a business that affects the lives of other people. It follows that it doesn't take long for an interested party to learn a lot about us from those we deal with regularly. If you mistreat your employees or suppliers, they'll spread the bad news. Similarly, if you go out of your way to treat these people well, the good word spreads. Sometimes this interconnectedness is hard to believe, because just about all small business owners feel pretty isolated at times. And it's true that the word about your business (good or bad) may be dormant for a while, but when someone does inquire about your business reputation, it will wake up and promptly continue its journey from person to person.

Rasberry was at the local Hospice Thrift Store one rainy afternoon and the popular store was filled with shoppers. A young woman lugged a vacuum to the checkout stand and the person next to her commented, "You don't want that vacuum." She preceded to tell a horror story of her motor conking out in the same model after only two months of use, and that when she read the small print in the warranty it excluded the motor. Other customers starting putting in their two cents worth, and at the end of ten minutes the thrift store put the vacuum in the trash out back.

James, a well-known author, had worked on a book for over six years and in the process interviewed several hundred people. A publisher was mentioned to him by several people as being "just perfect" for this book. Having published many books in the past, he could pretty much choose his publisher but decided to give this one a try. Imagine his dismay when

his manuscript was returned after three days with the most perfunctory two-sentence rejection form letter. The pages of his manuscript appeared to have been untouched and they forgot to take out his cover letter. Needless to say an outraged James has told everyone this story, including other authors.

How often have you been asked if another business pays its bills to suppliers on time? We know dozens of smaller companies that are reported to have poor employment practices, slow or erratic payments to suppliers and bad records when it comes to dealing with independent contractors. These poor business practices are not an infrequent conversation topic among businesspeople at trade fairs, coffee shops or over lunch, and for good reason; most small business owners can't afford to deal with people who don't pay their bills on time or who otherwise treat them badly.

B. How Employees Spread the Word

One of the easiest ways for anyone to learn about how you run your business is by talking to your employees. Because your employees' lives are so intertwined with yours, and because you affect them so directly, your treatment of them will almost automatically be communicated to their friends and family, even if inadvertently. And remember, because your employees spend more time with you than anyone outside of their immediate family, they know about you and your business in a way few others ever can.

How you run your business may be reported indirectly when employees make such statements as:

- "I'm exhausted; the inventory is such a mess that I had to work late last night."
- "I don't know when I'll get a vacation; no one has made an entry in the general ledger in three months."
- "Don't phone this week; everyone's nerves are on edge. Two people quit a few weeks ago, and we are trying to do their work as well as our own, and it looks like the boss isn't going to replace them."
- "The boss poor-mouths all the time, but he's always getting twenties out of the cash box."
- "I have to hold my paycheck for a day because there isn't enough money in the bank to cover it."

If you have any doubt about how fast word of your treatment of employees is passed along, consider these examples:

- Many American Jews, as late as the 1950s, avoided one major brand of gasoline because of their belief that the company had an anti-Jewish employment policy in the 1930s.
- TWA was one of the first major airlines to hire black pilots. Years after other airlines had also broken the color barrier, many black Americans still went out of their way to patronize TWA.

- Whole Foods operates with a wide-open financial system. Sensitive figures on store sales, team sales, profit margins, even salaries, are available to employees in every location. The company shares so much information so widely that the SEC has designated all 6,500 employees "insiders" for stock-trading purposes.

To return to our Coors beer example from Chapter 1, in an amazing series of public statements, the Golden, Colorado, company so alienated many of its Chicano employees that their union led a boycott against the company.

Syndicated business columnist Milton Moskowitz, along with co-authors Robert Levering and Michael Katz, responded to the concern so many Americans feel about the quality of the companies they work for by writing a best-selling book. In *The 100 Best Companies to Work For in America* (Doubleday, 1993), the authors describe the practices of 100 American companies in detail. Working conditions, pay, benefits, firing and promotions policies and all sorts of other information of importance to employees are discussed.

How did the authors get all their "inside" information? While the task was time-consuming, it wasn't as difficult as it might seem. The reputations of businesses, even those with only a few hundred employees, such as Celestial Seasonings and Odetics (both of which were included in the 100 best list) are really quite well known.

Not only do employees know a lot about their own employers, they know a great deal about the employment practices of others in their line of business. For example, Moskovitz, Levering and Katz learned that companies with outstanding reputations in promoting blacks (Cummings Engine, Levi Strauss and Polaroid) and women (Hallmark Cards, Federal Express and Nordstrom) were widely known and respected for their practices. The same was true for companies with policies that encouraged employees to study for advanced degrees (Bell Labs), companies where retirement policies are outstanding (Johnson Wax), and even companies that have great parties (Advanced Micro Devices) or employee gardens (Control Data).

Cody's Bookstore: "Finding Good People and Keeping Them"

Cody's Bookstore in Berkeley, California, is as much an institution as the university in whose shadow it sits. Its fame for diversity and completeness of stock is rivaled only by the reputation for erudition and expertise its employees enjoy.

The bookstore trade has traditionally been noted for low-paying salaries. The work is desirable, and employees are often viewed as an "easy come, easy go" proposition. This causes high turnover, low morale and a perpetually inexperienced staff. Anti-traditionalist Andy Ross, owner of Cody's, is a believer in paying as high a wage as possible and treating his employees as his most valuable resource. He even did several surveys to make sure that his wages are high relative to other bookstores. And this kind of care for employees pays off in healthy sales, high employee morale and customer loyalty.

At a time when many small bookstores are going out of business due to the so-called "superstores," Cody's continues to grow. Ross's perspective is that "bookselling at its best is not just a job. Independent booksellers bring their own unique sensibilities rooted in the communities they serve which includes treating employees fairly."

Ross is pleased that his 60 employees elected to join a union, because "it keeps management more professional and consistent in our treatment of employees." He thinks that encouraging good, experienced staff to stay by paying a decent wage is money very well spent. "In a bookstore with over 140,000 titles," he says, "new employees just aren't very valuable. Finding good people and keeping them is the key to a store's success." In keeping with this theory, Cody's employees receive, besides a relatively high salary, a profit-sharing plan in the form of a healthy annual bonus based on merit (judged by Ross and the five employee managers) as well as the store's profits.

Another way Ross has found to maintain good employee relations is to encourage their participation in the store's operations by delegating responsibility while trying not to look over too many shoulders. "Besides the fact that employees come up with great ideas, their morale is an important ingredient for the business to run right—a factor that is often overlooked in the bookstore business," he says.

In a small business, the payment of wages and benefits takes on particular importance. Employees need to feel they are being treated fairly. An open book policy in which everyone knows what everyone else makes, from the boss to the teenaged delivery boy, is an excellent idea, especially when the business genuinely tries to pay people fairly. (See the discussion of "openness" in Chapter 6.)

We all know of companies (big and small) where most of the employees scrape by on minimum wage while the owner keeps the amount of his own pay and benefits a secret, plays golf twice a week during business hours and drives a Mercedes to work. This kind of behavior almost always results in low employee morale and gives pause to customers. Customers will consciously or unconsciously ask themselves whether the fact that the employees are treated unfairly means that when push comes to shove, their concerns will also be held hostage to the owner's needs. On a more positive note, we know of more than one small business owner who regularly checks on wages paid by similar businesses in their community and then pays at least slightly more, even if they have to cut their own income to do it. They reason correctly that their employees will be proud of the fact that they are valued highly and as a result will not only work harder but spread the good word.

Malden Mills, in Massachusetts, produces Polartec®, a fabric made from recycled plastic bottles. It is an exemplary company known to be a trend-setter in employee/employer relations and to have an incredibly high rate of employee productivity. Aaron Feuerstein, the owner, a spry man of 70-something who quotes Shakespeare, is dedicated to improving the earth's environment and pays his employees well. Some years ago there was a big fire at the mill, and business was shut down. Feuerstein informed his worried employees that their wages and salaries would be paid through the period of reconstruction. Needless to say, his employees love their boss, and the mill was up and running within the month. The feelings of the employees toward Feuerstein, the mill and the product is demonstrated through high productivity, love of the company mission and incredible loyalty.

Job Applicants Deserve Good Treatment, Too

Don't forget to extend good practices to your hiring process. Unfortunately, when it comes to interviewing prospective employees, many companies don't pay much attention to people's feelings. They forget that each applicant will learn enough about their business to form an opinion and spread it. Pay attention to this in the light of its effects on personal recommendations. For example, one small electronics manufacturing company we know gives a nice sample as a gift to everyone applying for a job. This helps cushion the fact that, inevitably, a majority of those interviewed are not offered a job. Another very effective approach is used by a printer we know, who shows job applicants examples of his monotypeset work and then gives them a gift of a hand-pulled page done by a famous typographer. Other creative businesspeople develop similar techniques to be sure the people they consider for a job have a good interview experience.

These gestures make a great deal of sense for two reasons. First, they acquaint others in a personal way with your business and let them know you care about people. Second, a large proportion of the people interviewed may find work in your field, and you are very likely to have to deal with them in the future.

Use the same concerned approach with occasional and part-time workers, freelancers and others who come into contact with your business on an occasional basis.

C. Common Employee Complaints

The most common areas of employee complaint are unequal treatment, arbitrariness of management and exploitation. Let's examine the causes of each of these briefly, and look at some suggestions that should help avoid, or at least ameliorate, problems.

1. Unequal Treatment

An unequal treatment complaint is a synonym for any differences in pay, work rules, expense accounts, job opportunities and perks that an employee doesn't understand or accept. The best medicine to both cure and prevent the recurrence of this nasty infection of your workplace is to embrace a system of open books and an open management style, complete with well-defined personnel policies and frequent performance reviews. And keep in mind that, legally, company policies on vacation, sick leave, promotions and other important matters must be applied in a nondiscriminatory manner.

2. Arbitrariness of Management

A complaint that management is arbitrary stems from much the same problems, but also usually signals that important business policies are being developed in secrecy, so that employees don't know what the business is doing and why.

One good example is a public relations firm whose top management decided to drop one client, whom their financial records showed was unprofitable, and put extra energy into another one which was more profitable. Unfortunately, the information was secret and the decision was never explained to the rest of the staff. The company dropped by the P.R. firm was in the recreation business and was respected by the staff for a number of good policies, while the one that got the extra attention was in a business that several employees of the P.R. firm didn't respect. Because the reasons for the decision were never explained or discussed, several employees quit.

An open management style, involving employees in decision-making to the maximum extent possible, is the best way to prevent this sort of complaint from developing in the first place and curing it if it does (see Chapter 6).

3. Exploitation

In the small business world, complaints that management is exploitive usually point to an atmosphere in which financial data is kept secret and there is a perception that some employees (often the owners) get a disproportionate share of the financial returns. This sort of complaint also commonly occurs when employees observe customers and suppliers complaining about the treatment they receive from management with no apparent redress or explanation from the company. You'll often hear this kind of complaint in businesses where it is routine to use highly competitive language like:

- "No matter what else you do, you have to win."
- "A lot of people are out to screw you; the only way to handle that is to screw them first."
- "As long as the bottom line is healthy, there is nothing to worry about."
- "What they don't know won't hurt them."
- "If we didn't do it, someone else would."

Again, the best methods of prevention and cure for employee feelings of exploitation include a commitment to open financial records and an effort to compensate employees fairly.

One company that successfully follows these practices operates a resort/conference facility near Tucson, Arizona. When it began, the company took over and remodeled an old and respected hotel. The existing staff was initially careless and did not respond to the new management group. Finally, the resort manager, with the approval of the owners, posted the monthly financial report in the kitchen area, where employees could see it. Not one employee asked any questions for almost two months. Finally, at a newly organized bimonthly staff meeting, one of the oldest workers asked why the figures showed the business was losing money and expressed concern that the business could not survive the coming months. The key financial issues were discussed, and the concerns of management that sloppy staff performance was contributing to the problem were aired and fully understood by every employee. Morale changed overnight. Worker productivity improved so much it amazed even the workers themselves. The outcome was visible in the quality of upkeep of the grounds, the dining room service, and particularly in the behavior of the front desk staff. Before long the figures posted on the kitchen wall showed a healthy profit.

The Employer's Legal Handbook, by Fred Steingold (Nolo), explains your legal responsibilities as an employer, including your duty to treat employees in a fair, nondiscriminatory manner.

D. Handling Employee Complaints

How you handle employee complaints is central to how your business is viewed by employees and ultimately the public, which hears about how you treat them. Creating a positive way to encourage and deal with complaints is a sign to your employees that you care about them and that they are appreciated. Again, the idea is simple. If employees truly feel that their concerns are taken seriously, they will walk an extra mile (or maybe even ten) for your business because they will regard it as their business too.

Perhaps the best example of the value of a procedure for handling employee complaints is a company with one of the worst records: the United States Postal Service (USPS), a semi-private organization that was partially separated from the U.S. government in the late 1960s. Because the USPS was originally a government bureaucracy it retained a rigid structure that was inappropriate for the type of employee relations that prevails in the commercial market. The consequence became evident in the late 1980s and well into the 1990s when several USPS employees killed their supervisors and other employees in the workplace. The American public became greatly alarmed as the horrors of workplace homicide spread to other industries. During this time the phrase "going postal" was commonly used to mean workplace homicide. TV comedians suggested that when a flag flew at half mast over a Post Office this was a sign that it was hiring new personnel.

All of this changed when the USPS introduced employee mediation services in the late 1990s. Throughout the United States, in hundreds of cases per week, postal employees are offered free mediation services, with paid time off to mediate all disputes and disagreements with managers, supervisors and fellow employees. The consequences have been very positive and as the success becomes recognized, similar commercial enterprises have copied the Postal Service.

In most small businesses, there is an informal complaint structure. An employee who doesn't like something tells the boss or a supervisor face-to-face. This process is generally workable as long as the problems are minor and the business small. However, when a business employs more than five or six people, a formal process, including personnel reviews, makes it easier to deal with a wide array of problems that are not so minor.

Even in very small businesses, a formal employee grievance process should be written, posted and given to each employee to sign. The grievance procedure should specify where and how to complain about all types of potential problems. It should discuss in detail how the complaint will be investigated and, if necessary, be formally considered and resolved.

Finally, a tight procedure to keep complaints confidential is obviously a crucial part of any formal complaint procedure. In the best circumstances, an employee complaint process should also include an appeals process for serious matters where management's judgment may warrant a second opinion.

If you don't have a good grievance procedure, an employee who feels there is no internal structure to deal with a problem about termination, demotion or salary may seek help outside the business. This can often mean either that employees will sue you, or try to organize a union. For example, we know a small wholesale business which recently—unilaterally and without consultation—changed a series of employee rights and benefits. In the view of management, the benefits conferred on the employees by the change were much greater than what the employees lost in perks. So when the employees turned to the Teamsters Union, management was initially both flabbergasted and angry. It never occurred to them that the employees, suddenly facing a whole new set of work rules, some of which they thought were very unfair (for example, loss of pay for lunch hour), went outside the company for help because there was no fair grievance and appeal procedure or, for that matter, any process that allowed them to communicate their position to management.

Sample Employee Grievance Procedure

Here is material excerpted from the formal grievance procedure of a 20-person software development company. It isn't a complete grievance plan, but illustrates some of the issues that should be covered.

Grievances concerning personnel reviews: The person with a grievance is to write a letter to the chair of the grievance committee requesting a hearing time and date. The chair will hear the matter, put comments in writing for the employee personnel file and take whatever actions are necessary in the matter. No further appeals are provided. If the chair of the grievance committee is a direct supervisor of a party involved, the latter shall be sent to a company lawyer who is the alternative chairperson.

Grievance concerning salary, benefits or office working conditions: Same as above except that the grievance committee chair shall include in the deliberations the company president and another employee chosen by the person filing the grievance. There is no appeal for final decisions of this group.

Grievances concerning ethical behavior of employees or management concerning termination of employment, matters of illegality, public issues, discrimination: The procedures shall be the same as above, except that the full grievance committee shall be called. The person filing the grievance letter can specify individuals to be excluded from the committee where their presence would directly bear on the grievance matter. Appeal on the decision of the committee can be filed with the Chairperson of the Board, within two weeks of the final decision of the grievance committee, and the Board shall as a whole make a final decision at its earliest convenience.

All personnel involved in the grievance process are expected to maintain confidentiality when requested.

E. Finding Out What Employees Are Thinking

One good way to find out what your employees think about you and the practice of your business is to ask. If you have only a few employees, you may want to talk to each individually or have a series of meetings, taking care to establish an environment of trust so that your employees will feel confident in saying negative as well as positive things.

If your business is larger, you may want to rely, at least to some extent, on a written questionnaire. Here is a sample which you can adapt to your needs. Give it to employees and allow anonymous responses.

Employee Questionnaire

	POOR	ADEQUATE	EXCELLENT
The working conditions here are generally…	☐	☐	☐
The working conditions, compared to other jobs I've had, are…	☐	☐	☐
Handling of serious employee problems that are brought to managers is…	☐	☐	☐
When most employees describe the business management they say…	☐	☐	☐

I know the established policy for handling employee problems and grievances.

☐ YES ☐ NO ☐ THERE ISN'T ONE   It is…   ☐ ☐ ☐

I know the established policy for handling employee wage disputes.

☐ YES ☐ NO ☐ THERE ISN'T ONE   It is…   ☐ ☐ ☐

I know the established policy for handling conflicts between employees.

☐ YES ☐ NO ☐ THERE ISN'T ONE   It is…   ☐ ☐ ☐

When someone is fired most fellow workers know the circumstances
in which the employee can appeal the decision within the company.

☐ YES ☐ NO ☐ THERE ISN'T ONE   The appeal process is…   ☐ ☐ ☐

	YES	NO
I am paid fairly.	☐	☐
I know what others are paid.	☐	☐
Most employees know their jobs.	☐	☐
Most employees understand the direction, policies and goals of the business.	☐	☐

Comments and suggestions for improving working conditions:

_____

_____

_____

_____

F. Suppliers

It has long been remarked that the tallest buildings in a society reflect its central concerns. Only a century ago, church spires defined the skyline. They were replaced by the buildings of major industrial concerns. Today, bank buildings, insurance companies and office towers filled with investment companies and law firms dominate the rest. A focus of all these businesses is credit and credit-worthiness.

As a nation we have been taught to trust the integrity of these giant financial enterprises because of their track records. However, some of these institutions, such as savings and loans, have proved themselves unworthy of trust. A number of huge but financially troubled banks have been sold to other huge banks to avoid failure. It may not be too soon to wonder what institutions will replace the banks on the top floor of urban America.

When it comes to small businesses, people are judged more on how they treat their creditors than on how big their headquarters is. Having a good record in paying bills is insurance against negative stories being circulated about your small business. Having an extra-good record can be a positive marketing tool that can work to improve your business when the people you deal with spread the positive word, as they inevitably will.

Every business has suppliers. They vary greatly depending on the business, but almost everyone must deal with lawyers, accountants, bankers, maintenance people, office supply stores and a variety of neighborhood businesses. Those of you in retail, wholesale or restaurant businesses must relate to many more.

From the marketing vantage point, suppliers can be seen as similar to family members who share the same house. Your actions have immediate and important effects on each other. When at home a child leaves the cap off the toothpaste, the next person must deal with the dried-up glob on the end of the tube. Similarly, your failure to pay a printing bill on time means your printer may have to deal with the nasty mess of not having enough money to pay his bills.

Both at home and in the business community, how you handle problems is quickly noticed by others. At home, if you yell and scream and make the erring child feel miserable, chances are she will act out her resentment in some way. The same is true when problems develop in business. If you make little or no effort to view problems from your suppliers' point of view, you have no right to be surprised if your relationships with them deteriorate. The surprising thing is that people so often ignore their suppliers' needs—in spite of the fact that even a modest effort to communicate about your business difficulty will go a long way towards solving it.

The worst mistake a small business owner or manager can make is to ignore the fact that many of your primary business concerns are, at bottom, the same as those of the businesses you deal with. This is particularly true when it comes to taking in enough money to meet payroll on time, pay off bank loans and generally fulfill financial obligations. Far too often, small businesspeople become so manic about making their accounts balance at the end of the month that they forget that their suppliers have the same needs, that their accounts payable are someone else's accounts receivable.

Think of it this way: When it comes to economic survival, businesses, especially small ones, are like links in a fence. If one business doesn't fulfill its obligations, the fence is weakened. If a large number don't, the fence collapses. For this reason, every small business owner knows which accounts pay promptly, carefully and considerately. Surely, in your business, even small accounts take on disproportionate prominence if they pay you slowly and always make excuses. By the same token, you can safely assume that, though you may be only a small account to someone else, they know very well how you treat them. The criteria they use in judging you are the same ones you use: how promptly you pay, and how honest and forthcoming you are in explaining the reasons for any delays.

How does all of this directly affect marketing? Let's consider the book business. Small publishers, of which there are literally tens of thousands, often pay the printer late. Part of the reason for this is that many of these publishers depend on sales from the first few thousand copies of a new title to pay the printing bill. Given this somewhat marginal financing scheme, it is not surprising that printers who deal with small publishers routinely keep tabs on how each is doing. They constantly tune into the book business grapevine to check on who is keeping up on their accounts payable and, more important, who isn't. It's amazing how quickly word gets around when someone begins to slip up. The reason that this word-of-mouth system works so well is that all sorts of people (bookstores, wholesalers, graphic artists, freelance editors and dozens of others) in addition to printers absolutely need to know that they are dealing with a solvent publishing house, and take the time to find out.

When even a modest amount of negative information about a particular publisher is spread, the results can be disastrous to that business. Part of the reason for this is that books (unlike most types of merchandise) are typically returnable by a bookstore to the publisher for at least a year after purchase—but obviously not if a publisher declares bankruptcy. If a bookstore, or worse, a large chain of stores, learns that a particular publisher is way behind in its bills, they are likely to make a special effort to quickly return all of that company's overstock, hoping there is still time to be reimbursed.

This sort of loss of trust can quickly snowball; we've seen it sink several publishing companies that might otherwise have been able to cope with their short-term financial problems. For example, the computer book field went from boom to bust between 1982 and 1984. Several small publishers failed and others teetered on the brink of insolvency as nervous bookstores quickly returned perfectly salable books to companies rumored to be in trouble. The bookstores sensibly feared that if they delayed and the books didn't sell, the publisher would be out of business.

Two revolutions have occurred in the book business that reflect the way that commerce and technology have responded to these supplier trust problems. The first was implemented by the pioneer of online book sales, Amazon.com, who established a fully automated online publisher accounting system. The system orders a small number of books to be kept in Amazon warehouses, and automatically reorders by e-mail as books sell. The system pays automatically every 60 days and the publisher can track the entire accounting online. The second innovation has been publishing-on-demand. Publishing-on-demand uses computer printing technology to print one book at a time. The publisher pays the printer for the set-up costs for a book, and then orders any number of books as the books sell. This has fit in perfectly for the niche markets of small publishers with small market books. Both of these revolutions occurred in response to the problems of supplier trust and credit.

Of course, most businesses face a cash flow problem at one time or another, and suppliers help finance these periods. There is nothing wrong with this as long as all concerned are honest and open with each other. Accordingly, whenever we give advice to small businesses with cash flow problems, we urge them to immediately notify their suppliers, by phone, about the problem, explain their plan to solve it, and ask for permission to delay or modify payments. We have never seen a reasonable request along these lines refused. Often, this sort of interaction actually improves relationships. We know of several instances in which the positive communications that developed during a crisis resulted in suppliers helping their customers finance their expansion once the crisis was past. In one instance, when the Japanese economy declined for five years in the early 1990s, an American company that sold pre-fab houses to the Japanese was encouraged by the cooperative Japanese distributor to shift the business in several directions, all of which resulted in new and rapid expansion when the Japanese economy finally picked up in 1996. In other instances, suppliers who were kept in the picture liked what they learned and actually invested in the business.

If you want to know how your suppliers feel about you, why not ask? Here is a questionnaire you may want to give to several of them.

Questionnaire for Suppliers

I have found in my dealing with _____

NAME OF YOUR BUSINESS

that you and your key employees are generally:

	POOR	ADEQUATE	EXCELLENT
Accessible when I need you…	☐	☐	☐
Reliable in your payments and financial projections…	☐	☐	☐
Polite in your general business dealings…	☐	☐	☐
Reliable in doing what you promise on time…	☐	☐	☐
Able to handle any problems with your product and services satisfactorily…	☐	☐	☐
Careful and neat when it comes to recordkeeping…	☐	☐	☐
Generally trustworthy in all dealings…	☐	☐	☐

Comments:

_____

_____

_____

_____

_____

_____

_____

_____

G. Business Friends and Acquaintances

There is a direct connection between a good small business marketing plan and how your friends think about and understand your business.

A friend is someone who is connected to you by mutual esteem, respect and affection. Acquaintances are people to whom you have been introduced and are socially free to speak with again by recalling an earlier encounter. This latter group includes, for example, school classmates, fellow employees, members of the same military unit and people you come into friendly contact with at trade meetings, conventions and continuing education courses.

Satisfied customers have some of the qualities of friends. In at least one important way they share values with you, since you both view your business with esteem. However, because your relationship is probably limited by a business context, they are in most instances more like acquaintances. Certainly, like acquaintances, they have the right to approach you without a new introduction. They just call up or walk up and say, "You fixed my plumbing a few years ago and did a wonderful job. How've you been doing lately?" They even have the right to subject us to bad jokes. "You're the guy with the shade shop. I'm glad to see you hanging in there."

All of your friends, family and acquaintances should be involved in your marketing strategy because they have a predisposition, often a strong one, toward seeing your business prosper. Unfortunately, despite this predisposition, we often hear friends, or even business acquaintances, say something like this: "I don't really understand what you do or how your business as a public health research (or solar energy, land use, or waste disposal, etc.) consultant works." Or, "I know you distribute shoes (or books, candy, tape recorders or trees), but what that really means is a mystery to me."

The point should be clear: Friends can be extremely important in your effort to market your product effectively, but only if you give them a reasonable chance to help. How do you do this? By keeping your social network aware of your operation—your joys and disappointments as well as the nuts and bolts of how your business works. Sometimes months go by without talking with our friends about business. In order for friends to recommend us we have to make the effort to keep them current. It's worth the effort to periodically make a phone call or fax a poem or cartoon you think a friend would enjoy along with an update about any changes in your business. An added benefit is that it helps keep your friendship network healthy. When you e-mail business associates news about your business be sure to include your friends on the list. Friends will often let you know when you are going in the wrong direction, and will be there to listen and help put your problems in perspective.

Just as important, they will know enough to really appreciate your successes and celebrations. And, of course, they will actually help you sell your product or service.

For example, if you are a landscape architect and often lunch with the lawyer in the next office who shares your enthusiasm for soccer, don't forget to make her knowledgeable about the nitty-gritty of what you do, how you get business, how much you charge and so on. Sooner or later your lawyer friend will find herself in contact with someone who needs some landscaping done—perhaps a business which consults her about zoning problems connected with a new building. When this occurs, you want her to be able to mention your business confidently and knowledgeably. Be sure to remember to tell others that your business benefits from referrals and to show appreciation when they give you one by expressing thanks in person or by sending a note, flowers, a gift certificate or whatever is appropriate.

The opinion your business peers have of you is also very important to your business. Being in contact with people in your field is one of the best ways of learning about new products and innovations that may be directly useful to you. In addition, consulting people in your peer group network is one of the common ways potential customers check out your business as part of deciding whether or not to patronize you. For some businesses (for example, a new pediatrician or chiropractor in town), it may be difficult to create good personal recommendations without a strong friendship and peer group network. For others (say a drain cleaning service or a butcher shop), the good opinion of friends may not be so crucial as is listing the availability of your service in all the right places, but it is still helpful.

Even a dentist, however, can do a great deal to establish a good friendship network in a hurry. One extremely kind and good-hearted dentist we know did just this by following his best instincts. New to a strange town, with few friends and very limited resources, he spent every spare moment visiting old people's homes and fixing the teeth of the indigent residents free. After a few months, when it was apparent that he was sincere, some of the people who worked at the convalescent homes began to call him for appointments and refer their friends. The local dental society was so proud of his work that established dentists began to refer their overflow. Within a couple of years, our public-spirited friend had enough patients that he was able to buy the old Mercedes he had always coveted. To his credit, however, he still drives it over to one or another of the old people's homes a couple of afternoons a month and fixes teeth for free.

La Blue's Cleaners in Sebastopol, California, has been in business for more than 40 years. In addition to providing pick-up and delivery service to homes and offices, they are known in the community for extending a hand to the temporarily unemployed. If you are out of work they will custom dry-clean and press one suit or one dress and launder two shirts or blouses at no charge. This information is posted on a sign inside the store which says "This is our gift to you so you will look your best at your next job interview." Customers really appreciate it, and you can be sure that when they are back among the employed they bring their business to La Blue's.

H. Individuals Who Spread Negative Word of Mouth About Your Business

Most of us want to be liked, if not considered perfect or adorable. However, unless you are a very rare person indeed, you probably have at least a person or two buried somewhere in your network of personal relationships who consider you the first cousin to a scorpion. It's important to have a strategy for dealing with those few misguided souls who have chosen you or your business for their hostility. This is important, of course, because negative word of mouth about a business, especially when someone goes out of his way to spread the bad word, can have truly bad long-term consequences to your business.

Here are two strategies that often work well:

First, emphasize the positive attributes of the person who dislikes you whenever possible. When you emphasize the positive attributes of someone who is hostile

to you, you usually decrease the effect of her malice. You also let others know that you are objective about the problems in your relationships. Finally, your efforts to be more than fair will probably get back to the person and may cause her to treat you more fairly in turn.

Second, mediate or arbitrate your differences with this person, if it's appropriate. Mediation is a process in which arguing parties select someone who helps them reach their own agreement. In arbitration, the parties agree in advance to let someone else make the final decision. Both techniques are good ways to avoid long-term hostility and the negative word of mouth that flows from it. And when a business openly promotes these alternative dispute resolution techniques in an honest effort to resolve differences without initiating a formal court action, it gains a reputation for honesty and fairness.

Even if the person who dislikes you won't try to resolve a dispute through mediation or arbitration, at least others affected by the dispute will know you have done your best. It takes a thick-skinned individual to resist the pressure of his peers to work things out.

Despite this good advice, many people find it hard to admit some people feel negatively about them. A four-year-old friend, Joshua, has a philosophy that may be helpful in encouraging you to do this exercise. One day Joshua came home from pre-school and told his parents about a kid who had called him a series of truly ugly names. The parents, who were themselves somewhat upset, were surprised when Joshua indicated very little concern. When the parents questioned him about his feelings, Joshua replied, "He just needed someone to pick on. He really doesn't know me."

We also like the approach of Virginia Simons, an independent paralegal in Bakersfield, California, who has had a lot of experience dealing with attacks from bar associations. She was sued by a bankruptcy trustee in federal court, charged with practicing law without a license because she had helped customers prepare their own bankruptcy forms. She told each of her customers what was going on and that the suit was being brought in a effort to put her out of business, not because of incompetence on her part. Several of her colleagues, who were also targeted by the local bar, joined forces with Simons. They got their clients to sign petitions on their behalf. They went to bankruptcy court when it was in session and took notes as to any unequal treatment given to non-lawyers representing themselves. Twenty-five people from all over California showed up in court to support them, and they won their case.

Instead of gloating or spreading negative word of mouth about the bar association, they decided to open up the lines of communication with their opponents and convince individual lawyers that many people couldn't afford them and needed the services of paralegals. They contacted the District Attorney and judges in their county and even the lawyers who had sued them. Simons and her colleagues invited one of the lawyers to the local meetings of the California Association of Independent Paralegals. They had him to lunch. They invited him to speak at their meetings. He invited them to speak to a bar association lunch. They told him that if he thought they were doing a bad job that they were open to having him teach them to do better. The District Attorney's office is now a member of their advisory committee.

I. Your Behavior in Public

Two people were sitting behind us on an airplane talking about a client in very negative terms. The conversation was so vitriolic that our ears perked up. When they mentioned the name of the client and the name of their own firm (a national accounting organization), we were shocked. It didn't speak very well of their own company to be so negative about a client in a public place, and some of the mud they were slinging stuck to their company.

A far more blatant example of how important our public behavior can be to our business success occurred during a San Francisco restaurant strike, when a psychotherapist punched a picketer. A prominent newspaper columnist picked up the item. It certainly wasn't good for his word of mouth in the psychotherapy business.

It's often difficult to think of ourselves in a public sense, always being a representative of our business; to know that our language, appearance and personal dealings shape our customers' attitudes. But it's true, from small town America to the largest city.

A businessperson must always be "on," to a certain extent. For example, if when making copies at the local self-serve copy shop, you lose 50 cents in the coin slot and respond by beating up the offending machine, anyone present who recognizes you will probably view you as a highly volatile person. (This, of course, is unfortunate, we hasten to add, because kicking a machine that has done you wrong can sometimes feel very good.) In the back of their mind they may hold this image of you for a long time, and it may shape their future dealings with you. ■

Chapter 6

Openness: The Basis of Trust

*O*penness in business is definitely not a strategy taught in business school. Sadly, the currently prevailing view is that it's best to "play your cards close to your chest" about almost everything from the way a product is made or a service delivered to profits to pay scales to who qualifies for what business perks. This is a serious mistake. Openness builds customer trust, which, as you should know by now, is the prime requisite of any marketing without advertising campaign.

If you doubt that openness leads to trust, consider the public sector. These days we require public officials to report their campaign finances and top officers in publicly held corporations to report their salaries and stock transactions. Similarly, nonprofit organizations that receive tax subsidies must file a public financial statement; and even private corporations that seek to raise funds in the financial markets must publish much of their financial data and supply the Securities and Exchange Commission with even more. In short, openness in financial dealings is fast becoming a fundamental legal requirement in all sorts of contexts.

Despite this powerful trend, and despite the fact that openness obviously contributes to building customer trust, many small businesspeople still try to hide as much as they can about their financial and operating affairs. This is a miserable policy, especially from a marketing perspective. Nothing destroys trust as fast as an atmosphere of secrecy. On the other hand, a business that is obviously open with its customers is so refreshing that this policy itself stimulates positive recommendations.

Promoting openness in your business counters the accurate public perception that most businesses watch out for their own interests while often ignoring those of their customers. For many years, this tradition found support in our law under the doctrine of caveat emptor, or "let the buyer beware." These days, courts and legislatures have shifted much of the responsibility for selling safe products to business, but there is still a widespread feeling in the business community that if consumers aren't canny enough to watch out for their own interests, they deserve to be taken advantage of.

As a result, customers tend to be wary both when dealing with individual businesses and the business community generally. For example, these days, someone who reads in the newspaper that a local Merchants' Association favors a particular political position is likely to conclude that the position promotes the merchants'—not the public—interest. And although this is not always true, it is an understandable assumption when you consider how many industries, from those making birth control devices and drugs to those making autos and insulation, have at times cynically placed their own interests before those of their customers.

How open is your business? Can people see what you do and how and where you do it? When they are interested, do you explain the technical parts of it they don't understand, or do you jealously guard this information as a "trade secret"? Is your profit-and-loss information generally available to your customers? Do you let your customers know in advance what they can expect of you if there is a problem with your product or service?

An attitude of openness should be built into all of the details of the way you conduct your business: your pricing, your treatment of employees and your willingness to answer questions about your products and services.

A. Financial Openness

The few leading-edge businesses that actually post or publish their financial information where their customers can monitor it constantly get surprised and pleased reactions from customers. It's one of those simple, excellent ideas that customers intuitively understand and respond to. It should be standard procedure for all topnotch small businesses. If you don't know how powerful this technique can be, consider this example from our book *Honest Business* (Clear Glass, San Francisco, 2000):

> Howard publishes the finest bicycle repair manual for the 6,000 bicycle repair shops in the United States. He was ready to print his second edition

when he ran into several problems. The first was that he had borrowed to the limit of his personal credit to keep his business going, and the second was that the printer still had an outstanding bill from the first edition. Howard had pre-sold some of the new editions at less than $12, and that was the break-even point by later calculations. What was he to do?

Howard first considered and rejected accepting advertising in the manual. Although it would have bailed him out of his financial problems, it would have been at the expense of credibility among his readers. What he did, instead, was to announce that he had a problem and described it to a group of bicycle product manufacturers at a trade show. They too thought it was a bad idea to take ads. After his announcement, two people came to him and offered to co-sign a loan for him.

Small businesspeople are reluctant to open their books for much the same reason many people are timid about appearing in a bathing suit. They don't want people to know that they're in less than perfect condition. This sort of shyness is unwarranted, because openness is reassuring regardless of the actual financial condition of the business.

This point is clearly illustrated by Chris Andersen, who runs a construction company in Stockholm, Sweden. Chris prominently posts his financial records on the work shed near his current construction site. When asked at a recent small business conference, "Doesn't your smallness worry your customers?" he answered with a resounding "No. People can see from my balance sheet that I can afford to finish their project," he explained, "and that's what they primarily care about. When they occasionally see that I have underbid a job and am not making money on it, they rave to their friends about what a great deal they got. And when I make a profit, they always say they are coming back to me for the next job and they expect a lower bid."

One effective open marketing approach was initiated by a store that opened a few years ago in Tokyo called "No Brand." It now has over 200 locations throughout Japan. No Brand sells a wide range of products and, true to its name, none of them have brand names. We might call it "generic" in English, but it really isn't, since all products are top-of-the-line quality and the "generic" concept in the U.S. has generally been marketed as bottom-of-the-line or economy quality. The Japanese stores are very small, 600 square feet, but very efficient. Clothing is of the highest quality and the materials are all natural: cotton, wool, linen or silk. The packaged foods are organic, with no additives. Paper and cardboard products are from recycled material. All products come in limited colors: black, brown, beige, tan, white or natural. The whole store is designed to give the sense that you can completely trust what you buy. Nothing secret is added, nothing harmful lurks in unknown ingredients, and even the electrical appliances are the most durable ones on the market. This is openness of a unique form. The products themselves cry out, in an organic, simple way, to be trusted.

A fascinating San Diego, California, company with 240 employees, Action Instruments, has a unique explanation for its commitment to openness, which it calls "the rights of ownership." Action, which began in the early 1970s and expects to pass $100 million in annual sales soon, has a five-part openness program:

1. In the center of its main building, which houses a cafeteria and meeting rooms, is the InfoCenter, where each department posts all of its current financial and operating reports.

2. Each employee has an "Owner's Manual," which explains how the company works and how to read the InfoCenter reports. Not all employees are, in fact, owners, but most are.

3. Daily at 9 a.m. there are announcements over the public address system about crucial issues of the day and about visitors expected that day.

4. A newsletter keeping everyone abreast of important company news comes with each paycheck.

5. On Fridays, starting precisely at 4 p.m. and ending precisely at 5, is the $100 Million Club, which anyone can attend (50 to 75 employees come regularly). It's an informal talk by an outside guest about business, management, the industry or related subjects.

B. Physical Openness

One of the most interesting business developments in the United States has been an increased physical openness in the workplace, which has been enthusiastically supported by customers. For instance, small photo developing shops have sprung up where customers can watch the machine that processes their film. It's also reassuring and fun to watch your car via video as it's being repaired. Restaurants and bakeries that have designed their kitchens to be clearly visible to their customers announce that they have nothing to hide. Hospitals invite fathers and other close relatives into the delivery room during childbirth so they can see exactly what is going on.

Can this approach be made to work in your business? Absolutely. A Step Ahead in Petaluma is California's oldest shoe store, and we can see why it's been in business so long. Instead of just the ordinary displays and the rather mysterious curtained-off stock room of most shoe stores, boxes of shoes line the walls so that their entire stock is out in the open. You know for a fact if they have your color and size.

Or consider the case of Berkeley Fish. Since this small store moved its sushi-making area from the back of the store to the front window, people gather to watch the Japanese delicacy being prepared. Many are so impressed that they come in and purchase some for the first time.

This strategy could be followed with success by all sorts of other retailers, but for the most part, it isn't. Most businesses still prefer to do much of their work in a back room, far from public view. Are we alone in suspecting that this is often for good (or should we say bad) reason?

Whether you run a garage or small radio station or fish hatchery or beauty salon, ask yourself how you can change the physical layout of your business to let your customers better see what you do. The harder this is to do, the more they are sure to appreciate your efforts and the more likely they are to comment favorably about your business to others.

A STEP AHEAD
40 BRANDS
115 Petaluma Blvd., No. • Petaluma, CA 94952
Robert Yocom   (707) 763-0880
California's Oldest Shoe Store

Avoiding Conflict by Being Open With Clients

Jim Sullivan is an activist in the land preservation movement, writer and landscape contractor/designer who lives and works in Sonoma County, California. He has found that being open with clients is essential to the success of his business. He describes it like this:

"Often a client approaches me with a design idea he wants a bid on, and a problem can arise when they don't have enough money to implement their plan. If you can be open with your client and create a good atmosphere, usually you can mutually redesign to reduce costs. One problem is that in the landscape business most of the money a client spends is not visible. The actual plants, for instance, are only a small part of the cost. The bulk of the cost actually goes into planning, overhead, soil reconditioning, irrigation, transporting materials, site preparation and labor. Because these costs are invisible, the client must have trust in the landscaper or conflicts are likely to develop.

"To develop trust, I try to be absolutely open about everything I do. I put all the specs of the particular job into every contract, and write the contract on a computer. Then I print it out and read the entire four or five pages to my client. While this may sound tedious, I have learned the clearer our understanding, the fewer problems that will arise. Reading aloud with the client makes it easy to discuss any questions they may have and make necessary corrections before work begins. The more precise description we work out the better. It also gives me a chance to explain all the 'hidden' work that must be done for a really excellent job."

A building contractor we know does all of the above and also adds his profit and overhead on the estimate instead of the usual practice of "hiding" these figures in the bid.

C. Openness in Management

In addition to building trust, openness has the great advantage of increasing business efficiency. When each employee has to be given detailed instructions and requires careful supervision, a large hierarchy of middle management is inevitable, and so are mistakes. When employees have an overall perspective on the business operation, they can make better decisions where it most counts: at the lowest level of operation.

The Open-Book "Revolution"

Here's what *Inc.* magazine (cover story, June 1995) had to say about the radical idea of giving employees lots of financial information about the companies they work for:

"Companies large and small have been inventing an approach to making money that is as radical as it is simple. The open-book revolution. More and more CEOs have discovered what was missing from all the past decade's management cures—and have invented a new way of running a company that overturns a hundred years of managerial thinking. The new system gets every employee to think and act like a businessperson—and it gets astonishing results....

"There are a few basic principles and by now, a lot of people...have experience putting those principles to work in companies.

"Get the information out there...not only what they need to know to do their jobs effectively but how the division or the company as a whole is doing.

"Teach the basics of business.... Some [employees] believe that revenues are the same as profits. Or that profits are whatever a company has in the bank. Not many employees can tick off the expenses a company must pay.

"Empower people to make decisions based on what they know...at Foldcraft (a chair manufacturer in Minnesota) every unit is accountable for its own numbers— and every man and woman in that unit shares in the accountability.

"Make sure everyone—everyone!— shares directly in the company's success, and in the risk of failure....

"Manco, a box manufacturer in Baltimore, sets annual targets for net earnings and return on operating assets. If employees hit both targets, the company 'Makes bonus,' meaning that employees collect payouts ranging from 10% to 50% of their total compensation. Want to know the prospects? Check out that lunchroom wall."

A wonderful example of this kind of openness is Scandinavian Airlines (SAS). SAS "study circles" were created so that each employee can learn about basic management issues, such as the long-range plans of the company. In the first year's study circles, there are ten topics covered, with about six hours of tapes and study per topic. Topics range from "A Functional Organization" to "An Introduction to Systems Development." The second year's subjects range from "Strategic Development" to "Planning for the Next Generation of Aircraft."

Even more important than bringing management-level issues directly to each employee, SAS publishes a weekly newspaper that presents and explains current financial information about the company's operations. In one edition, the financial information was even broken down into subsidiaries such as hotel and catering services that the company operates.

The newsletter includes letters from customers (including complaints) and an open forum for staffers. For instance, in one issue Jan Sorenson complains that a company brochure "is pure nonsense" and Nancy Johnson, in reservations, suggests a better way to handle prepaid tickets.

The paper has very detailed operational information as well. For example, a chart on the back page shows the amount of available seating on various routes for the coming three weeks.

D. Openness With Information

More and more businesses sell information instead of, or at least in addition to, tangible products. Think about why you go to optometrists, lawyers, stockbrokers, banks or real estate agents: you need the specialized information only they have access to.

If you're in a business or profession that trades in information, being open about your finances and how you organize your workspace, while important, are clearly not the only elements in your efforts to be open. Your real task is to be open with your customers by giving them the maximum amount of information about what you do. If you trust your customers

enough to demystify your precious information, they will feel more comfortable, satisfied and appreciative of what you're doing for them.

Few people outside the particular profession understand how a dentist, lawyer or architect evaluates a particular problem. Too often, the professional works like a "black box": the client feeds in a problem and out comes an answer. The client has no real understanding of what a root canal, temporary injunction or soils test is all about.

To change this situation, a doctor can stock the waiting room with material (written, audio cassette or, increasingly, computerized) that answers medical questions. A real estate broker's office can hand out information going into detail on all procedures for selling a house. A bank can explain how its policies make its loans or checking accounts a better deal than other banks.

If you find yourself reluctant to give out free information about the details of what you do, you should rethink what you're charging your customers for. Are you afraid that if you give them information they'll realize they don't need you? If so, perhaps openness isn't for you unless you are willing to change some fundamental aspects of how you work. However, if you come out from behind the professional jargon your colleagues hide behind and let your customers in on the maximum amount of useful information without paying you to interpret it for them, you will find that your work satisfaction will improve because you are now helping educated participants rather than ignorant skeptics. And at least as important, your income will go up too, because your clients will surely tell many others about your refreshingly open and honest business practices.

Here is a questionnaire to help you measure how open your business is. This is important and well worth the time it will take to complete. The authors' years of consulting experience with small business clearly demonstrate that the more boxes marked with an "X" on the right-hand side of the page, the more effective the marketing program. Few "X" marks is a red flag indicating serious problems.

Advice by E-mail

Michael's offer to do telephone consultation in the first edition of this book now has a new twist, thanks to one of his phone clients, The Center for Traditional Medicine in Cambridge, Massachusetts. When the Center decided to plan a new marketing event, instead of phoning Michael again for advice, they sent him a postcard asking three questions and offering multiple choice answers for each. Michael cried "brilliant!" and instantly added the Postcard Question Service to his repertoire. Soon afterwards, he began offering this service by e-mail.

You can obtain an e-mail Multiple Choice Consultation for just $10. (Because of the background information required—see the information on telephone consulting in the Appendix—this offer applies only to businesses who consult with Michael on the telephone first.) For information on how this service works, see Michael's website at http://www.well.com/user/mp/mwa.html. This is also a new form of accessibility (see Chapter 9).

How Open Is Your Business?

We are willing to answer the following specific
questions about our business to:

	FAMILY	FRIENDS	EMPLOYEES	ACCOUNTANT	ATTORNEY	SOME CUSTOMERS	ALL CUSTOMERS
wages...	☐	☐	☐	☐	☐	☐	☐
rent...	☐	☐	☐	☐	☐	☐	☐
cost of goods...	☐	☐	☐	☐	☐	☐	☐
source of supplies...	☐	☐	☐	☐	☐	☐	☐
financial problems...	☐	☐	☐	☐	☐	☐	☐
profits and losses...	☐	☐	☐	☐	☐	☐	☐
specific techniques...	☐	☐	☐	☐	☐	☐	☐

I personally will show or explain in detail:

	FAMILY	FRIENDS	EMPLOYEES	ACCOUNTANT	ATTORNEY	SOME CUSTOMERS	ALL CUSTOMERS
How I do what I do...	☐	☐	☐	☐	☐	☐	☐
How my equipment works...	☐	☐	☐	☐	☐	☐	☐
How I price a product or service...	☐	☐	☐	☐	☐	☐	☐
How I keep track of time...	☐	☐	☐	☐	☐	☐	☐
How I keep track of costs...	☐	☐	☐	☐	☐	☐	☐

My financial statements are available to anyone
who wishes to see them...   YES ☐   NO ☐

E. Openness With Ideas

Many businesses deal in what has become known as "intellectual property." Intellectual property consists of ideas, designs, trade secrets and practices, as well as patents, copyrights and trademarks that you own.

Licensing is the main way that ownership of intellectual property is shared. For example, books are licensed to filmmakers, films are licensed to video cassette distributors, toy designs are licensed to manufacturers, promotional advertisements are licensed to local TV stations and inventions are licensed to manufacturers.

Another way that intellectual property can be made available to others, of course, is simply to give it to them. A restaurant can make its recipes available to its customers, a computer programmer can post a program online for public use and an author can give away his poem.

Many businesses, of course, neither license nor give away their legally protected property but try to monopolize it for their own gain. The world is full of secret formulas, patented inventions and fiercely defended trademarks. Like other sorts of secrecy in business, most businesspeople never question their monopolistic practices.

They should. A small business that tries to monopolize intellectual property treads a very dangerous course. To illustrate this point, let's look at a big business example of a product that most people are familiar with.

In 1977, RCA developed a video player requiring a specialized video disc. It did not license this product to others and tried to monopolize what it correctly saw as a phenomenal new business. Unfortunately for RCA, Matsushita and Sony developed videotape players that produced similar results (the Beta and VHS systems). Both were licensed to many manufacturers. By 1983, RCA's basically excellent product was so isolated in the marketplace that the company canceled it. A few years later it was clear that of the two surviving systems, the one which had been licensed most widely (the VHS system) was scooping up the lion's share of the business.

There are lots of similar examples of companies refusing to license their intellectual property losing out to others who were more open. Audio tape is one, where reel-to-reel and eight-track systems lost out to small cassettes because the Dutch Philips company licensed the systems for making and playing the tapes to virtually anyone interested at a very reasonable rate.

Two Internet businesses offer the best and most recent examples. The Web-browsing boom was virtually created by the founders of Netscape who gave their Web browser software free to consumers and only charged businesses for the licenses. The Internet server business has been revolutionized by Linux, a free software program that has become a major force in the formerly closed server market dominated by Microsoft. Linux is served by the community of "volunteer" programmers around the world and by commercial businesses that have also grown up to provide service to large corporations.

What is the moral of this for small businesses that develop intellectual property?

Simply that those who are most open to including others in what they are doing are far more likely to prosper than those who don't.

Generous Marketing Proves Historic Success

The late Andrew Fluegelman, formerly editor of *PC World* and senior editor of *MacWorld,* prominent computer magazines, authored a program to allow certain types of computers to talk to each other, called "PC Talk." Instead of selling this program, Fluegelman gave it away, in the process refining a marketing strategy now known as "freeware." Those who were given a copy of "PC Talk" were encouraged to voluntarily send a licensing fee to Fluegelman. If they did, they qualified for free program updates. The result is a computer business legend. With no advertising, Fluegelman's program became a substantial success, bringing in over $200,000 in 1984 alone. Indeed, until his untimely death in 1985, Fluegelman's total revenues from "PC Talk" exceeded the net return of all directly comparable programs, many of which were marketed with expensive advertising hoopla.

Fluegelman's program allowed computers to link to networks, which in the early 1980s were new and limited. By 1993, computer networks were beginning to grow and the Internet had several million active users. Into this environment stepped one of the most astounding marketing achievements in history. Marc Andreeson started distributing, free, a program called Netscape. Netscape was elegantly simple at the outset and allowed good graphics, direct access to files that were made public on the Internet and easy movement to other distant files. The new environment was quickly called the World Wide Web, and Netscape became the standard.

Netscape charged commercial users for its program and sold its services for internal corporate use. The company sold public shares of stock in early 1995 and created a sensation that played a direct role in lifting the whole domestic American stock market nearly 30% in one year. Then Andreeson's company achieved another historic first by generating revenues in excess of $100 million in its first year of existence.

Marketing Without Advertising deserves a tiny amount of credit. The 1986 edition of this book was the first published account of generous marketing, the RCA, Dutch Philips and Fluegelman stories.

At this point you may be saying, "Great story, but what's the point for my small business? I don't write software, splice genes or have a pantry full of secret recipes." While the issue of licensing and the principle of generosity in marketing doesn't come up often for small businesses, something very similar does commonly occur for all providers of goods (and sometimes, services) under the guise of exclusive marketing agreements and exclusive territory agreements.

We have seen many businesses confronted with a retailer or wholesaler who says, "I'll carry your product only if I can have an exclusive agreement in this area for selling it." At first examination, it makes sense: The retailer or wholesaler may make a greater effort to sell it if she has an exclusive deal. In reality, the small manufacturer, artist or craftsperson faces the same situation as do giants like RCA and Philips. The exclusive agreement makes it much harder for your ultimate clients to find and buy your product or service because it inevitably results in severe restriction of the many ways it can be sold, displayed and marketed. Indeed, no matter what the incentive, it is almost never worth signing an exclusive agreement of any sort. Sometimes this means making a tough decision to turn down what seems like a very lucrative deal. Do it. Never let short-term greed get in the way of long-term good business practices. ■

Chapter 7

Deciding How to Educate Potential Customers

or the most powerful marketing force—positive recommendations—to work, most businesses have a major communication job to do. After all, if people don't know the details of the goods and services you offer, they are unlikely to be effective in recommending your services to their friends. But before you can design an effective marketing plan, you must decide:

1. The general kind of information people need to know about your business so that they can tell others about you, and

2. What specific groups of people you want to target for your educational efforts so that your marketing plan based on positive recommendations will be maximally effective.

This chapter helps you focus on these issues. Once you've decided them, Chapter 8 deals with the specifics of getting your message across effectively.

Before we get into the details of how to best spread the word about your business, however, we suggest you run a little test as to how accomplished you already are in disseminating information about your business. Ask ten friends and acquaintances—people you live near, or participate in sports with or know from the PTA or a social club—to give a brief description of your business. How well do they describe what you do? Could they convincingly tell others about what you do? Or do they need more information to really recommend you?

A. What Does Your Business Do?

Before you can sensibly design a marketing plan based on personal recommendations, you need to articulate a clear, easily understandable statement of what your business is about.

A statement of what your business is may seem so obvious to you as to not bear mention. It isn't. After working with many small businesses, we have learned that the business owner who can clearly communicate what he does is the exception. When many of us are asked what we do, we make statements such as, "What don't I do?" or "Isn't it obvious?" or "You know—pretty much what the average small office CPA (financier, vet, etc.) does." This sort of vagueness usually exists even in seemingly straightforward operations such as bicycle repair or independent grocery store businesses.

Charmian Anderson is a therapist who is excellent at marketing her services. She started her practice in San Francisco with the few clients she acquired while finishing graduate school, but needed more.

Anderson discovered early on that mentioning the fact that she was a therapist with a Jungian bent didn't generate much business, so she decided to concentrate on describing her business in a way her friends and potential clients could easily understand. To do this, she created and memorized a simple 25-word statement: "I help successful people with executive jobs or their own businesses who have short-term emotional problems such as divorce, family stress or trauma." She includes it in her written flyers and other materials and delivers it orally at all sorts of gatherings, including meetings of businesspeople—the kind where you stand up and tell who you are and what you do.

The brevity and clarity of her statement allow Anderson's friends and supporters to actually find potential clients for her because they have a concrete way to communicate what she does. By contrast, her earlier definition of "I'm a therapist" was virtually useless.

Obviously, to create a good description of your business, you must thoroughly understand it yourself. Surprisingly, many businesspeople, even those who have worked in a field for a long time, haven't fully thought out all aspects of their business.

One place to start is by developing a clear understanding of the broader domain in which your business functions. Let's take an example. Suppose you manufacture a cooking pot. It would be easy, but only partially correct, to say you are in the business of making cooking pots. To develop a meaningful description of your business—one that will help you develop a marketing strategy—you must consider the role of the pot in the lives of your customers. The idea is to look at all the possible ways your business touches customers' lives. Pots are for cooking, so any marketing strategy should presumably be based on this fact. The truth is, however, if you assume that your business has to do only with cooking, you will consider only a part of your possible market.

Let's see what happens to your marketing options if you consider these additional facts:

- Your pots are stored somewhere, so you are also part of the "kitchen storage" domain.
- Your pots must be cleaned, so you can add the "cleaning" domain.
- If some cooking methods, such as boiling and steaming, work in your pot while others, such as frying, don't, you might conclude that you are in the "health" business.
- Your pots (their color, shape, finish, etc.) will play an aesthetic role in the kitchen, so you are in the decorating domain.

By broadening your own thinking about what your business is, you may well end up defining it in ways you haven't thought of before. Some of these new ways may turn out to be keys to developing a successful marketing action plan.

Each of our businesses is dependent on other businesses. This interdependence is pervasive and shapes our activities. Thinking about that interdependence can help improve your self-definition as well as help others place you in the spectrum of commerce. An architect is a cog on a big wheel that includes her graduate educational institution and the contractors, engineers, landscapers, decorators, lawyers and graphics people she works with.

Consider another example. In 1850, the quill pen used by secretaries to copy documents could be repaired by a wide range of semi-skilled craftspeople using many readily available materials. By contrast, keeping a contemporary copy machine in operation is a far more complex task. To start with, the copier is dependent on the proper electric power supply. It functions within a limited temperature and humidity range and requires a certain type of paper and very precisely manufactured fluids and powders. Further, it needs highly specialized maintenance by people who show up with a trunk full of replacement parts that are impossible to get any-place else.

The copier, then, is clearly in many domains: repair service, complex parts maintenance, reproduction, electrical apparatus, information transfer, chemistry, xerography, aesthetics and toxicology (some fluids are poisonous). Each of these domains has an impact on the marketing of copy machine manufacturers, wholesalers, retailers, consultants and repair people.

To understand all the aspects of your business and define the wide range of domains in which you can legitimately sell what you do, ask yourself these questions:

- What exactly is the role of my business in the life of my customer?
- How many domains does it touch?

For example, suppose you own a small grocery store and your only marketing technique is having periodic sales, featuring discounted items. When you do this, your business attracts attention only in the price domain. Many grocery stores never go much beyond this sort of marketing. In other words, they implicitly describe their business as "food for sale at reasonable or low prices."

But what about broadening the definition of your grocery store to include the fact that the food your customers buy they must cook, clean and store. And when you think about cooking, don't forget that a significant percentage of your customers regard the preparation and eating of food as an important hobby, and a few elevate it to the status of a religion. Thinking about all of this might prompt you to:

- Put on a demonstration of how to cook an unusual vegetable currently in season. This would be an excellent way to both focus attention on a produce department aware enough to carry the vegetable in the first place and to show your customers that you think of food in ways other than how much it costs.
- If you are located in a congenial neighborhood or a small town where such events are popular, you might invite some local chefs to make their favorite barbecue sauce. Pass out samples of chicken dipped in the sauce as part of a contest to crown the local Barbecue King or Queen.
- Invite a nutritionist to autograph books inside your store.
- Set up a display of kitchen storage systems.

- Demonstrate how to make a casserole in a microwave oven.
- Have your local Tupperware distributor set up the food storage containers and explain how they keep food fresh.
- Invite a cookbook author to sign copies of his book in the store.

Many of these things are done by stores that understand how to view their product in domains other than price. By broadening their view of their business, they are able to broaden their marketing plan. Unfortunately, the great majority of businesses have yet to really take advantage of the concept. In other words, they define what they do too narrowly.

Boiling Down What You Do

When we are approached by friends whose small service businesses are slow, we often suggest a very simple technique that draws on the principles discussed in this chapter. We ask the service provider to list four things she does on a 3x5 card and include her name, phone number, hourly rate and available hours. Their next step is to duplicate the card and give it to friends and acquaintances. Even this simple type of description always generates business.

For example, a bookkeeper friend who needed more customers listed:
- check reconciliation
- preparation and filing of quarterly tax returns
- general ledger posting, and
- making budget projections.

A photographer's card read as follows:
- photograph valuables for insurance records
- am very patient with babies and small children
- frame photos, and
- make home visits.

Within two weeks after each of these people sent their cards to twenty friends, both were busy.

One reason this simple card approach is effective is that it forces you to describe your business in terms that make sense to potential customers. Your description tends to fit the customers' language and speak to their immediate needs better than a nondescriptive title like "bookkeeper," "photographer" or "therapist."

What My Business Does

The following is a definition of what my business does, in about 35 words:

We support—with information, training, and equipment and whatever
else is needed for greater safety and enjoyment—individuals who are interested in kayaking. We offer good storage and beach areas, help them
form clubs, offer trips and support others in the industry.

What My Business Does

The following is a definition of what my business does, in about 35 words:

We help individuals and businesses effectively define their aesthetic
and spatial desires. We use our skills and talents to organize the relevant businesses, products and technologies to create the desired
goals. We work best with groups of five to 50 people.

B. Defining the Domains in Which Your Business Operates

By now you should be convinced that a clear, creative definition of your business is an essential basis for a marketing action plan, and that you simply cannot develop concrete marketing steps until you know who you are aiming at and what, exactly, you offer. Once you know what your business does, you can focus on those elements that make it unique.

Start by listing the domains your business operates in. To help in this process, examine your list of payables to see with whom you really work on a continuing basis. Now, review your checkbook to see what consultants you use, and make a list of them. Last, think over the general functions you fulfill (the major domains in which you operate) from a customer's perspective. Below are two examples.

Now, put your lists together, think about them and refine them. Once you do, you should be able to describe your business.

If your business has a Web page you will find this domain exercise has an additional value. The current structure of the Web allows websites to list key words called "meta-tags" on their website that are not visible on the Web page itself. The meta-tag is read by search engines and in many cases can be useful in helping customers find you. The "meta-tag" is a perfect place to put the relevant words that define the domain of your business.

The Domains in Which Your Business Operates

The major domains in which I operate (taken from my payables) are:

water safety equipment, marine suppliers, sports clothes,

navigation equipment, equipment storage, imported kayaks

The major domains in which I operate (from looking at checks paid to my consultants) are:

sports clubs, emergency first aid, environmental science, fabric technology,

salt water lore and tradition, water safety education

The general functions I fulfill (the major domains in which I operate)
from a customer's perspective are:

recreation, health, stress reduction, weight control, travel,

family fun

EXAMPLE FOR A WATER SPORTS EQUIPMENT BUSINESS

The Domains in Which Your Business Operates

The major domains in which I operate (taken from my payables) are:

lumber yards, hardware stores, paint suppliers, specialty catalogs, county

refuse site, insurance companies, electrical sub-contractors, plumbing sub-

contractors, moulding company

The major domains in which I operate (from looking at checks paid to my consultants) are:

accountant, law firm, materials specialists, architects, painters, mac-users

group, computer programmers

The general functions I fulfill (the major domains in which I operate) from a customer's perspective are:

bring dreams to reality, create an efficient, utilitarian, aesthetically pleasing

environment, child safe play areas and entertainment centers for the family

EXAMPLE FOR A CONSTRUCTION COMPANY

Bob Schwartz's Tarrytown Conference Center

Bob Schwartz incorporated his vision of a business conference center into a larger domain than just meeting facilities: the domain of ideas and issues. Bob took over a beautiful country estate in the rolling hills just north of New York City and turned it into the Tarrytown Conference Center. By the beginning of the 1980s, he had made it into one of the most successful and prestigious corporate meeting centers in the U.S. Bob's background was in journalism, working for Time-Life and helping found *New York* magazine; also, along with his wife, he opened a small Japanese inn in the Catskill mountains, long before there was a single sushi bar in the U.S.

All these experiences combined to give Schwartz the necessary skill to create the Tarrytown success. In his favor, the bases were well covered from the start—the estate was beautiful, and he hired superb people to run the hotel and dining facilities. But plenty of conference centers have both of these attributes and still fail. Schwartz's genius was to realize that corporate executives, who were his principal market, were high energy people like himself, interested in the world, ideas and the excitement of social issues. While other conference centers focused on "strictly business" in the narrowest bottom-line sense, Schwartz organized a wide range of conferences at Tarrytown, including the friends of Margaret Mead discussing anthropological issues, Judith Crist with weekends on film and a number of creative thinkers discussing the social concerns of business. Tarrytown's reputation began to grow.

To this Schwartz added a School for Entrepreneurs and later a School for Intrapreneurs (see Chapter 8). He also created a 15,000-subscriber mailing list for a Tarrytown newsletter, which reported on the exciting diversity of the conference center's activities and provided background material on guest speakers and their ideas.

As Schwartz's view of his business broadened, he continued to add new projects. For example, he organized a conference and a group—The Tarrytown 100—made up of many of the most innovative entrepreneurs in the U.S. This project is not only glamorous and fun, but also will enhance his primary market as many of the young entrepreneurs take their places at the heads of future Fortune 500 companies. Says Schwartz: "The power of an idea or a vision is the driving force behind a successful marketing strategy, and the 'whole' has to fit together perfectly."

C. Providing Information on Businesses in Established Fields

Those of you who are in well-established fields—anything from a grocery or bakery to a television repair shop or retail clothing store—normally need not be concerned with communicating the basics of what you do. You are fortunate because the public has a pretty good knowledge of your type of business. If you show a group of strangers your business card, you can expect the great majority of them will generally understand your business and know at least some of the reasons why they need you. Obviously, however, these people won't know what special services and extras you offer, such as the women's clothing shop that does minor alterations at no extra charge, the grocery store that delivers, the laundromat that serves free coffee, the used auto parts company that delivers to commercial accounts, the bakery that accepts phone orders for specialty cakes and so on. To fully enlist the positive energy of your friends and acquaintances, you must give them something to talk about. Your job is to make sure they are aware of the things that set you apart.

A business Michael consulted with, Joseph's Sewer Rooter of Los Angeles, has been in business more than a decade and makes service calls 24 hours a day, seven days a week. Joseph's problem is convincing a skeptical public that it really does

provide such exceptional service. Skeptical customers are like amateurs; they know enough to doubt. Michael suggested that they develop five humorous stories about service calls made at odd hours and recount them on radio talk shows and at real estate luncheons, chamber of commerce meetings and similar occasions. The real message of the stories, of course, is that Joseph's really does make house calls at any hour; that message will come through the humor of the stories.

It's not too difficult to figure out what a bed store might offer, but the Berkeley Design Shop offers a whole lot more than the usual mattresses and box springs. Michael Lavin, the owner, is in the business of selling a good night's sleep. He has done extensive research during his 25 years in the business on how to make a comfortable mattress and is extremely knowledgeable. Lavin usually spends an hour and sometimes two with a customer as they try out different mattresses and learn about what goes into a comfortable night's sleep. As part of his initial research he gave away beds to physical therapists in exchange for their feedback. He also had them come into the store two nights a week for a year to answer customers' questions. And later Lavin installed a pressure-mapping computer that greatly facilitates a custom match between mattress and customer. As you lie on the bed, Lavin receives an instant readout on the monitor indicating your particular pressure points.

When you leave the Berkeley Design Shop you are a truly educated customer, and after a night's sleep on your new mattress will probably tell all of your friends.

To take another example, almost everyone has some idea of what a bail bondsman does. Just the same, a bondsman who provides better service can do a lot to gain the business, if not the affection, of potential customers. A bondsman who accepts collect calls, takes personal checks or jewelry in an emergency, is open 24 hours and has a radio dispatched car and national service should emphasize these facts.

A bank is another business that doesn't need to be explained to potential customers. So, rather than bore people with explanations of check cashing services or safe deposit boxes, a wise banker will emphasize unique services. Take, for example, the National Bank of the Redwoods, headquartered in Santa Rosa, California. This locally owned bank specializes in providing services to small businesspersons and tells customers that its commitment is "to bring the bank to you." For example, bank personnel often go to the borrower's place of business by appointment. In addition, the bank underwrites a messenger/courier service to deliver paperwork and pick up deposits and other important documents, making banking less time-consuming. To make changing from other banks easier, NBR sends out an account executive to work with the business's accounting personnel. This includes helping them with the forms, endorsement stamps and other paperwork needed to complete the switch.

When the woman in charge of New Accounts was asked how the National Bank of the Redwoods (NBR) informs customers of these services, she commented: "I sit down with every new customer and assess their needs, suggesting services that seem appropriate for them. In addition, I give

2 YOU CAN'T GET COMFORTABLE

Comfort is closely related to pressure distribution. If your mattress yields too much, not enough, or unevenly, pressure imbalance can cause your sleeping posture to become unnatural. You contort your body-- twisting spine, waist, shoulders, hips or legs-- trying to find relief.

Every body shift causes a mini-awakening. Whether you remember them or not, these awakenings disturb the sleep cycle and contribute to morning fatigue.

In addition, you may be plagued by lower back ache or stiff shoulders and neck because your bed was not able to provide a comfortable, natural body alignment during the night.

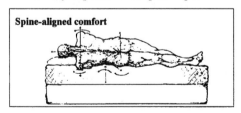
Spine-aligned comfort

*The **European Sleep Works** at the **Berkeley Design Shop** carries exclusively 100% natural latex foam rubber mattresses, which offer the greatest comfort and natural body alignment we have found. We also dual-adjust mattresses for couples, to provide a comfortable night's sleep for each person.*

them pamphlets that explain our services and charges. Of course, we are continually working on new services such as online banking, having grown from our original, innovative electronic banking which required a different approach. In the first case, we formed a focus group of customers and did role-playing exercises to help figure out what customers might require. We then devised a questionnaire that we sent to 170 customers. From their feedback, we now have ten questions we can ask potential customers to help them decide if this is a useful service. We use those questions for our online banking product, phoning customers we think might be interested in online banking and offering to go to their place of business to give them a demonstration."

Salli banks at the Sebastopol branch of NBR and notes that in addition to offering personalized service to the small businessperson, the bank employees make the trip to the bank a pleasurable experience. Unlike many austere banking institutions where the tellers and bank managers treat their customers impersonally, the staff is cheerful, friendly and genuinely helpful. They even provide dog biscuits and, on the last Friday of the month, cookies for humans.

There are many ways an established business can inform customers about these kinds of extra services. For example, the 7-11 convenience store chain brilliantly chose a name that told its customers that it was open earlier and later than traditional grocery stores. More typical methods include flyers sent out to your mailing list

$ BUY - RENT - HIRE $

- tractors are expensive to purchase
- associated implements can double that
- add 10-15% for operation + maintenance

PURCHASE

- with rare exceptions, the most expensive choice both short-term and long-term
- ties up many thousands of dollars saves a few hundred
- requires maintenance and repair
- makes financial sense only if you have several hundred hours work per year

RENT

- dramatically cheaper than owning
- still must learn to operate
- still must pay for fuel (and any breakage)
- have to haul it home or pay for delivery

HIRE

- costs similar to renting, minus fuel
- experienced, skilled operator
- includes ALL equipment costs

the Gentleman Farmer

is the most reliable, cost-effective way to get the right job done
with the right tool
at the right time.

and signs in retail stores or office waiting rooms. You can also note an extra service or two on your business card and personally explain the availability of extra services when customers visit your business. In occupations where you deal with a relatively few people, you can even call them to let them know about a particularly valuable new service. Chapter 8 discusses many more strategies.

D. Businesses in New or Obscure Fields

It's one thing to market an established business by convincing customers that you do a better job or offer extra service, and quite another to let people know about a business in a field they have never heard of. For example, if you are a businessperson who sells wholesale lapidary supplies or structural mylar members, very few people will know what you do from a quick perusal of a business card. Even if your business isn't quite this obscure—say you are a freelance video technician, a computer-aided drafting firm or the operator of a papermaking studio—exactly what you do may not be clearly understood.

Don't assume that your business is immune from the need to educate existing and potential customers because it has been in operation for some time. For instance, even today there are many people who don't take advantage of the services of specialized travel agents, services that buy airline seats in bulk and negotiate low rates at no charge to the customer. Specialized agents can get flights to Hong Kong, Tokyo and Amsterdam at rates that are half of published fares.

Many owners of new types of businesses do realize they must educate people about their field in order to create customers. Take the tofu business as an example. For the uninitiated, tofu is a Japanese soybean extract: the cottage cheese of soybean milk. It was introduced in the United States in the early 1970s as part of the health food movement.

Bill Schurtleif and his wife, Akiko Aoyagi, were among the pioneers in creating the first small market for the product with their *Book of Tofu* (Ballentine), which they promoted with a nationwide media tour. On their tour, they gave order forms to interested people to buy "do-it-yourself" tofu-making kits. Schurtleif and Aoyagi understood that if they were to sell many books, people needed more and better information about tofu, the most important of which was what it tastes like.

Now, several decades later, many people in the food business take it for granted that everyone knows what tofu is. This, of course, is nonsense; probably a majority of Americans have yet to taste tofu. In other words, people in the tofu business, even after years of educating potential customers, have barely scratched the surface. To further expand their market, they still have a major teaching job to do.

Redwood Hill Farm, an award-winning goat dairy that has the greatest variety of goat milk products of any dairy in the United States, has been in business in Sonoma County, California, for over 20 years. Not only is it in a rather obscure field, it also has the added challenge of overcoming buyer resistance to its product. Even though the dairy is successful, it never lets up on efforts to educate both existing and potential customers. The most effective way that owners Jennifer Bice and the late Steven Schack found was to give out samples of their yogurt, milk and a wide variety of cheeses so customers can taste for themselves. Jennifer brings some of her 400 goats to fairs and invites the public to "Open Farm" days during the summer to milk the dairy goats and play with the babies and enjoy goat milk yogurt and cheese. The animals are extremely friendly, and the public can see that the operation is immaculate. Along with the samples, they hand out recipes and literature at fairs informing customers that the farm uses organic feed whenever available, does not use hormones such as BST to increase milk production and is committed to producing the best-tasting, least-processed goat milk products possible.

Steve Halpern is a composer and performer of a very specialized type of soothing and meditative electronic music. In the early 1970s, he was a pioneer in a field that later attracted many musicians (of course, Ravel and others had done it earlier with traditional instruments). Halpern chose to put his music on cassettes, a medium which had almost no retail market at the time. After questioning a number of people who responded favorably to his music, he found that many patronized natural food stores. One by one he called on these stores and played his tapes for the owners. Sure enough, they liked it, stocked them and even played the tapes as background music for their own enjoyment. Not surprisingly, the tapes slowly began to sell. Each tape had an address and price for additional ordering. Several years later, when FM radio stations began playing his music, Halpern's audience grew even more rapidly.

Ambica, a potter, was among the first Americans to work successfully with low-fired raku, a process of firing pottery that was relatively unknown and unappreciated among art, craft and pottery buyers. To help people understand it, she scheduled regular evening events where she served tea and snacks in her studio. Generally, she was able to attract ten to 15 guests a month. At each event, she encouraged people to make an object of clay which she would glaze and fire. For those who were shy, she had ready-made pieces that they could engrave or personalize. Nearly everyone came back to pick up their pieces after the firing and looked around the studio at Ambica's work as well. The market developed, and her work sold.

Charmoon Richardson, the owner of Wild About Mushrooms, has developed an excellent marketing plan based on educating potential clients. Many people are leery about eating mushrooms other than the ordinary kind found in supermarkets, and the more adventurous often have no idea how to prepare the exotic mushroom varieties. Charmoon has figured out how to educate both kinds of clients.

Salli first met Charmoon at an environmental gathering where he was cooking exotic mushrooms with a delicious marinade, giving out samples and answering questions. She loved his samples and attended his Feast of Forest Mushrooms held at Mistrail, a popular eatery. The event included an introductory talk and slide show and displays of fresh wild and exotic mushrooms, followed by a five-course dinner featuring a variety of forest mushrooms. Some of Charmoon's other events include mushroom identification walks, the Wine and Mushroom Festival, weekend forays for mushroom gathering, and mushroom dying and paper making.

Some businesses, if not exactly obscure, are traditionally very low-profile. Good Vibrations, a San Francisco and Berkeley store that sells sex toys, video and audio tapes, guides to safer sex and books, has broken out of the sleazy sex-shop mold and now, after two decades of operation, is recognized world-wide. Education is central to putting potential customers at ease. The business does public outreach at human sexuality courses and clinics, sponsors workshops, hosts book signings and acts as a resource in the community. It publishes informative and humorous catalogues and newsletters that discuss the products. The Good Vibrations motto is, "If you want something done right, do it yourself," so it is fitting that it is the sponsor of Masturbation Month, which has been picked up by national magazines. Within the catalogue they make sure customers know just what they will be getting by clearly marking each category. In the book section, for example, under Family Sexuality are titles such as *Talking With Your Child About Sex* and *Period*; in the smut series there are titles like *Modern Lust* and *Lusty Lesbians*.

The business also makes potential customers, who would never patronize the typical store that sells sex toys, comfortable by assuring them of confidentiality. It never sells, rents or gives customers' names to anyone else, and all items and literature are shipped in plain brown packaging with their corporate name (Open Enterprises) on the return label. To encourage customers to tell their friends, they offer to send them a brochure. The mature approach taken by founder Joanie Blank and adopted by the current worker/owner cooperative sets Good Vibrations apart from others in the field.

E. Whom to Educate

Once people in a new business face up to the need to educate their customers, the next question becomes whom to educate. Don't assume, as many small businesspersons do, that this is a trivial

VIDEOS

Woman-centered. Focuses on female orgasm, identification with women's arousal and satisfaction.

Superior film making, particularly in areas of script and acting. You will not want to fast forward.

Hot sex scenes

Lesbian theme

Unconventional sexual content, scenes of or focus on sexual activity other than traditional foreplay, intercourse and oral sex.

Demonstration or display of safer sex techniques for avoiding transmission of body fluids.

Primarily educational or enlightening with erotic component.

Underground or art picture, not readily available through commercial X-rated outlets.

question. The key to getting a good personal recommendation marketing plan in motion is to get your message before the eyes and ears (and in some instances, the noses and mouths) of the right people as efficiently as possible. To put it another way, because all small businesses have finite (often painfully finite) resources, you must concentrate your educational energies on the people most likely to respond positively.

The following chart illustrates categories of potential customers.

Categories of Potential Customers

	NAIVE	AMATEUR	STANDARD	EXPERT
Non-user				
Light user				
Medium user				
Heavy user				

Where are your current customers?
          potential customers?
          potential sources of referrals?

It may be surprising to you to learn that many users do not fall along the diagonal, increasing their usage of your business as they become more expert about what you do. This is important to know, because most marketing strategies are based on moving people along this diagonal—teaching them more about your business as they increase their use of your product or service, with the idea of increasing use even more. There is nothing wrong with this strategy unless you overlook the facts that lots of potential customers also exist in other categories (the boxes on our chart), and that catering to the needs of these customers can also produce excellent results. For example, there are people who don't use a product but have expert knowledge, such as an aerodynamics engineer who doesn't fly, or a professor of criminal law who rarely, if ever, sees the inside of a courtroom. Both of these people are surely asked by friends and relatives (and maybe even by business or government, if they are retained as consultants) for recommendations about businesses or people who provide services in their fields.

Similarly, there are heavy product users who are naive, such as the wealthy champagne drinker who just loves "those happy little bubbles," or the person who orders large bouquets for the home each week because it's expected, but doesn't know the names of most of the flowers. People in these groups may have no interest in increasing their sophistication about the product. The naive user of a flower service may care a lot more about whether the business will deliver on short notice than about whether it publishes a newsletter full of interesting horticultural facts.

The point is that any good marketing strategy must communicate with customers who have a number of different levels of expertise. If you own a mountaineering shop and concentrate on communicating with your class 5 climber customers, you are likely to talk over the heads of, and perhaps even alienate, the much larger number of weekend backpackers.

Similarly, if you own a men's clothing store and concentrate all of your marketing strategy on educating people about fabric, you may totally lose the interest of the many men who simply want a decent suit that won't wrinkle on airplanes.

If you have ever been to a typical audio store where the salespeople (if you can find one) don't have a clue about the equipment and the music plays at full blast as you try to figure out what's what, you will appreciate The Good Guys. They hire salespeople who understand their products and will give you an educated opinion about what to expect for the price. The mood is low-key and calming, and there is no pressure to buy until you are ready. For the high-end user there are sound-proof rooms available for you to test out the various speakers and other components, and the salespeople will help you put together the system that is right for your level of expertise and budget. For the low-end user, there is a vast array of products available.

To make this point in a different but important way, consider how often people who are naive about a particular product or service purchase it as a gift, as is often the case when a man buys a woman jewelry, or someone who knows a relative is into photography buys her a camera lens.

Businesses that traditionally cater only to men or only to women should be particularly aware of changing societal gender roles and broaden their marketing accordingly. Thirty years ago, men bought most cars. Today, women buy cars (and trucks) by the millions. If you're selling pickup trucks and assume that women are only picking out the color after some man decides on the model, you're going to overlook a lot of potential customers who are probably eager for helpful information about what you're selling. Similarly, today men buy skin lotion, cookware and diapers in numbers that would have seemed amazing less than a generation ago.

Osmosis, a company that marketed the first enzyme bath in America, got immediate results by directing its marketing at expert non-users. Owner Michael Stusser printed a brochure explaining the enzyme bath to potential customers:

"A remarkable form of heat therapy from Japan, which relaxes, soothes and energizes the body, mind and spirit. Unlike other heat treatments, the enzyme bath generates heat biologically, through fermentation, nature's purification process. The bath is composed of fragrant antiseptic cedar fiber, rice bran and over 600 active enzymes. The action of the enzymes produces a special quality of heat that improves circulation and metabolism, helps the body to break down toxins, and thoroughly cleanses and beautifies the skin. The bath often relieves aches and pains, and is especially beneficial for people suffering from tension, fatigue and high stress."

Since the enzyme bath is almost unknown in the United States (even though it's been enjoyed by the Japanese for over 40 years), Stusser clearly must teach people a good deal about this product before they are likely to buy it. In this case, trying to move a lot of people up the diagonal line on the marketing chart from naive/light user to expert/heavy user would almost surely be both incredibly time-consuming and expensive, probably involving writing a book (and a number of magazine and journal articles), doing extensive public relations to sell the book and giving public demonstrations and teaching classes, to mention just a few.

Perhaps eventually Stusser will find the time to do many, or even all, of these, but because he needed customers right away, he decided instead to concentrate his marketing effort not on informing potential users, but experts in the field of body work. These people are primarily health professionals who practice alternative healing methods and have studied Asian medicine. Some of them had heard about the enzyme baths but had never had a chance to experience them. Stusser provided them with an opportunity to take a complimentary bath. Many of those who responded loved the enzyme bath and immediately began referring their clients who they felt would benefit from the relaxation and penetrating heat.

Sylvana LaRocca owns Made to Order, an Italian delicatessen in Berkeley, California. She concentrates on educating non-users about Italian delicacies. In addition to fresh pasta and imported cheese and wines, LaRocca stocks a wide array of Italian delicacies, many flown to her fresh. Realizing that her customers are unlikely to purchase things they can't pronounce and have never tasted, she follows the fairly standard practice of placing samples of many items on the counter. In addition, however, she hand-prints large colorful signs, which she hangs on the wall behind the counter, which say things like, "Mascarpone: made from fresh cream. A heavenly cheese from Italy that can be eaten with fish, fruit or spread on chocolate cake—perfect on bread with olive oil and salt."

LaRocca's idea is to stimulate her customers to ask about these products. She then has the chance to enthusiastically educate her customers about Italian delicacies, her favorite subject. Most people who hear her share her excitement and take home a bag or two of goodies they hadn't planned to buy when they entered the store. Eventually, many even learn the correct pronunciations, which they use to impress their friends, thus educating a whole new group of potential customers.

Byerly's is a prospering chain of grocery stores that almost never advertises. The manager of each store in the Minnesota-based chain has considerable leeway to provide services in the particular neighborhood. Every store has a full-time home economist who helps customers with nutrition and menus. A wonderful example of its superior service and education of customers in this health conscious age is Byerly's color-coding of foods for special diets. For example, all low-cholesterol foods in the store might have a blue tag, and customers can also get a list of them from the store's home economist.

The enzyme bath treatment consists of three parts and lasts an hour and a half. It begins in our Japanese tea garden where you are served an herbal tea blended especially for Osmosis. The tea is mixed with enzymes made from over 25 different organically-grown plants. This preparation is a digestive aid that is soothing to the whole body and works with the metabolic processes that occur during the bath.

Working With Knowledgeable Customers

Nan Hohenstein, a skilled publicist whose one-person San Francisco agency specializes in handling publicity for the publishing industry (such as author appearances on radio and TV shows) and also publicizes events such as fairs and trade shows, concentrates on knowledgeable businesspeople in the field—for example, small publishers with an even smaller budget. Many people in this group, because they have been only light users of publicity services, fear that comprehensive public relations (P.R.) services will be too expensive. Holstein's goal is to help these people become medium or heavy users by explaining to them how she can lay out an overall campaign but allow them to do many of the time-consuming P.R. tasks themselves at a very reasonable cost.

Hohenstein explains, "I'm really good at what I do but have a difficult time with certain kinds of clients—the worst client for me being someone who has rarely used a publicist. These people really don't know enough to appreciate the work that goes into what I will do for them. If lots of people show up at an event I organize, those clients tend to assume that it's in the nature of things, not acknowledging how much my getting the word out contributed. That's why I prefer to concentrate on clients who know a good deal about how the publicity business works, say someone who has worked in an arm's-length relationship with a big P.R. firm that has charged them high prices. While these people are generally knowledgeable, they don't know how to use my more personal and flexible services, which allow the client to save a great deal of money by doing their own envelope stuffing, follow-up calls, etc. My job is to educate this second group on how to use my services effectively. Once I do this, it's usually relatively easy to produce positive results at a moderate cost and I naturally get repeat business."

Allen/Vanness, which began by selling elegant woven fabric available in a wide range of patterns at craft fairs, decided its best marketing strategy was to educate clients in the "naive heavy users" category. It expanded to include scarves, shawls, wraps and ties, selling to expensive designer stores in San Francisco, Los Angeles and New York. Initially, the people who patronized these pricey outlets had little real appreciation of the extraordinary quality of the handwoven fabrics used in the garments; they just liked them. To increase sales, Allen/Vanness decided to help customers understand why they liked woven products so much. They taught the salespeople in the various shops about how their handwoven goods were made and why they offered such a superior value. When this information was passed along to the customers, sales went up.

Consider how educating customers can lead to better business. Pastorale, a Freestone, California, business that emphasizes natural fibers, sells beautiful clothing made of silk, rayon and wool. Larry and Nancy Rowinsky, the proprietors, go to great lengths to educate their customers about the care of what they buy. Their main concern, however, is that light users are often naive about taking care of fine wool garments and exotic silks and rayons. For instance, they put a wet wool cap on a hat rack or sweater in a clothes dryer—and when the hat stretches and the sweater shrinks, uneducated customers typically blame everyone but themselves. To deal with this, Larry and Nancy put a lot of effort into teaching new customers how to care for their fabric. In addition to the tab inside each garment and the hang tag, they believe in verbally informing each customer of the safest and surest way to care for their purchase. The time spent with each purchaser makes for satisfied customers who feel confident in buying and caring for their items.

Recently they have branched out into clothing products that are environmentally friendly and made in the USA, so they have the job of educating customers about an entire new field. An example is Polartec® jackets, made of a fabric made from recycled plastic bottles. They inform each customer that the quality of the product is unsurpassed. Not only do they come in stunning colors, it's a friendly plastic. It doesn't pill and doesn't get itchy. It stays soft and comfy; it is rain repellent, can be treated with Scotchguard for waterproofing and lasts and looks great for a long time. Technically speaking, all clothing on the American market must pass rigid tests for flammability. This one is no exception. Now and then you hear about a recall; there have been none on this product. Customers take pride in wearing the jackets because they feel they are participating in recycling.

Our favorite yarn store follows the traditional approach of converting novices to amateurs to encourage them to patronize the business more. The shop owner estimates that at one time or another, 40% of her customers depend on her to help them with a project. As they become better knitters and crocheters, many of her patrons move from naive/light users to amateur/medium users. Without instruction, business would surely suffer.

For another wonderful example of how helping your customers to become better-informed users can improve your business, let's again refer to the National Bank of the Redwoods. This bank has a credit analyst on hand to help unsophisticated small business owners put their financial information into a form the bank can deal with. This not only provides the bank with the correct information it needs to make loan decisions, it helps turn naive light and medium users of the bank's services into steady and profitable customers.

Do People Know What You Do?

At a party, ____% of the people who hear the name and a very brief description of my business will know a little about the details of what I really do. [For instance, 100% would know what a barber does, but only 3% would know that an oncologist studies tumors.]

At a meeting of business people generally (for example, the Chamber of Commerce), about ____% of the people who hear the name and a very brief description of my business will know a lot about it.

When a potential new customer approaches, how much does he or she really know about what I do?

☐ Doesn't know anything   ☐ Knows a little   ☐ Knows quite a bit and is very confident

Among new customers, ____% have used someone else in my field (or a similar product) before.

Are there experts in my field (or closely related fields) who have had little or no experience with my goods or services?

☐ YES ☐ NO

List by category: _____

Are there specific categories of people who would have less than an average level of knowledge about my field who might use my business if they knew more about it, such as people who seldom travel (about the travel business), landlords, commuters, etc.? List:

_____

_____

_____

_____

_____

_____

_____

_____

Do People Know What You Do? page 2

Do any of these categories of people include good prospects for my business? List:

_____

_____

_____

_____

_____

_____

_____

_____

_____

_____

_____

_____

_____

_____

_____

_____

I have available the following information about my business:

☐ Descriptive brochure   ☐ Guide book for new customers

☐ Descriptive label   ☐ General instructions or manuals

☐ References ☐ Articles   ☐ Order form for more general information
              ☐ Books
              ☐ Manuals

I provide:

☐ Personalized instruction   ☐ Classes

☐ Examples of other customers   ☐ Samples

☐ Introductory discussion   ☐ Free first lesson

Chapter 8

How to Let Customers Know Your Business Is Excellent

*W*e've just talked about the need to decide which groups of customers and friends to focus your marketing efforts on. This chapter discusses the best ways to give those people enough information about your business so that they will know why it is good and be able to communicate this to others. The point of doing this is obvious. To really become effective missionaries on your behalf, your customers, potential customers and friends need to know specifically what sets you apart from others in your field.

How do you make sure your customers have enough information about you to spread the word knowledgeably? One way is to tell them yourself. The way you run your business, of course, makes a strong statement. However, you should also make an effort to give your customers information that lets them judge the quality of your business for themselves.

For example, a plumber might say, "I'm glad you let me install 3/4-inch copper pipe instead of plastic, because I feel confident it will last two generations without giving you any problems. Also, it works so well that the pressure in your shower is now good enough that you can take a shower while washing the clothes and running the dishwasher, without loss in pressure."

Or, if you tell a customer in your boutique that the half-Dacron, half-cotton jumpsuit she is considering buying to bring on a trip will dry on a hanger in two hours without any wrinkles, and it does, that person has clear evidence that you and your business can be trusted. Or, if a respected financial columnist states that for a certain type of investment, a 15% return is excellent, and your personal finance advising service has just done substantially better than that, you will want to be sure your clients are aware of how you compare.

New Balance bases their marketing on the concept that high quality athletic shoes can be made in America at competitive prices. They include a hang tag with every purchase explaining their commitment to providing jobs for American workers and to support domestic manufacturers and suppliers where possible.

A second way to ensure that your customers have information is to have someone they trust tell them how good your business is. Positive validation by a trusted person can be extremely effective. For instance, think about how good you would feel if a fashion designer told you the suit you were wearing was beautifully tailored, or if your uncle who is a dentist looked into your mouth and assured you that your regular dentist did excellent work or if an award-winning architect remarked positively about the remodeling job you had just done on your kitchen.

You can and should, of course, use both of these methods to let your customers know that you run an excellent business. Once they know this, they will not only tend to patronize you more themselves, but will also surely recommend your business to others. Let's now look at these techniques in detail.

A. Tell Them Yourself

How can you effectively communicate your confidence and pride in what you do without boring people to death or appearing hopelessly egotistical? The most immediate way is to have your own genuine good feelings about what you do be so pervasive that your customers immediately pick up on them. Earlier in this book, we discussed the importance of having a clean business, enthusiastic employees, open books, honest pricing, and offering lots of extras as well as selling a quality product or service. All these things tell your customers that you are a first-class operation. In addition, it is extremely important to pay attention to details, such as how you finally present your product or service, including the wrapping, if any, clear instructions on use and what to do if something goes wrong with a product or a service proves disappointing.

Once these basic good business techniques are in place, you are ready for the next step: maintaining a high level of communication with your customers. Communication (oral when possible, written when not) should be built into the operation of your business. There is no need for this contact to be boastful. People are sick of being told by advertisements that a certain product or service is bigger, better, faster

or sexier. Make the communication meaningful and interesting—beyond a functional description of what you're selling. A catalogue can educate your customers about what you do, especially if you tie it to a story. We all love a good story, and are more likely to patronize a business that takes the time to tell us one. The following brief excerpts from mail order catalogues illustrate the technique.

Burgers' Smokehouse, located in the Ozark Mountains of Missouri, has this to say about its hams: "These are the hams our fathers, grandfathers, and their forefathers made. It is the ham that was made at the time of the Pilgrims and long before. They are cured the old-fashioned way— outdoors in a corn crib or, as in our case, in a special building which allows fresh country air to move continually around the hams—and aged for a year. Because it is so time consuming, most production of this type of ham is for private consumption, and we are virtually the only firm that makes it in commercial quantities."

The House of Tyrol in Cleveland, Georgia, sells beer steins to collectors. Its catalog contains not only detailed descriptions of the steins, but background information that is bound to captivate collectors. For example, with a description of a stein that depicts Frederick the Great and the Prussian eagle is the following story:

"His father thought him a weakling, beat him, and cast him into a dungeon for a spell. Indeed, Frederick II played the flute, corresponded with Voltaire for 42 years, was known as the philosopher king, and even anonymously published a refutation of Machiavelli. Yet, Frederick, inheriting an army of 100,000 giants, wrested Silesia from Maria Theresa, held off the combined forces of Austria, Russia, and France, and later joined in the first partition of Poland. When he died in 1786, he was known as the Great, and Prussia rivaled Austria for control of the German states."

Here are several other examples of businesses that tell their customers how good they are in creative and helpful ways:

- A delicatessen that makes sure all new customers know how to prepare the exotic foods they purchase.
- A caterer who has a favorite recipe printed on business cards.
- A craftsperson who includes a card with every piece of finished work, explaining how it was made and where the materials came from.
- A bakery that prints on its bags its policy about using only natural ingredients.
- A dentist who calls the evening that he performed a root canal to ask how you are feeling.

Here are some small businesses that do a good job of having others communicate favorable information about them:

- John Lande, a lawyer who specializes in mediation, publishes a newsletter/ bulletin to educate people about the reasons for choosing mediation over an adversarial approach to dispute resolution. This newsletter contains articles by people prominent in the field discussing the best mediation techniques and other important information about the field. Lande sends his newsletter to other lawyers who might refer mediation cases to him, as well as to a wide range of legal practitioners and former clients who might know of others who could use his services.
- The Redwood Funeral Society publishes an annual "Consumer Protection Price Survey on Death Arrangements" which lists prices broken down by services offered and whether they are an independent provider or part of a conglomerate.
- Mary's Flowers in Seattle sells special flowers, shears, decorative figurines and vases used for traditional Japanese flower arrangements. She always has a fresh arrangement in the window created by a person skilled in the field. This subtly, but obviously, tells her customers that her flowers and other materials are first-class.

No matter what your business, you can offer a descriptive brochure about your goods or services, extensive descriptions on your label (if that is appropriate), guide books, instruction manuals or handouts containing basic information about your goods and services. Remember, if your business is truly a good one, the more your customers know about your field, the better you will stack up.

The options in providing general information about your field of business are very broad. The following questionnaire, though far from exhaustive, is designed to stimulate your thinking and imagination.

Do You "Tell Them Yourself"?

Do you give verbal assurance to customers about the quality of your goods or service?

☐ NEVER   ☐ SELDOM   ☐ OFTEN   ☐ ALWAYS

How? What kinds of things do you tell customers?

_____

_____

_____

_____

_____

_____

Is specific evidence given to customers to back up this assessment?
[Examples: "Call me back if you don't see a result in three days."
"Measure it before and after you put it in a cold wash to make sure it doesn't shrink."]

☐ YES   ☐ NO

Who usually tells the customer?

☐ I TELL THEM   ☐ SOME EMPLOYEES TELL THEM

☐ MOST EMPLOYEES TELL THEM   ☐ ALL EMPLOYEES TELL THEM

Is follow-up done to check new customer satisfaction?

☐ NEVER   ☐ SELDOM   ☐ OFTEN   ☐ ALWAYS

Is follow-up done to check regular customer satisfaction?

☐ NEVER   ☐ SELDOM   ☐ OFTEN   ☐ ALWAYS

Pinchot & Company

Selling a service to the top executives of Exxon, Xerox and DuPont can't be considered an easy job, especially when your first post-college business experience was blacksmithing. That is precisely what Gifford Pinchot III has done. His firm, on Vashon Island near Seattle, sells an Intrapreneurial training program. Included in Pinchot's sales packet is an "Innovation Audit" for major corporations designed to see if they are encouraging the development of new ideas. A full-scale audit can cost upwards of $50,000 and take several months. The company also offers a mini-audit for less.

Pinchot started with his own entreprenurial spirit and experience, first farming and then blacksmithing for eight years and running an inventor's brokerage. He had the respectable academic credentials necessary for many mainstream jobs but preferred running his own business.

In the late '70s, he participated in the School for Entrepreneurs at Bob Schwartz's Tarrytown Center (see Chapter 7). While there, he asked himself the question, "Could a large corporation keep the entrepreneurial spirit within itself?" As he said in USA Today (August 22, 1985): "One very large firm lost 37 people that they really thought were important. They discovered after five years that those 37 people had formed businesses which were 2.5 times as large as the company they had left."

Although Pinchot clearly had a good business idea, he had to do a number of things to appeal to major business clients. Many of them had to do with giving potential clients information with which to measure his work. To accomplish this, Pinchot first developed his direct support community—people experienced in the field, with whom he could brainstorm and learn. As it turned out, three men in Sweden (the Foresight Group) were taking a similar approach in helping Swedish and American companies, and Pinchot worked with them to learn how to deal with large corporate clients.

Next he, with the support of the Swedes and Norman Macrae, editor of the prestigious Economist magazine, gave the methodology a name: Intrapreneurship. With the name and the direct client experience, Pinchot opened the School for Intrapreneurs at Tarrytown Center and marketed the courses to the Center's big business community. In addition to instant credibility, this provided him with students.

Pinchot's next step was to begin to talk about his ideas with the American business press, which was eagerly soliciting information about his new ideas. As part of getting the word out, he wrote his own article on the material, published in International Management magazine, which led to further coverage by Inside R & D.

Simultaneous with the beginning of his publicity campaign, Pinchot started work on a book called Intrapreneuring, which was published in 1985 by Harper and Row. The book was based on interviews with "intrapreneurs" from major companies and provides examples for his prospective clients. When the book was published, Pinchot got widespread publicity in the general press and made special efforts to be covered by the business press. The result was large articles in Inc., Boardroom Reports, Business Week and other publications.

Finally, because he frequently used the 3M Corporation in Minneapolis as an example of an intrapreneuring company, Pinchot asked for permission to study the company. Not expecting payment, he was surprised when 3M felt it needed a new outside viewpoint and hired him for an audit. Word of Pinchot helping his best example spread widely among corporate executives and helped further expand the firm's business.

B. Help Customers Judge for Themselves

The best way to let your customers know your business is good is to provide them with the information they need to judge for themselves. You can give your customers four broad kinds of measures to accomplish this: Direct, Public, Education and Referrals.

1. Direct Measures

At the simplest level, you can tell your customers about special features of your goods or services. Examples of this technique include:

- A wine store that displays graphically attractive material telling customers how to judge a good wine and then gives them a list of ten "good buys" and asks them to judge how they stack up.
- A real estate company that demonstrates with a bar graph that it outsells other companies in the area and places this information in the local real estate guide and in the office.
- A brake shop that distributes information sheets explaining the various types of brake jobs it does and how long each should last.
- Rollerblade, an in-line skate manufacturer, which lays out a course and brings a van full of skates to an-

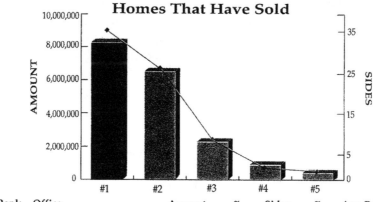

COMPANY COMPARISONS
Homes That Have Sold

Rank	Office	Amount	%	Sides	%	Avg. Price
#1	FRANK HOWARD ALLEN	8,259,500	25.34	35	25.74	235,985
#2	POLLEY, POLLEY MAD	6,522,350	20.01	26	19.12	250,859
#3	CREATIVE PROP. SERV.	2,296,750	7.05	10	7.35	229,675
#4	PRUDENTIAL CALIF.	906,750	2.78	3	2.21	302,250
#5	C 21 CRESTWOOD	440,000	1.35	2	1.47	220,000
	All other companies:	14,173,150		60		
	Total:	32,598,500		136		239,694

PART OF AN INFORMATION SHEET HANDED OUT BY REAL ESTATE AGENTS RANDY AND DIANA ROUSSEAU IN SONOMA COUNTY, CALIFORNIA

1996/97 **DRIVING TOUR**

ITALIANATE 1860 -1880

4353 24TH ST. - 1994
Awarded **first place**, exterior residential by the PDCA -1994
1944 WEBSTER - 1990
Awarded **second place**, exterior residential by the PDCA - 1990

EASTLAKE or STICK 1880 -1890

19 HENRY ST - 1983 & 1993
222 KELLER, PETALUMA - 1994

QUEEN ANNE TOWER 1890 -1910

722 STEINER ST. - 1994 (pictured)
Awarded **second place**, exterior residential by the PDCA - 1990
459 ASHBURY ST. - 1986
Awarded **first place**, exterior residential by the PDCA - 1987

QUEEN ANNE ROW 1890 - 1910

4319 22nd ST. - 1995
780 & 782 ELIZABETH - 1992

EDWARDIAN 1900 -1912

182 ARGUELLO ST - 1995
1901 PAGE - 1992

STUCCO STYLE

246 SEAVIEW - 1995
Julia Morgan Design: Piedmount, CA
711 MARINA BLVD. - 1989

INTERIORS

229 CASCADE
Dulce Murphy / Mill Valley
ZEN CENTER HOSPICE

nounced locations so customers can try before they buy.

These types of direct explanations offer a concise measurement that your customers can easily evaluate. Let's now look at the specifics of how four businesses accomplish this.

Bruce Nelson of Local Color Inc. in Mill Valley, California, specializes in exterior paint jobs for older houses. He has developed a one-page checklist that details the elements of a quality house-painting job. He gives this form to all prospective customers when he bids for a job. This gives them a chance to understand all that his work entails so they can have a sensible basis on which to compare other painters' bids. More to the point we are discussing here, it also provides them with the background information necessary to evaluate the quality of Nelson's work when the job is complete. Local Color also gives potential customers a list of buildings it has painted. Divided into "Driving Tours" of different neighborhoods and house styles, this provides a convenient way for anyone interested to check out Local Color's work in advance. In 1994, Local Color painted two houses on the famous Post Card Row—a street in San Francisco lined with historic Victorian homes—and won first and second place in the "Picture It Painted Professionally" contest sponsored annually by Painting and Decorating Contractors of America.

The House Cleaners of Memphis, Tennessee, specializes in cleaning apartments when tenants vacate. When its employees finish, they leave a detailed checklist for the landlord, marking off such items as "cleaned venetian blinds," "oiled hinges" and "cleaned refrigerator coils." Many landlords who would never think of cleaning some of these items still feel very good to learn about what they see as an extra service.

In a similar vein, Barbara, a mother of school-aged children, needed to supplement her income and decided to clean houses so she could control her schedule and be home when her children arrived after school. Barbara has evolved a method that makes new customers both knowledgeable and satisfied. Initially, Barbara comes to a potential customer's house to determine, specifically, what is expected of her. She then sits down with the customer and draws up a short contract which specifically states what will be cleaned, how often, who will provide necessary supplies and how much this will cost. Then, Barbara comes and cleans everything at the agreed-upon price, even if it takes her a little longer than estimated. She then leaves the homeowner a note asking him to call if he has any problems and suggesting any adjustments in the arrangement. If she doesn't hear from the person within a few days, she calls to make absolutely certain he is happy with her service and to discuss whether he wants to add or subtract anything from the agreement. From then on, she comes as scheduled and keeps to the

agreement. Needless to say, Barbara is so valued by the people she works for that she commands a premium price and has a waiting list for her services.

Written agreements are particularly important in many consulting and personal service businesses where customers often don't know just what it is you do. In addition to defining the specific task to be accomplished (for example, designing a computer program to track sales calls), it is also important to use a contract to tell the customer exactly how you charge. For example, many professionals charge for missed appointments in some circumstances. If you do, letting your clients know in writing as part of your contract about the specifics of your billing practices, such as the fact that "Travel time is charged at one-half the standard hourly rate," or "Phone calls of more than five minutes' duration are charged for a quarter of an hour," is a direct and beneficial way to both give them necessary information about your business and to indicate that your time is valuable.

In the home contracting business it is very common for the home owner to keep adding on to the job without realizing that the cost is going up with each addition. The savvy contractor anticipates this by explaining verbally and in writing that anything not included in the original contract requires an extra work order signed by the home owner.

Typically, a letter of agreement such as this works well:

Sample Letter of Agreement

Ms. Nancy Lowell
Compu-Consultants
24360 9th Street
Berkeley, CA 94710

Ms. Jeanne Pierson
Butterfly Boutique
1234 Mountain Blvd.
Montclair, CA 94725

Dear Ms. Pierson,
The object of this consulting project is for Compu-Consultants to help you, the owner of Butterfly Boutique, to set up an operating financial reporting system that will allow you to travel for periods of up to six months with confidence that the accounting and bookkeeping aspect of your business will be well run while you are gone. This should be accomplished in three months, using no more than 90 hours of consulting time.

The technical specifications of all software necessary to accomplish this goal and a detailed statement of what the software will accomplish are appended to this agreement. Consulting time shall be billed monthly at $75 per hour. If you agree with these terms and find them satisfactory, please sign under my signature below on both copies; keep one of them for your files and return the other to me.
Sincerely,
Nancy Lowell
President

2. Public Measures

Another important way your customers gain knowledge about your business is through your creative use of public communication. Public communication can include almost any source of authority, such as a trustworthy media outlet or consumer rating service that your customers know makes judgments that are reliable, objective and, most important, independent of your control.

For example, when you offer something that has been evaluated favorably in *Consumer Reports* magazine or by any other consumer rating organization, it's good business to post a copy at your place of business. (*Consumer Reports* discourages use of its ratings in ads, for obvious reasons, but their use as part of direct marketing efforts by your business is acceptable.)

Similarly, listing the FDA minimum daily nutrition requirements side by side with the contents of your food products allows your customers to intelligently judge your product. Where relevant, Environmental Protection Agency (EPA) warnings are certainly important for your customers to be aware of so they can evaluate how you have dealt with any potential health risks. For example, if you run a garden shop and know the EPA has listed several types of pesticides as being particularly dangerous, you would be wise to post a notice to this effect along with a list of the substitute products you recommend to accomplish the same pest control purpose.

Here are some other examples:

- "The following is a list of five negative traits associated with religious cults by *Time* magazine—please judge for yourself if our spiritual center has any of them."
- "Following are the important characteristics of a fine woolen sweater as established by the National Wool Bureau. Notice how our sweaters compare."
- *"Tennis International* magazine has published the following criteria for a well-strung tennis racket. Please check to see that we meet or exceed all of these requirements."

Similarly, if you are in the insulation business, you want to let your customers know about the products you sell that work as well as asbestos, without the health risks. One way to do this is to make available the recommendations of a prominent architect associated with the environmental movement. Besides the educational value, your customers will appreciate your awareness of these matters.

Articles in newspapers, magazines or professional journals that evaluate your business or products also give the public readily available measures of quality they can use for their own purposes and pass along to others. It's important to be aware of such articles and make them available on a regular basis. For example, if you sell appliances, electronic equipment or hardware, all products that are top rated should be marked accordingly. In addition to placing informative signs on the goods themselves, consider creating a display where you post the actual reviews and articles commenting objectively (and ideally, favorably) on the products you sell.

The Internet has a plethora of sites that evaluate products and services. If you have a website, you can add a page that has evaluations of the products you sell. Even better, you can provide a page of links to other sites that provide evaluations and measurement tools.

The Industry Standard, a magazine on the Internet economy, has a Secret Shopper column that rates websites for accuracy. In one instance, the Secret Shopper ordered a dozen clothing products from online stores in order to compare the actual color of the clothing with the Web graphic examples. If your company obtained a good rating, it would be worth noting publicly.

The Sonoma Land Trust in Santa Rosa, California has devised a Partners in Nature program with local business owners. As part of helping participating businesses market their services, the land trust provides a logo that the businesses can use to show their commitment to land protection and conservation.

In the May 1996 issue of *Money* magazine, in the "Wise Up" column, there is an article entitled "The Post Office's Priority Mail Flunks Our Five-City Test." The article is prominently displayed on the counter of our local mail service that handles Fed Ex and UPS packages.

Don't assume that providing convenient ways for customers to measure the quality of your goods and services may work well for some types of businesses but not for yours. For example, even dentists—hardly a group that normally engages in creative marketing—are sometimes evaluated. A San Francisco Bay area publication, *Consumer Checkbook,* sent a questionnaire to thousands of Bay Area citizens and asked them to rate their dentists. Two of the questions were: "My dentist explains what he/she is doing," and "My dentist encourages patients to look at their own dental files." The magazine published the tabulated results, which contained information on costs, dental specialty and other matters. One Palo Alto dentist, Daniel Armistead, who was rated at or near the top in all important categories, displays this rating in his waiting room, so that the majority of his customers who don't subscribe to *Consumer Checkbook* will know how he stacks up.

A dentist who isn't in a community where ratings are published can display articles and other information explaining new and improved techniques for teeth and gum care. This gives the patients valuable information about state of the art dental care and helps them understand that they are being cared for by a person who prides herself in keeping up with developments in her field.

In The Natural Bedroom in San Francisco, California, mail order catalogue customers are informed that their woolen products are "scrupulously cleaned and created without bleaches, formaldehydes, dyes or animal cruelty by more than 50 ranchers." Along with other information about the important attributes of wool they include the results of a study conducted by two leading European institutes that confirms wool's superior comfort (under both warm and cool sleeping conditions, wool-fill wicks away body moisture better than down, cotton or synthetic fibers) and demonstrating the lowering of heart rate, decrease in humidity and regulation of body temperature.

Offering customers something tangible is a good marketing strategy and can be another creative way to allow them to measure the quality of your goods and services. Pharmacies can provide charts that compare cost and potency of generic and branded medicines. This not only allows customers to save money, but also lets them know that the pharmacy is concerned with more than just its own bottom line. For businesses that sell things by weight, a cardboard slide rule that conveniently allows customers to compare volume to cost, or distance to weight, can be a wonderfully helpful device. It is both a useful tool and a reminder that the store wants to help customers get a good deal.

Nolo.com, the publisher of this book, does an impressive job of giving out information in a variety of ways, particularly at its website where an extensive Legal Encyclopedia offers free legal information for consumers.

How Customers Can Evaluate Your Business

My business provides clear verbal measurements of product/service effectiveness.

☐ NEVER   ☐ SELDOM   ☐ OFTEN   ☐ ALWAYS

My business provides training classes to new customers and prospects.

☐ NEVER   ☐ SELDOM   ☐ OFTEN   ☐ ALWAYS

My business provides clear written measurements of product/service effectiveness.

☐ NEVER   ☐ SELDOM   ☐ OFTEN   ☐ ALWAYS

We offer a

☐ Brochure   ☐ Specification sheet
☐ Checklist   ☐ Contract
☐ Informative label   ☐ Questionnaire
☐ Instructions   ☐ Evaluation form
☐ Worksheet   ☐ Physical measurement
☐ Website   ☐ Other online information (survey, newsletter, etc.)

We have:

☐ Displays/models   ☐ Samples/examples
☐ Photos of successful work   ☐ Other evidence of quality

3. Educational Measures

All the measures discussed in this chapter to communicate information to your customers and clients are, in a broad sense, educational. Here we focus on more traditional "educational" avenues: classes and workshops.

If you teach popular classes, you have a great marketing advantage over similar businesses because you have an enormous opportunity to communicate directly with both customers and interested prospective customers. And if you teach at a well-known school, it gives both you and, by extension, your business a valuable credential.

Most community college and university extension course catalogues include a wide array of courses in which businesspeople teach the public about their fields. The courses can generate clients and personal recommendations based on what the student learned. For example, a college extension catalogue that recently came our way lists the following evening courses, which are really just introductions to new business fields:

- Graphic Design for the World Wide Web
- Computer Ergonomics
- Mediating Business Disputes
- Ocean Kayaking
- Toxic Waste Safety
- How to Design Your Own Kitchen
- Coping With an Alcoholic in the Family
- Law for the Small Business Person
- Creative Divorce

Classes can also directly expose potential customers to your product. For example, auto dealers often lend cars to driver training classes, and customers are often exposed to computers, laser printers and other high-tech equipment through training classes. Indeed, this approach is so successful that the Apple Computer company bases much of its corporate marketing effort around making gifts and loans of computers and software to schools and nonprofit groups. Similarly, one of the reasons that Lincoln and Victor became the dominant names in the welding business was because they supplied trade schools with their equipment.

4. Referrals

The opinion of people in your field—professional peers, leaders in the field, knowledgeable suppliers, key employees or former students and apprentices—can make a huge difference to a successful personal recommendation marketing campaign.

In the small business context, one of the best references you can obtain for a service you offer is to send a customer to a respected peer for a second opinion or critical evaluation. For example, an architect might send a client to a solar expert for confirmation that his design is, in fact, solar efficient. A builder working in an area of earthquake risks can refer potential customers to a soils expert or structural engineer to review her plans.

The point is that it is extremely important, especially in service businesses, that you take the time to know others in your field and related fields. As they come to respect and trust you (and vice versa), there will be all sorts of ways you can help each other, one of which is to provide validation for each other's goods and services.

The Pickle Family Circus of San Francisco found an ingenious way to involve a former colleague. One of the clowns who helped found the circus in the early 1970s moved to New York and became a widely recognized performer. He even received a very prestigious MacArthur Foundation Award. In a well-publicized homecoming gala fundraiser, the circus was able to remind everyone that it is an important source of theatrical talent and an exciting place to be.

Similarly, a good strategy for a dance school would be to have a top student perform at a party held by a board member of an important ballet company.

Whenever we think of apprentices, Hal Howard comes to mind. Hal, a floor sander, has trained numerous assistants throughout the years, passing along his expertise and love of fine craftsmanship. Now, when Hal's apprentices have jobs that are technically too difficult for them, they refer those customers to their "master." If you have been involved with apprentices, let them know if you are available to back them up or help with complicated jobs.

Dear Friends and Associates,

I am writing to introduce you to a Naturopathic Doctor in Sebastopol. Michael Lipelt has recently opened a practice at 523 S. Main Street in downtown Sebastopol. The very tastefully redecorated office is welcoming as soon as you walk in the door.

I have been a patient of Dr. Lipelt since he first opened and am pleased to recommend him to you. Formerly a dentist in Santa Rosa, Dr. Lipelt returned to school and received extensive education in both acupuncture and Naturopathic medicine. His focus is on wellness and prevention.

In addition to being highly trained and skilled, Dr. Lipelt takes the time to listen and to get to know you and your history -- a trait I find very important in a health care provider. He offers a free introductory consultation, so you can see for yourself! An Open House with music, wine and refreshments will be held on Friday, May 17 from 4:30 to 7:00 PM.

Please review the brochure sent with this letter to learn more specifics about Dr. Lipelt's practice. Then call him for that free consultation -- and tell him I sent you.

Sincerely,

Marty Roberts

Marty Roberts

Referrals

My business is:			by:
KNOWN	RESPECTED	RECOMMENDED	
			Others in the same business
☐	☐	☐	Some
☐	☐	☐	Most
			Locals in the same business
☐	☐	☐	Some
☐	☐	☐	Most
			Others in closely related businesses
☐	☐	☐	Some
☐	☐	☐	Most
			Leaders in my business
☐	☐	☐	Some
☐	☐	☐	Most
			Students and former employees
☐	☐	☐	Some
☐	☐	☐	Most

C. Giving Customers Authority for Your Claims

While it can be very effective for you to communicate your pride in your work or product to your customers directly, it is usually even more effective to have someone else do it for you. There are many ways you can provide the authority of others to help customers realize that your product or service is of high quality.

Chances are you already use some of these techniques and are familiar with others. For example, displaying diplomas, awards and certificates of course completion are traditional ways to let clients and customers know that you have the "seal of approval" of the educational or licensing institutions in your field. Similarly, wine bottles often have an "appellation"; marmalades and mustards often tell us they won "First Prize in the Cloverdale Fair"; film posters and book jackets tell us about awards won and display favorable critics' comments and electrical products have the "Underwriter's Labs Seal of Approval." Web pages may note that they've been named "One of the top 5 Yahoo sites on the Net." If you are an author or small publisher, a high rating by readers on Amazon.com can be useful in your marketing.

Ways to use third party testimony to tell your customers that you do a good job are almost limitless. Even the smallest business should be able to create a healthy range of this type of information. For example, in some businesses such as consulting, graphics, interior design and advertising, it is customary to list one's clients in a portfolio. This idea can be carried further by not only presenting a bare list, but including descriptions of each client, as well as quotes from them about your business. It is also a good idea to give special potential clients the phone number of an existing client (with permission, of course) to call for more information about your work, as long as you don't overdo it. Architects, interior designers, graphic artists and landscapers are among the businesses that can offer portfolios of their work along with pictures of happy clients and letters of appreciation.

Many retail businesses display letters from enthusiastic customers, and some enlarge letters of special interest. For example, if a local photocopy store completes a huge rush job for a popular local business or a political figure and receives a note of thanks, it makes sense to display it on the bulletin board along with information about the speed and precision of its service. If you adopt this technique, however, be sure all letters and commendations are relatively recent and are changed often. Your regular customers won't be impressed the 37th time they see the same faded letter. Oh, and one more thing. Take the trouble to display all materials as nicely as possible. If you simply tape a review or commendation to a window or wall, you tell your customers that you have little imagination and don't value the accolade highly enough to present it well. A far better approach is to take all you want to display to a local framing shop and have them presented nicely.

Peter Martin, a Santa Cruz, California real estate broker, makes extensive use of statements from satisfied customers. When a customer compliments Martin after a job is done, Martin asks her to put the compliments in writing, on letterhead if possible. "It's important to ask clients when the good service they've received is fresh in their minds," he says. Martin sends prospective clients and friends well-designed and attractively printed brochures containing excerpts from the letters. The brochures, which are inexpensive to produce, serve the dual purpose of telling prospective clients about him and answering friends who ask "What can we say about you?"

Some businesses also display photos of local or national celebrities who patronize their business. If you do this, pay particular attention to both the quality of these photos and what they communicate to the viewer. While a photo of a top bike racer consulting on the repair of his bike at a local bike repair shop would be very effective, a 15-year-old picture of a former football player eating in a restaurant may subtly tell the customer that the restaurant is as out of date as the quarterback.

Another good approach to validating your expertise is to write a series of articles about your specialty or to contact publications and freelance writers to see if they are interested in telling your story for you. In almost every business or field of specialization, there are newsletters, journals or trade magazines that accept such articles. Once a favorable article is published about your innovative law practice, lawn repair service or language school, distribute reprints to your customers and have the original enlarged for display. Also, if you can, arrange to be interviewed on a local radio show, and have a friend photograph your appearance and display it at your business, or use it in your brochure. Newspaper articles about your business are, of course, an easy thing to display. Again, however, make sure that all material of this sort is reasonably up-to-date. People will be a lot more interested in the fact that you appeared on the Jay Leno show last month than the Merv Griffin Show in 1980.

Awards and displays explaining them can often be an authoritative way to tell your customers that others think well of you. For example, the Daily Scoop, a coffee and ice cream shop near our office, displays a newspaper article selecting it as the store with the best cafe latte in San Francisco. Written on the glass frame is "Chosen Number 1." Made to Order, the very successful delicatessen in Berkeley, California we referred to in the last chapter, let its customers know that its pesto was chosen Number 1 in Northern California by a well-known newspaper by enlarging the article, framing it with bright colored cardboard and putting it in the window with ribbons. After a month, the display was taken down and replaced with a list of new products. Made to Order, which regularly wins prizes and receives favorable reviews and awards, turns each into an exciting event, but never tries to milk any particular accolade or prize too long.

One of the most ingenious examples of giving customers positive information about a business was Zoah's Free Raffle Event. This popular Japanese luncheon spot in San Francisco opened during the late '70s and lasted into the early 1990s, catering to businesspeople. Zoah's asked each customer to present a business card to enter its annual raffle. Many hundreds did. Zoah's then awarded over 60 small but nice prizes (a beer mug or Japanese cookbook, for example). The name of each winner and his business was written carefully on long sheets of paper underneath his prize and posted on the restaurant wall. Zoah's crossed out the winners' names with light-colored ink when they claimed their prizes. The result, of course, is that all the restaurants' many customers, and even many people who work in the neighborhood who had never been to the restaurant, heard about the winner's names. Indeed, several prize winners reported being called by a number of friends telling them of their good fortune. Of course, in running this little event, Zoah's not only provided fun and prizes for its customers, but the roster of winners posted on the wall allowed others to see how many prominent and interesting people patronized their restaurant.

Unfortunately, Zoah's didn't do an adequate job of keeping the place clean, and Japanese food is known for its ultra-cleanliness. Word got out, and Zoah's early marketing could not overcome the effects.

Customer Referrals

I offer new customers the names and phone numbers of other customers.

    ☐ SOMETIMES   ☐ USUALLY

I refer customers to others for second opinions or evaluations.

    ☐ SOMETIMES   ☐ USUALLY

I have available:

    ☐ Printed lists of customer referrals

    ☐ Letters from satisfied customers

    ☐ Evidence of awards or certificates for my product

    ☐ Newsletter with customer comments

I display:

    ☐ Articles

    ☐ Photos of customers enjoying my product or service

    ☐ Certificates and awards

    ☐ Any other evidence of accomplishments

Chapter 9

Helping Customers Find You

*H*aving the best product or service in your area won't do you any good if potential customers can't find you. If you run a small animal hospital, how does a person whose cat gets violently ill in the middle of the night find you? If you fix Apple computers, how does a writer with a balky Macintosh and an unforgiving editor get your phone number in a hurry? If you operate a language school to teach English as a second language, how do potential customers who may not know enough English to use traditional listing services such as the phone book locate you?

To begin with, ask yourself two questions. The first is obvious: Do the maximum possible number of potential customers know how to find your business? Depending on what kind of business you own, the second question can be far more subtle: Assuming a potential customer knows where you are, can he actually get to your goods and services with reasonable ease?

Answering these important questions can involve thinking about everything from your business name, your product packaging, the signs on your building and vehicles and the wording on your business cards and flyers, to deciding to distribute a humorous T-shirt or poster to your good customers. It also involves determining whether or not you are listed in the appropriate and logical places—for example, in the Yellow Pages, Internet search engines, all appropriate professional reference manuals or with the Chamber of Commerce.

At this point, you may be thinking about skimming or skipping this chapter; after all, if you have been in business for a while, you probably believe that you have already dealt with all the obvious accessibility issues. It is our observation that many established and otherwise efficient businesses have a lot of room to improve in this area. And don't dismiss concerns about accessibility because yours isn't a retail business. Even if you only have a relatively few loyal clients, as is true of many wholesalers and small consulting businesses, it is imperative for you to attract new ones if your business is to thrive. To do this, you must make it easy for new people to find you.

For example, suppose a visitor from another country reads an article you wrote in a trade journal about how to efficiently use variable speed electric motors in generators, and asks the State Department for an introduction. You will never meet the person if you can't be found fairly easily. Similarly, imagine the former spouse of a loyal customer who now has a thriving business of her own and needs the services of your employee benefits consulting business but doesn't want to communicate with her ex-spouse—will she be able to find you on her own? What if someone from your college hears from a former professor that you are a hot-shot Web page designer; will he find you easily or give up in frustration?

A. Finding Your Business

Particularly for retail businesses, letting potential customers know where your business is located is extremely important. Often, businesses use well-known landmarks to help clients find and remember their location. Such slogans as "Bridgeman's, across from the main entrance to the University of Minnesota," or "Matthews, Top of the Hill, Daly City," can be very helpful for the new customer. Think about how landmarks can help you. For example, if your knife sharpening shop happens to be at the crest of the hill on Main Street, your business cards, Yellow Page listing or delivery truck might say "Main Street Saw & Knife Shop—Get an edge at the Top of the Hill." This approach may be corny, but if it's effective, so what?

Your business name can also be an important tool. The "24-Hour Pet Emergency Clinic" clearly lets people know that they can get help in the middle of the night and is a far better name than "Miller Veterinary Clinic" when it comes to promoting your business. Similarly, the "Cosmetic Dentistry Clinic" tells potential customers what you specialize in. Of course, business names can serve a number of other valuable purposes, but in choosing or changing a name don't overlook the potential in terms of helping customers find you.

Never assume that customers will find you easily—or at all—once they get your address from the phone book. How many times have you looked for someone's office or shop a little longer than you wished to? Have you ever quit in disgust? Probably, most of the time you kept searching until you found your elusive quarry, but weren't in the best of moods when you finally arrived. Enough said, we hope. You don't want new customers to struggle to find you and to pass the word that you are "really out of the way" or "impossible to find at night."

Normally, it is fairly easy to eliminate problems people have in finding you even if your location is out of the way. For example, Santa Rosa Dodge capitalizes on the fact it is difficult to find through its Yellow Pages listing, "Hardest Place in Town to Find…But Worth It!" and then prints a map so customers can in fact easily locate it. It is an excellent practice for businesses to print maps in the Yellow Pages as well as on any flyers or brochures. If you are hard to find, or if you draw customers from out of town, it behooves you to do this.

We like The First Light Cafe, whose name tells customers that it is open early and which provides very clear directions, in the Yellow Pages, to its location.

Accessibility includes many obvious things beyond telling people where you are located, such as making sure your working hours are posted at your place of business and that you keep to those times. Being unpredictable is a rapid way to erode customer trust. Imagine how you would feel if you got up early on a Saturday morning, packed up the car for a long awaited ski trip, and, arriving at the tire chain rental store promptly at eight, no one was there, even though the sign clearly says, "Open at 8:00." You get a cup of coffee and return at 8:30, and still no one is there. You pace around, trying to rationalize traveling without chains, when finally at 8:45 someone comes to open up. If you have a choice, you probably won't ever again patronize that business and certainly won't recommend it to fellow ski buffs.

A number of retail businesses in all sorts of fields, from books to baby clothes, have found that staying open longer hours, especially at times when most people are not working, results in more than enough sales to cover the increased overhead costs. Your customers will tell others that there is one place in town where you can buy a bridal gown, lawnmower or a guppy on Tuesday evening or Sunday afternoon. Many businesses that have profitably extended their hours have done so by hiring reasonably priced part-time Sunday and evening help. Even professionals and others who traditionally work 9 to 5 should consider keeping their businesses open longer hours, or at least making some services available during times when others in their field are closed.

Using modern communications equipment creatively often makes it possible to offer extended access to at least some services at a reasonable cost. For example, one attorney we know of put a small advertisement in the phone book emphasizing that his office took messages 24 hours a day from people who had suffered personal injuries. He signed up over 30 new cases within a few months. Similarly, some dentists and many therapists are now taking evening appointments, and one friend very successfully offers 24-hour emergency dental care for his patients.

Having a website can be very helpful in directing your customers to your business. A website can provide vivid and accurate directions, maps, electronic coordinates

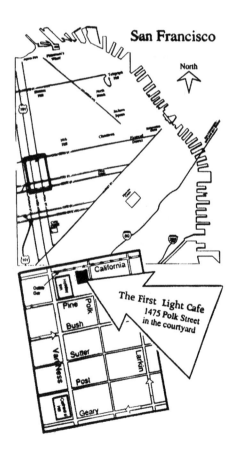

(for a global positioning system (GPS), a tool that uses satellites to find ground locations) and details about parking. As the Internet becomes increasingly connected with mobile phones, more and more people check a business's website to find its geographic location.

B. Convenience of Access

You probably know businesses that are easy to find, but located where parking is such a problem that you rarely go there. Indeed, shopping centers, which offer free convenient parking, grew in large part because shoppers got fed up with driving around the block. Parking should be seen as an integral part of access to your business. Unless you are in a shopping center, are lucky enough to have plenty of parking or depend entirely on walk-by traffic (such as a gift shop in a hotel), you should go to great lengths to see that parking is reasonably available.

If parking is a potential problem for your customers, you should take affirmative steps to help them locate what is available. The fact that most businesses don't bother to do this is even more reason for you to set yourself apart by going out of your way to help your customers.

Some creative businesses offer validated parking privileges at nearby lots, give out maps showing where parking spaces in their neighborhood are most likely to be found, or print maps with public transit lines clearly marked. All of these are good ideas. The important thing is that you analyze the parking needs of your customers and try to meet them, even if doing so costs you a little extra.

For example, the Counseling Center in downtown Westwood, California is in a neighborhood with very difficult parking, including 4 p.m. tow-away zones and half-hour meters. It printed a map showing all the various parking zones, including free spaces, metered ones and parking garages, within a four-block radius. It's been very popular with customers.

The Franz Valley Gardens in Calistoga, California specializes in growing and introducing new and unusual plants. It turned a huge problem with accessibility into a flourishing business. The nursery is small, remote and has limited parking, so it instituted a shop-by-mail program for clients. In addition, it sends out a newsletter listing the local Farmers' Markets where you can purchase its plants; it also has a display garden of ornamental grasses and various plants which may be seen by appointment. When the items that you order arrive, the nursery calls and sets up a mutually agreeable delivery time or a time when you can pick them up at the nursery if you wish.

Providing parking information isn't the only way to get your product and your customers together. Indeed, it may make sense to reverse the normal process and take the product to the customer. Home delivery, of course, is a tradition in a few businesses, such as pizza and Chinese restaurants. Other businesses, especially service ones, make house calls but often charge a lot to do it. Certainly, many businesses could gain customer trust and expand their business by flouting tradition and offering free or low-cost deliveries and service calls.

This raises an important point: Providing accessibility to your customers at their homes or businesses should never mean punishing them by charging outrageously for the service. Take stock of your business. If offering low-cost or free home delivery would increase sales, consider buying a clean second-hand pickup, hiring a retired truck driver at a reasonable rate and of course purchasing the necessary insurance. This expense shouldn't be huge and may be more than offset by the improvement in sales.

Here are some examples of interesting solutions to the problem of getting product and customer together:

- The Fit Lab, a clean, bright, well-staffed exercise facility with branches in Albany and Oakland, California, fairly bubbles over with innovative marketing without advertising techniques. One of its best is to open at least part of the day on major holidays such as Christmas, Thanksgiving and Easter. You are just bound to brag about a gym that cares enough about your well-being to let you exercise on the days when you eat the most. Fit Lab also has brochures available in a rack outside its door. Curious passers-by, who can see all the exercise equipment through the sparkling window-front, can get more information instantly without going in. This is good not only after hours, but also allows people to "browse" without risking a hard sell (which they wouldn't get anyway).

- Hansen's Mill of Kromforsh, Sweden, runs a portable sawmill operation and serves rural customers by milling logs right on their property. When the tree feller finishes his job, Olaf and his brother Torbjorn level a spot, set up their equipment and start to work, milling lumber to the customer's specifications. It's not only convenient for the customer, but extremely satisfying for her to build a deck or outbuilding using lumber from her own land.

- A masseuse might bring her specially designed chair and magic hands to your workplace, offering 15-minute neck and shoulder massages for a minimum of four people. What better Friday afternoon bonus?

- Many small office, auto and hardware supply stores have found that they can successfully compete with large discount warehouses by emphasizing fast delivery service.

- Many drug stores will make deliveries when necessary, especially to new mothers or the elderly and, in an emergency, will meet you at the drug store at any hour.

- A young friend of ours has many auto repair customers who live in rather remote areas. He customized his truck so he could do many repairs at their homes, often saving them costly towing charges and inconvenience.
- Bookstores that allow customers to order current titles over the phone or online and ship the same day are providing a service to the elderly and handicapped as well as researchers and other busy customers.
- Tilley Endurables makes the supersturdy, squashable, rain and mildew resistant, wide-brimmed cotton duck hat that floats and comes with a forever guarantee—"Put it in your will." It also sports a "Brag Tag" in the crown of the hat for the owner to give people who inquire about the hat.

Our Guarantee

If you ever find the workmanship or materials to be less than the best, your money will be refunded. If your (unbleached) Tilley Hat ever wears out, we'll replace it free! Bring it to any store that sells the Hat and you'll be given a new one.

Lastly, in the crown of your Hat is a "Brag Tag". *It could get you into trouble!* Open it up and you'll see what we mean! When you run out of them, phone us and we'll send you more at no charge.

Enjoy your Tilley!
Pass it on!

Alex Tilley

- The small business owner who refinishes clients' bathroom fixtures in their homes is certain to benefit from personal recommendations. In the same vein is the mobile dog grooming and bathing service, which is an especially great boon for owners of large dogs.
- A lawyer or tax preparer who makes house calls at no extra charge to deal with the problems of the ill and elderly opens up a whole new market for herself.
- The Mad Matter in Port Townsend, Washington is a framing business whose owner brings her mat and frame samples to the clients' homes for truly individualized service.

A business that operates online offers additional accessibility. See Chapter 11.

C. Signs

Drive down any commercial street in America and look at the signs. How many do you like? How many do you hate? If you are like most people, the ones you are attracted to are probably a distinct minority.

What makes a good sign? There is no one answer. While many people hate neon, it can be very effective in some circumstances. Other materials and styles of typefaces can be effective or not depending on how they are used. Our bias is toward signs that are simple, easy to read, and communicate the essence of the particular business.

For example, the Pacific Basin School of Textile Design flies an exquisite woven flag from the front of its building, telling thousands of people who pass on the busy road more about the business than a hundred conventional signs ever could. Similarly, we know of several locksmiths who use large cut-out wooden keys to quickly alert passers-by to the nature of their business.

The Internet has its own kind of signs. Businesses that rely on the World Wide Web for a good part of their business should invest in domain names (their online addresses) that describe their business (such as Salli's Creativecenter.com) and are very easy to remember. Other businesses may, in effect, put up signs pointing to your online site; if they think people would be interested in it, they may link their site to yours, allowing browsers to jump to your site almost instantly. More about this in Marketing on the Internet, Chapter 11.

D. Telephone Accessibility

For any small business, the telephone is a very important tool; your number should be listed in all places a customer is likely to look. This is especially crucial for service businesses and others who do a large part of their business by phone.

1. Yellow Pages Listings

An independent study done for Pacific Telephone determined that 95% of the people interviewed found the Yellow Pages helpful and 78% of them had contacted a firm located there. One-half of those in the study made a purchase or used a service as a result of their inquiry.

Some businesses, however, waste their money having a listing or display ad in the Yellow Pages and similar books. For instance, while escort services, 24-hour plumbers and bail bondsmen depend almost entirely on customers who see their Yellow Pages listing, industrial broom suppliers, nonprofit trade organizations, artists and economic research firms typically get few if any new customers from this source.

Van Entriken is an example of a businessperson who found advertising in the Yellow Pages to be ineffective. The owner of an interior design business in Reno, Nevada, he laments that "all that ever came to me from my Yellow Pages listing was a knowledge of the street layout of the city." This knowledge came about the hard way, when homeowners who found his Yellow Pages listing under Interior Designers invited him over for an estimate as an excuse to get a free consultation.

If you question whether the Yellow Pages are appropriate for your business, it's helpful to see what others in your field have decided. If lots of similar businesses use listings, it's probably wise to give it a try. If you find only a few listings, check old directories, which can usually be found in public libraries, to see if others in the field have tried listing. If you notice people trying it at various times and then dropping it, that's an important clue that it probably won't work for you.

Many businesses fall under more than one Yellow Pages category. For example, a word processing service can be found under that title as well as under "Secretarial Services" and even "Typing." When you check the Yellow Pages, it is a reasonable assumption that if all large displays or boldface listings are in only one category, this is where customers look most often. Spending money to appear in a related category will probably be a waste unless you are in a rapidly changing field featuring new terminology. For example, a number of years ago computer sales and service were listed under "data processing." The first businesses to escape from this category and be listed under "computers" did very well.

If you decide that your business will benefit from more than a listing and want to pay for a display ad, the question of ad size (and price) is important. The best guideline is to start at a price level you can afford even if the ad doesn't generate any business at all. No response would naturally be painful, but if you've been cautious it won't put a financial strain on your business, forcing you to work longer hours or significantly increase your debt. If you do get a positive response, you can always increase your display size next year, or even sooner in directories for adjacent geographic areas.

If you do decide that a display ad makes sense for your business, keep in mind certain considerations:

- **Emphasize your specialties.** Describe goods and services that distinguish you from others in your field. One charter boat company we know originally omitted the fact that it had sailboats for hire, even though it was the only company in the Yellow Pages that offered this service (others were power boat charterers). A change in the display ad copy increased business by 20%.

- **Put in as much access information as you can.** Include credit cards you accept, hours of operation, whether you respond to calls at night or on weekends (businesses that do so usually do particularly well in the Yellow Pages), whether you deliver (another big plus in this kind of listing) and, of course, detailed instructions about how to find you.

- **Don't be cutesy or try to win a graphic design award.** Information that answers customers' questions as clearly as possible is what counts. Also, if your business has been in existence a long time or has just won an award, mention it briefly. Customers who don't know you will appreciate the reassurance provided by this information.

2. Phone Technology

Because of rapid technological change, it is worthwhile to review your telephone-related marketing needs at regular intervals. While staying current isn't always cheap, failing to do so often undermines customer confidence in your business. As a general rule, anything that significantly improves the way your customers can reach your business is worth the money.

A back-up telephone answering machine or voice mail service is essential so you can be accessible even when you aren't there. Calling a business and having no one answer turns customers off. We recently called a large drug store in our area and the phone just rang and rang. Needless to say, the drug store that gave its address and hours of operation got our business. We are continually surprised at businesses that let the phone ring and ring, passing up a great opportunity to provide important information to potential customers. Letting the phone ring also raises the question in potential customers' minds that if you are that remiss about the phone, what about the rest of your business?

When you use an answering machine or voice mail service, let people know approximately when you will be returning their call. If you are out of town, say so, and have some system for dealing with calls during that time.

 Answering Machine and Voice Mail Rules

- Keep your message short. By now everyone knows how to use the machines and doesn't want a long explanation before getting a chance to speak. Something like, "Hello, this is Tandy Belew Graphic Designs. Please leave a message of any length, and I'll get back to you within 24 hours. Thanks," is all you need.

- If you have an old-fashioned answering machine that cuts off after a certain number of seconds, throw it out and buy one that will let callers talk as long as they wish.

- If you tell callers when you will be back, keep the message current. "I'll be out Tuesday afternoon" sounds dumb on Thursday.

- Get the best quality machine and fix it or replace it immediately if it breaks. Answering machines generally rank as cost-effective investments.

- If you have voice mail with multiple mail boxes, say so immediately so callers know what to listen for.

Here are a few more useful phone techniques:

- Three-way calling, which allows you to connect an incoming customer's call with someone at another location so that all three of you can talk, is available in many parts of the country. This service is essential for lawyers, consultants, accountants and others who regularly must communicate with more than one person at a time.

- "800" and "888" numbers, which let your customers call you at no expense to them, may be absolutely necessary if you take phone orders. If you are too small to contract for your own service, there are "800" residential services.
- Credit card billing for telephone sales is a growing practice. It offers many types of retailers and others the opportunity to send catalogues to their good customers, take orders over the phone and send out the product via UPS or other delivery service the same day.
- Worldwide telex services are now available for anyone with a computer and modem to attach to a telephone.
- Fax machines have become standard in a wide variety of businesses. A separate line is often a necessity, as may be 24-hour high-speed automated transmission.

For many businesses, the telephone is the primary access point people have with you. It's very irritating to call a business and be transferred by the person who answers the phone to someone else without even a "one moment please." Even worse is just being put on hold without permission. This is especially annoying when you are calling long distance. If you ask for someone or a department and then hear nothing but a click, you may not be sure whether you've been transferred, put on hold or cut off. Not a great beginning for your contact with a company.

The one thing worse is to get trapped in a telephone branching system, the kind that says: "If you want our hours press 1, if you want sales press 2" and so on, but never gets you to the place you want or gets you to the wrong place. Nearly every American can tell a story about a terrible telephone branching experience.

 A good telephone branching requires three vital elements:

1. Explain the branching system immediately. For example, "You will be given four choices, including an in-house directory."
2. Make sure that every branching route will get to a logical place. If you have five products, and inquiries about two of them go to line one and two go to line two but there is no line three, you have made a common mistake.
3. Always let people talk to a real live human being if they are confused or can't find their choice among the ones you offer.

Many imaginative business services are becoming available over the phone. For example, Michael, one of the authors of this book, offers personalized marketing consulting over the phone. For details, see the back of the book.

Phone Accessibility Checklist

WE OFFER   UPDATED YEARLY

☐   White pages listing in appropriate areas   ☐

☐   Yellow Pages listing under applicable topics and in appropriate geographical areas   ☐

☐   Answering service/system with clear instructions   ☐

☐   "800" numbers   ☐

☐   Numbers listed on cards, receipts, order forms, mailers, vehicles, repair labels and publications   ☐

Mail Accessibility Checklist

WE OFFER

☐   Clear, stable address

☐   Return address on everything we distribute

☐   Mail forwarding up-to-date

☐   Personal relationship with mail delivery person to avoid mistakes

☐   Clearly identifiable mailbox, with alternative places to deliver packages and postage-due mail

☐   If in out-of-way location, maps are included in mailings

Walk-In Accessibility Checklist

WE OFFER

☐ Clear, distinct signs not blocked by trees

☐ Neighbors given an invitation to visit so they know where we are and what our business involves

☐ Parking available or clearly designated

☐ Safe places for bicycles

☐ Door that opens easily, bell in working order

☐ Convenient hours

☐ Convenient parking

E. Listing Your Services Creatively and Widely

As you might guess, there is no one way to list information about your business in a way everyone will find it; each business is unique and requires an analysis specific to its needs. Just the same, there are always a number of sensible steps you can take to make it easier and more pleasant for potential customers to find your business. These include the obvious such as listing in general phone books, specialized phone books (for seniors, disabled, ethnic Yellow Pages, and "green" pages, to name a few), and trade and professional association directories. Don't forget Chamber of Commerce publications, public library listings, city directories, locally produced maps, tourist publications, international directories and publications of county, state and federal government agencies that operate in specialized fields. Online listings on electronic bulletin boards may also be useful. Remember also that local training schools (such as a culinary academy), trade schools and wholesalers commonly publish directories, some of which may be appropriate for your business.

Once the obvious listings are covered, it's time to be a bit more creative: to think of the kinds of listings that are seen by significant numbers of people who might overlook traditional listing places. As an exercise to get your mind focused in the right direction, assume that all of the following people are trying to locate your business. Where are you listed, posted or known that they are likely to look?

- An old school chum whom you last saw five years ago before you opened your own business.

To help this person locate you, inform your alumni associations as well as former employers and employees of your location. It's a good idea to do this more than once. This can be done by a friendly letter—be sure to include your business card. Also, when communicating with an alumni organization, always provide information about what you are doing in a way that is suitable for use in its publication. For example, if you open a wharf-side retail store featuring fresh fish, you might include a picture of yourself in a wetsuit with a spear gun, captioned, "Our fish is so fresh, I haven't caught it yet," or some such. Alumni magazines thrive on this sort of good-natured silliness and will surely run your picture and accompanying information, telling a number of old friends (great potential customers all) where you are.

- One of your first customers, a person you haven't seen since you moved your business five years ago.

If you have a customer mailing list, write to old customers informing them of your move. Do this more than once; people often don't focus on this sort of information unless they need your service right then. For example, if you have your wood floors refinished, you may not need the "Floor Doctor" again for a number of years. If he has moved and changed his name to the "Floor Surgeon," you may never find him unless he notifies you of the change a couple of times. In addition, anyone associated with your product or service (invoice, label or container suppliers, for instance) should have your up-to-date address and phone numbers. People who run neighboring businesses should also be informed of your new location when you move and, if possible, you should arrange with your old landlord to display a small sign giving your new address. You might offer to pay a few dollars or provide the landlord a free service in exchange for displaying the sign for an extended period.

- A person who heard about your unique skill from a former client and knows only your last name and city.

You should be listed in all local professional and trade association directories, including those of trade groups and schools related to your work. Others in your city who do related work should know who you are and where you are located. It's a good practice to periodically bring others up-to-date on your location as well as the current nature of your business. This is true even for a civil engineer, painter or author working out of his home.

Spend a few hours online with this chapter open in front of you. Sending e-mails to business contacts, associates, friends and acquaintances will help ensure that people you know will in fact be able to find you when they want to.

Salli lives in a little-known rural area 60 miles north of San Francisco. Because she knows being accessible to the media helps her market her books, she is listed in the San Francisco phone book so that radio and TV talk show producers and newspaper reporters who remember she is from the Bay Area can easily locate her.

F. Getting Referrals From People in Related Fields

Many people in service businesses, from yoga teachers to optometrists to piano teachers, rely on referrals for many of their new customers. Listing the availability of your services far and wide is crucial to getting those referrals. For example, if you're an independent paralegal, someone who helps people prepare legal forms for divorces, bankruptcies and adoptions, you might want to list your services with the following types of groups:

- Legal services (legal aid) offices
- Battered women's shelters
- Immigrants' help organizations
- Law school "pro per" assistance centers
- Law libraries
- Community service agencies and directories
- Drug treatment centers
- Marriage counselors and family therapists
- Social services offices
- College student assistance offices
- Gray Panthers and other senior advocacy organizations
- Major corporation personnel departments
- Parents Without Partners and other singles groups
- Law enforcement (including the sheriff's office and county jail)
- Consumer organizations
- The state Employment Office
- Women's organizations
- Collection agencies
- Child care centers
- Military bases, including Judge Advocate General offices

Listing Questionnaire

We are listed in:

☐   All appropriate professional journals and directories

_____
_____
_____
_____

☐   Our alumni organizations' directories

_____
_____
_____
_____

☐   Local business organizations' publications

_____
_____
_____
_____

☐   Trade associations' directories

_____
_____
_____
_____

☐   Appropriate online databases

_____
_____
_____
_____

Unique Marketing Accessibility Problems

There are, of course, some businesses where marketing accessibility is a built-in problem. With custom-designed dresses that are sold through boutiques, for instance, the retailer is likely to allow labels with only the designer's name and the store's name and not the designer's or manufacturer's address. The same holds true with some craft items such as custom-made chairs. The retail stores don't want the customers to bypass them and go directly to the source.

From the specialized manufacturer's or craftsperson's point of view, a good solution to this problem is to include the name of a city as part of your designer name and logo. Suppose you run Sasha Designs and are located in San Diego, California. Your designs are sold all over the country, but it's very hard for people, even other retailers, to locate you directly. An easy solution is to change your name to Sasha/San Diego or otherwise work your location into your name. Now potential customers can simply call information in San Diego to find Sasha. Even if Sasha is located in a neighboring suburb, you could list the name in the San Diego directory.

G. Trade Shows and Conferences

In some industries and for some businesses, the trade show is the primary marketing event. A customer who can't buy from you there probably won't buy from you at all. Such is the case for many products sold through gift shops, bookstores, boutiques, small groceries, and for businesses selling to interior designers, school districts, college lecture organizers and many more.

Especially for a new small business, a trade show offers a unique opportunity. Typically, retailers, wholesalers, sales reps, industry press, importers, exporters and agents are all under one roof, and business is conducted in a myriad of ways. If you have a good product and display it well, one trade show can put your business on the map.

Conferences of people in a particular field often offer a similar opportunity. For example, people who purchase equipment for electronics companies and hospital x-ray departments might be in one place for several days, and if you have a product or service of interest to them it behooves you to be there too. But before you rent a booth and set up a display, take the time to educate yourself about how the show operates and what activities are appropriate and customary.

All the marketing advice in this book is applicable to trade shows; re-read it with your exhibition booth in mind. Especially keep in mind the general advice we discussed in Chapter 1: Don't recruit customers until you can properly serve them. Often, sales orders taken at a trade show cannot be filled on time, and word spreads to the rest of the industry with laser-like speed.

Here are some trade show tips to keep in mind:

- Get to know the old pros in your business and study what they do. If possible, get their advice on display, location and promotional offers.

- Have enough supplies and back-up personnel, and don't attempt demonstrations unless you are sure it will go smoothly. A sample (whether it's a toy or a bulldozer) that doesn't work will be the topic of far more comment than will a hundred products that do work.

- Try to set up your display early, and design it to be flexible enough to adjust to the surroundings. It's hard to know who or what will be next to you and what visual, technical or other complications can arise. At one booksellers' trade fair, for example, the booth of a publisher of books on human sexuality was located between those of a Bible company and a publisher of children's books. Clearly, adjustment was in order.

- Get a list of the trade shows scheduled for all convention centers near you. Consider displaying not only at those in your field, but also at those which are in any way connected with what you do. For example, an architect who likes to design kitchens might take a booth at a gourmet food trade show, or a lawyer who specializes in employment problems might set up a small display at a personnel executives' conference.

Using Trade Shows to Launch Your Business

Vivien Feyer is a trained psychologist. Several years ago on a trip to Bali she was struck by the fact that the Balinese are a happy people who view work as a service to the gods. Attracted also to Balinese jewelry, and knowing that she had a talent for design, Feyer decided to experiment with the idea of having fine jewelry of silver, gold, shell and other natural materials manufactured in Bali to her design.

One of the many questions Feyer had to face as part of launching her business (which she named Paradiso: Jewels of Bali), was the basic one that all new businesspeople must confront. Was there a genuine demand for the product she wished to bring to market? To find out, she decided to attend some trade shows. Here are a few of her comments.

"My first show was the International Fashion and Boutique Show in New York City. I was completely naïve, but I knew I needed to see if I was kidding myself or if my designs would work. Even though I had a sad little booth, retailers, reps and others were interested in my jewelry and were very complimentary. I sold enough to pay for the show, met a lot of people at all levels of the business and saw what others were doing. Best of all I found out in just a few days that my basic business concept was sound.

"In later shows, I improved my display and had many more products. Many of my first customers reordered and I met many more retailers. I also met a lot of charlatans who wanted to order but not pay, and learned quickly that if you don't check credit references very strictly, you don't stay in business. Through people I met at the shows, I was able to sign up a good crew of regional sales representatives.

"To tell you the truth, despite the fact that as I did more shows I recruited a wonderful crew of people to help with the booth (dropped-out lawyers, many of them) and had good business access, I don't really enjoying doing trade shows. It's all so overblown, full of hype, and, in the jewelry business, a little paranoid, in that you have a lot of valuable goods in a place where security isn't always so great. These days I do very few."

One interesting recent development is that trade fairs have become so successful for some businesses that they have led to the development of permanent national wholesale showrooms, normally located in a sales mart devoted to the products of similar types of businesses. While this sort of sales center has been popular with furniture, jewelry and gifts for some time, it has now spread to many other areas, including crafts. National Craft Showroom opened in New York, primarily as a response to the growing success of crafts fairs throughout the country. The invited exhibitors for the showroom are selected from the best craftspeople who have displayed in regional crafts fairs. These can be a very cost-effective way for a small business to display its wares. Obviously, the main advantage of this sort of display is that the type of customer who would attend a trade fair (wholesalers, store buyers, sales reps) now has access to your product throughout the year. ■

Customer Recourse

*H*ow often are you disappointed with a business transaction? Have you ever bought a shirt that had to be taken back because of a flaw? Have you ever returned a car to the repair shop because it wasn't fixed right? Have you ever ordered something from a catalogue or the Web only to be told a month later that it won't be available for many more months? Have you waited hours or days for someone to show up to work on your house? Have you spent months trying to have a billing error corrected, meanwhile getting new bills that contain the same mistake plus penalty charges? Have you ever authorized a business to automatically debit your account and months after you have terminated your relationship they are still debiting your account?

When these sorts of problems occur, your reaction probably varies from mild annoyance over the minor ones, some of which are not even worth the hassle to correct, to anxiety and sometimes anger over major problems. Chances are you will be reluctant to patronize a business that won't correct a problem or one that you think will be reluctant to do so and will create more hassles for you than the transaction is worth. Certainly, you are unlikely to recommend such a business to your friends.

Slip-ups are inevitable in any business. To avoid losing customers (and referrals) over mistakes, you need to establish an effective recourse policy. Providing recourse to customers simply means giving them a way to get a fair resolution of their complaints. It's essential that you make a very strong recourse statement to your customers and back it up with an immediate response to their needs.

It's almost essential that a small business go out of its way to emphasize recourse policy, especially in the light of the mistaken public presumption that because larger businesses have more assets, they are more responsible to their customers. While most customers appreciate the personalized service they receive from a small company, they sometimes worry that, should something go wrong, their recourse is more limited than if they dealt with a major corporation. They might assume, for example, that a business that does lots of advertising is a substantial company with plenty of money behind it, and that if something serious involving legal liability occurs, it has the resources to make it good. In fact, small businesses, because they are closer to their customers, often offer better recourse than do larger ones. Your job is not only to establish an excellent recourse policy but to make sure your customers understand and trust what you offer.

Although recourse is a potentially difficult and unpleasant topic, it is at the heart of long-term business health because it protects the supportive customers who make personal recommendations. Relatively small efforts, well-thought-out from the customer's point of view, cost very little and do much in protecting our total investment in public trust. In fact, when you promptly and attentively make sure the customer is treated right, you can gain their loyalty. It feels so good to have the transaction turn out right that the customer naturally tells their friends.

On the Internet, recourse is equally important—perhaps even more so. A survey of Internet shoppers found that 85% considered "product returns" a key to their online shopping decisions. (*The Industry Standard,* August 14, 2000.)

The Industry Standard magazine has a secret shopper who reports on Internet transactions. In May of 2000, the shopper ordered clothing from ten well-known retailers' online outlets. Only the products from two of the ten sites—Nordstrom and Victoria's Secret—matched the descriptions and images as presented at the websites.

Much of the difficulty in developing a recourse policy is not designing good mechanisms to catch and correct errors, but applying them in a context where your customers are mad, disappointed, anxious or all three. Unless you set up a recourse policy in advance, there is little hope that you can do this effectively. Unfortunately, many small businesses attempt to handle individual problems as they arise.

We strongly suggest that this is a mistake. It confuses both your customers and your employees. For example, you may give the impression you will repair your product only in limited situations, yet retain the discretion to actually be more generous if you feel a good customer deserves more attention. But a customer who doesn't know that you will try to solve the problem if confronted is likely to give up in disgust and never discuss it with you. If that happens, you risk losing a valued customer who is very likely to pass negative feelings on to others.

In a retail business, a reputation for quick exchanges or refunds is a key ingredient in customer loyalty. For example, you probably know which retail stores you deal with allow returns without question, which businesses have complicated procedures to return an item and which stores make it so difficult to return an item that it's not worth the hassle. Many good neighborhood businesses have built a lot of their following based on customers' confidence that the business will stand behind its product or service.

In this context, it's worth remembering that your customer has recourse to public measures if you don't handle the dispute satisfactorily. In extreme cases, a determined customer can picket your business or hold a press conference. More typically, customers appeal to local consumer action groups, TV reporters or newspaper columnists, put postings on the Web or just tell their friends. You may not think of customers spreading negative feelings about your business to their friends as "going public," but it surely is. Now that many people browse the Internet and are part of online newsgroups, negative word of mouth can be sent to literally thousands of people instantaneously. Consider how many times you have remarked to a friend that you plan to try a particular restaurant, optician or computer store only to be told about a negative experience that your friend (or maybe even your friend's friend or someone your Aunt Hilda's neighbor knows) had with that particular establishment. Did you still plan to patronize the business? Probably not.

An extreme but slightly humorous example of this aspect of negative word of mouth involved an acquaintance who was cheated by a 12-hour photo processing merchant and couldn't get suitable recourse from the manager. His frustration was so great that he pounded on the counter, inadvertently scattering merchandise around the store. The manager called the police and the customer, while standing around waiting for the police to come, gathered support from other customers who thoroughly enjoyed seeing someone make a business "pay." When the police arrived, they listened to both sides and then talked to each party separately. They informed the store owner to mend his ways or face possible prosecution and then, smiling the whole time, told our friend not to damage property again.

A. Elements of a Good Recourse Policy

The best recourse policies give your customers as much control as possible, as early in the relationship with you as pos-

sible. When people feel they are in control from the start, they are much less likely to get upset. As you design your recourse policy, ask yourself: What role do my customers play in deciding whether my product or service is substandard?

An example of a situation where a customer enjoys a high degree of control is a fine restaurant where the discovery of a hair in the salad immediately results in delivery of a new salad, a sincere apology and often a free bottle of wine or some other extra. In this situation, the customer is at least implicitly in control, the assumption being that when dining in that restaurant, every effort will be made to provide first-class service and take care of even small problems.

An example of little customer control is when you attempt to deal with a mistake in your checking account balance at a bank, where the typical attitude is that you are wrong. Incidentally, in this era of bank deregulation, treating customers with more respect would seem to be a much better strategy than giving free teddy bears to everyone opening a new account (especially since the majority of accounts acquired with a premium offer don't stay open a year). Sadly, most banks are so focused on their own bottom line that they resist spending even modest sums to treat their customers decently. This situation appears to be getting worse instead of better with the advent of ATM machines and electronic banking; it's not easy to work things out with a machine. One of these days someone in the banking business will do the things necessary to give customers more control and will revolutionize the business.

Not many years ago, an even more frustrating recourse problem involved trying to enforce the provisions of the warranty on any new American car. Indeed, some customers became so frustrated about the lack of automobile company response when their cars broke that they painted them yellow to look like lemons and call attention to their plight. It proved to be a very effective way to get the message across, and eventually a number of states stepped in and passed "lemon laws" to force manufacturers to arbitrate the most serious warranty disputes. In other words, the need for recourse became so great that laws had to be passed to take care of it. In the meantime, of course, close to one-third of Americans began purchasing imported cars, particularly Japanese ones, which had fewer problems in the first place and whose makers offered mediation and arbitration to solve customer disputes.

Today a similar situation has developed in the insurance business, where company after company is canceling the insurance of long-time policy holders or raising rates outrageously, with no meaningful opportunity for customers to appeal what they believe is arbitrary treatment.

The worst instances where customers lack control over recourse result in lawsuits. Lawsuits are expensive, slow and unpredictable. Even if a favorable judgment is entered in your lifetime, it may be impossible to collect if the person you sued is insolvent. Because most people understand these drawbacks, it means that if your business has been sued, or even threatened with suit, it is a sure sign that your recourse policy is seriously deficient.

B. Designing a Good Recourse Policy

When designing or improving your recourse system, remember that customers care most about:

- Promptness. The amount of time it takes—or your customers think it will take—to correct a problem is crucial. Fast resolution of disputes is not good enough if you can think of a way to do it faster.
- Responsibility. Is your customer presumed (even implicitly) to be the cause of the problem when a complaint is made? If so, your policy is a poor one. Clearly, the responsibility for dealing with a real or perceived mistake should be on your business.

No two businesses are exactly alike. For this reason, we can't lay out a policy that you can clip out and apply to your situation. But whether you are a stonecutter, a storekeeper or a stress-reduction clinic, there are a number of proven techniques to help communicate that your recourse policy is very responsive to your customers' needs. Here are several of the best.

1. Consult Advisors

Invite well-known and respected people to serve as a board of advisors to your business and get them to help you make your business better—which, of course, involves developing a recourse policy. These advisors should not be merely names used to impress, but trusted associates. By doing this you are borrowing a technique that has been used by nonprofit organizations for years. As long as you truly run an honest business dedicated to serving your customers, it will work for you. Be sure to list your advisors on your letterhead. (We discuss the value of this sort of association in other contexts in Chapter 11.) When it comes to recourse, associating prominent, well-thought-of people with your business is a subtle but direct way of assuring your customers that in the event of a problem, you will make it good. Your customers know that your respected advisors wouldn't associate themselves with your business if it weren't trustworthy. If you can actually involve one or two of your prominent friends in a formal mediation procedure to deal with occasional serious complaints, so much the better.

A board of advisors was used effectively by Dick Rolm, an independent film producer working in New England who contracted to make a film for a local public TV station. The station was dissatisfied with the results, which led to a very uncomfortable situation for both parties. The matter was resolved when two of the most promi-nent board members of the TV station took the time to get together with two of the film company's advisors. The film was re-edited, and the station was charged somewhat less for it. The happy result was that Rolm got paid, no lawsuit was necessary, the parties are still on good terms and the public got to see a good film.

Small businesses can tell customers about a board of advisors in various ways:

- A motorcycle shop could hang photos of the owner together with a few racing celebrities on the wall. Alongside the photos would appear the list of advisors, including the people pictured.
- A computer consultant could print a list of business advisors along with a short list of current and former clients (after getting their approval, of course) on all brochures and on the cover sheet for bids.
- A graphics supply wholesaler might use some examples of design work done by prominent local artists in its catalog in addition to listing them as advisors.
- A textile teacher could display his latest fabric design along with photos of his finished upholstery in the homes of his well-known advisors.

2. Join an Established Ethical Business Group

It is also wise to join an organization that already handles customer problems.

If a truly active Better Business Bureau exists in your locale, consider joining. Better yet are local Consumer Action organizations and mediation services. Merely adding your name to their membership roster is not enough. If you participate in the group's activities, you will learn a great deal about how to handle recourse problems and solutions at the same time you are doing your bit to promote public trust in small business and helping to assure honest business principles in your community. A fringe benefit is that word of your involvement in good business groups often spreads, which, of course, is good for your business.

3. Involve Employees

Consider forming a customer service committee of employees. No one knows what your customers need more than the people who deal with them daily. And no one has more incentive to make changes in the way the business operates and to avoid complaints before they are made.

Nolo.com decided to try to get every individual book and software mail order out the door the same day, or the next day if the order comes after noon Pacific Time. While this sometimes takes almost super-human effort from its customer service representatives, it has turned out to be well worth it, if for no other reason than the fact that the reps now waste very little time dealing with calls asking, "Where is my book?" Before customers can wonder where their books are, they have them.

4. Ask for Public Participation

Include as wide a range of community members as possible in the design and decision-making of your recourse policy. A good example of this is the Pike Place Market in Seattle, which houses many small businesses. This group has wisely created a committee of both business operators and members of the general public, which meets periodically to review specific complaints about consumer problems. This is a marvelous process, as it both allows many different points of view to be aired and creative solutions to be developed.

You may doubt that your customers really care enough about your small business to participate. This is rarely true. The people who deal with a particular business on a regular basis, such as professional gardeners who buy from a particular nursery or graphic artists who patronize a particular typesetter, care a great deal about how the business operates and probably have all sorts of ideas for improvement, including how to develop a better or more flexible recourse policy. If you ask them to share their ideas with you, they probably will.

Good Recourse Policies

Here are some examples of businesses with good recourse policies:

- The Cross Corporation allows customers to return a pen for any reason, and stores that carry Cross products are provided with a supply of addressed envelopes to give to any customer who wishes a refund or a new pen. In other words, the decision of the Cross Corporation to guarantee its product is made evident to consumers by providing easy and convenience recourse.

- Sears Roebuck & Co., a huge company selling moderately priced goods, has a generally good reputation for customer satisfaction. For example, it has traditionally guaranteed its Craftsman Tools and replaces them years after purchase if they are defective. When Sears started selling computers, people correctly assumed that the same sort of replacement policy applied. This assumption was a key to Sears' early success in the computer market. Customers, knowing that there was little chance of getting good service from many computer retailers, preferred dealing with a store with a solid reputation for customer service.

C. Telling Customers About Your Recourse Policy

To ensure that your customers are always aware that should any problems arise they will be treated fairly, you must closely examine how you present your recourse policy.

- Is your recourse policy clear?
- Is it communicated to your customers early and often?
- Do your friends, employees and customers perceive your policy in the way you intended?
- Are customers with small complaints really encouraged to bring them to your attention?

A good recourse policy should be written and available to all customers and should be posted on your website. As noted, if your customers are educated in advance as to their rights in any potential situation, there will be far fewer problems and angry customers. Even customers who are a pain in the neck and enjoy making trouble will have a more difficult time if you adopt a fair recourse policy and go out of your way to let them know about it. And, of course, it is even more important to reach those customers who are reticent about voicing legitimate complaints. It is obviously much better to encourage these people to tell you about any problem with your goods or services than it is to have them avoid you in the future because of a problem you never even knew about.

A written policy is especially important in the mail order business, and the best mail order companies all have a guaranteed return policy. They do it for a simple reason: People are reluctant to buy something they can't see and touch, especially if they think it might be difficult to return. Thus, phrases such as "Return for any reason, any time within 30 days" have become common and have enabled people to shop through the mail and online with more confidence.

Recreational Equipment Inc., a cooperatively owned retail and mail order company headquartered in Seattle that specializes in outdoor apparel and equipment, does even better. Its order form states: "REI guarantees satisfaction on every item purchased. If you are unhappy with your purchase for any reason, please return it for a replacement or full refund." (Incidentally, this company is listed in The 100 Best Companies to Work for in America, discussed in Chapter 5.)

And the legendary L.L. Bean Co., a small business grown large, which built its reputation on quality clothing and outdoor equipment as well as excellent customer service, backs up its product with this statement in its catalogue and at its website: "All of our products are guaranteed to give 100% satisfaction in every way. Return anything purchased from us at any time if it proves otherwise. We will replace it, refund your purchase price or credit your credit card, as you wish. WE DO NOT WANT YOU TO HAVE ANYTHING FROM L.L. BEAN THAT IS NOT COMPLETELY SATISFACTORY." Not only do L.L. Bean customers get assurance that they will be satisfied, but Bean's recourse policy also works as an effective marketing message, because customers realize that only companies truly offering quality goods can make this type of promise.

D. Putting Your Recourse Policy in Writing

Lands' End sent out its first catalogue in 1964 from a basement along the river in Chicago's old tannery district. In one of the recent catalogues it printed the business's "Principles of Doing Business." Principle 3 states: "We accept any return, for any reason, at any time. Our products are guaranteed. No fine print. No arguments. We mean exactly what we say. GUARANTEED. PERIOD."

Reassured by this guarantee, Salli overcame her reluctance to buy a swimsuit through the mail. The swimsuit was shipped the same day, and she was very pleased with the quality and fit. One week after it arrived, Salli received a phone call from Lands' End asking if she was happy with the purchase. Not only was their recourse policy clearly stated, they followed up to make sure they had a happy cus-

Customer Recourse Policies and Practices

We have a written customer recourse policy.

☐ YES ☐ NO

Our written policy is:

☐ Given to all customers ☐ Given only upon request ☐ Displayed prominently on the premises

☐ Our policy identifies and deals with those areas and situations where customers are most likely to have problems with our goods or service.

☐ We have regular communication with our customers to be sure they understand our recourse policy and know that we implement it efficiently.

A customer who complains is:

☐ Always right   ☐ Almost always right   ☐ Seldom right   ☐ Rarely or never right

The most common complaints involve: _____
_____
_____

When the customer is right, he or she gets:

☐ Full refund or replacement when: _____
_____
_____

☐ Partial refund when: _____
_____
_____

☐ We send or give questionnaires to customers to evaluate their satisfaction with our service.

Our liability insurance covers the following customer problems: _____
_____

When a customer deals with our insurance company, it is:

☐ Very responsive   ☐ Responsive   ☐ Slow to respond   ☐ Don't know

When the customer disagrees with our recourse offer, we have available:

☐ Appeal process   ☐ Arbitration   ☐ Industry established board of review
☐ Mediation   ☐ Nothing
☐ Other _____

tomer. Recourse policies can't get any better than that.

Now, let's look at several other examples of how to put a recourse policy in writing. You will notice that these policies anticipate typical problem areas and establish a procedure to head them off before a dispute arises. For instance, a painting contractor we know prides himself on being extremely neat and doing quality work. However, because there is a lot of potential for paranoia among his customers about what their rights are if paint drips on their floors or furniture, he is especially clear about the precautions he takes to avoid this kind of problem and about what he will do to correct any that should arise. He not only promises in writing to correct the problem, but explains the type of insurance he carries and just what it covers. He also explains provisions made for outside evaluation and mediation should any dispute ever arise.

Another frequent problem for painting contractors is that a color a client chooses from a color key looks different than expected on the wall. All sorts of factors, from the nature of the surface being painted to lighting, can affect this. In anticipation of this common problem, this contractor puts on a first coat and then encourages his customers to live with it for a few days. He specifies in writing the number of days his client has to decide if the color is the correct shade. If the customer doesn't like the color, the contractor makes agreed-upon modifications in the second coat. If the customer assents to the color choice, the final coat is applied and after that no free repainting is done for reasons of color. If, however, the customer is legitimately dissatisfied with the quality of work, the contractor will do any repainting necessary at any time.

Ruth, who owns a garden and plant store, has a replacement policy should any plant she sell prove unsatisfactory. However, to help her customers avoid most common problems, she instructs them both orally and in writing as to what kind of care the plant they purchase requires. For example, Ruth goes out of her way to explain the symptoms of over-watering, letting a plant grow too large for its pot and become rootbound, and excess exposure to sunlight. Armed with this information, the customer is in a good position to evaluate and save a drooping or rootbound plant. One additional advantage of this kind of instruction is that Ruth gives her customers a reasonable standard against which to judge whether a problem with the plant was caused by their neglect or occurred because the plant was defective in the first place.

A carpet retailer we know in the Sacramento Valley of California not only guarantees in writing all carpets sold, but encourages customers with complaints to contact him so that problems can be remedied. As part of doing this, he sends every customer a postcard a few weeks after a carpet purchase, with a reminder of the store's "total satisfaction" policy. In addition, he includes a statement of customers' rights every time he communicates with them in writing. An amusing side result of this policy occurred as part of a Small Claims Court procedure initiated by the rug store against a customer who hadn't paid her bill. The customer showed up in court and said she failed to pay because the carpet was defective. The store owner was able to produce the written recourse policy, a copy of the postcard and several other communications explaining to the customer the "total satisfaction" policy. He then testified that, although a year had passed, the customer had never complained about the quality of the product until that day in court. The judge not only

ruled for the rug company but complimented its honest business practices before a courtroom full of people.

Kaiser Permanente, a huge health maintenance organization, invites some patients to fill out a card about the care they received. "If you're pleased," they advise, "Fill out the side of the card that says 'Great!' If you're not so happy fill out the 'Not so Great' side of the card to let us know how we didn't meet your expectations." Patients then have an opportunity to talk with the department manager or other administrator to get the problem resolved. If they want they can also receive a refund of their copayment, up to $25. Not only does this allow Kaiser to monitor service, it gives the patient control over service. ■

Chapter 11

Marketing on the Internet

*T*he Internet has been the subject of intense hope and speculation, bordering on national hysteria. It is well to remember the work of the great American Thomas Hughes, founder of the field of the history of technology, whose most famous book is *Technological Enthusiasm: The History of Technology in America.* The title summarizes Hughes's vivid observations on the subject; as a culture we have always been wildly enthusiastic about new technology and view our national future as commingled with its development.

Not only do Americans have a long and intense history of becoming enamored of the latest technology, we also have a propensity to believe that technology will solve most, if not all, social problems. The Internet is touted as the latest technological panacea that will welcome in a new era of democracy and social justice while also improving our sex lives and making the children behave. The Internet is perceived as having unlimited possibility in large part because we can't understand the possibilities.

Just as we are prone to accept that advertising works in other media, we are being seduced (or seducing ourselves) into believing that advertising on the Internet is the solution to our marketing needs. The best advice we can give is to evaluate the Internet as you do other media. All of the same issues, including where to be listed, accessibility, being transparent and educating customers, apply to marketing on the Internet.

Our job is to be clear-headed about the Internet, maintain our equilibrium as we examine it from a business perspective and report on successful marketing uses of this new medium. We believe the best way to consider the business marketing aspects of the Internet is to break it down into two approaches: passive Internet marketing and active Internet marketing.

The passive strategy focuses simply on creating a compelling online presence for your business for potential customers to visit—a site that offers them essential information about the business and perhaps entertains them as well. (When we say "online presence" it's simply another way of conceptualizing your website and any features it offers. In other words, your online presence comprises any and all ways your business exists online.) With a passive marketing approach, the emphasis is to create a website that essentially offers the same types of information as a comprehensive brochure or a very extensive Yellow Pages listing. Of course, unlike brochures or Yellow Pages listings, a website has the following essential qualities:

- it can provide many levels of depth for inquiring users;
- it is interactive, which allows more meaningful contact with potential customers.

Active online marketing, on the other hand, focuses on engaging in specific marketing activities online to generate business, such as sending out e-mail newsletters, promoting a contest at your website or publishing articles about your field at other related sites. Active Internet marketing is essentially the next step after nailing down your passive marketing strategy, and is an extra step that not all businesses need to take. While active online marketing is useful for some businesses, it's not essential for many of them.

As we discuss in more detail in the rest of this chapter, we strongly feel that all businesses should engage in passive Internet marketing by creating a solid website for their business. The majority of this chapter discusses how to go about doing this. At the end of the chapter, we briefly describe some active Internet markeing strategies for businesses that want (or need) to take the next step.

A. The Importance of Passive Internet Marketing

As of this publishing date, two-thirds of all American small businesses have a website. *(The Industry Standard,* July 31, 2000.) While the Internet does not produce miracles for most businesses, it is definitely a potentially powerful part of the marketing mix.

We believe that *all* businesses need a website—no exceptions. Think of it as a color brochure that, when people search for you, they can find out enough about your business to see if it suits their needs. In addition, when you meet potential clients at a trade show, chamber meeting or a party and let them know about your business, you can give them your card and suggest they check out your website. This reinforces your initial meeting and allows them to find out more about you at their convenience, if they choose. Having a Web presence is also an easy way for others to refer people to your business. And it's a convenient place to list your business's recourse policy and to cite positive recommendations.

Keep in mind that the passive strategy of maintaining a website should not in itself be expected to generate significant online revenue. For three-quarters of businesses, it doesn't and probably won't in the foreseeable future. Regardless, people expect an excellent business to have a website. If you don't, customers may wonder if you are not up-to-date in other aspects of your business.

What Exactly Is a Website?

Having a website (often known as a Web page) simply means having a computer file that is publicly accessible through the global computer network known as the Internet. The files that comprise your website are stored on servers, high-powered computers that are connected to the Internet 24 hours a day. Companies that run and maintain servers are often called Web hosts, or hosting services. Once you provide a hosting service with your files, they will put them on their servers and make sure that the servers are constantly running and connected to the Internet. Other companies, known as Internet service providers (ISPs), allow their customers to connect to the Internet by dialing in or through other technologies such as DSL. Often, ISPs offer hosting services as well.

Website files can include text, graphics, video and sound. It can be in color, animated and can automatically connect the viewer to other websites. The Web uses technology called hypertext markup language (HTML) that makes it easy to send images, photos and sound on the Internet.

"But Do I Really Need a Website?"

Two business friends of ours are not on the Internet and don't want to be. One is Al Pietsch, a master of the art of using a special old-fashioned multilith (an offset printing press) machine. To appreciate and use his work, designers and graphic artists need to see and touch it. In addition, Pietsch works alone and already has more work than he can handle. For his business, marketing on the Internet would appear to be irrelevant.

Bob G. is a brilliant class-action lawyer with more major victories than anyone in his field. He occasionally has room for a new client but doesn't dare to be listed on the Internet for fear he won't have time to answer his mail or screen the prospects. He feels that getting referrals from the few other lawyers who know his work and the kind of clients he is looking for is sufficient and efficient. His listing in the Yellow Pages, under Attorneys, is plain vanilla— just his name, so old friends can find him.

In our opinion, both of our friends need a website. Why? Al, the printer, needs one because customers want to recommend him and describe his work to their friends and associates. And most important, in the long run Al will need replacement clients. By that time, the Internet will be taken for granted and he will be seen as difficult to work with if he doesn't have a website. Bob G., the lawyer, needs a site because he needs to get a few highly specific clients. A website is a perfect place to explain the focus of his practice and his outstanding record, as well as screen potential clients. His site can also explain how busy he is (which in itself will reflect favorably upon his business), and make clear that he can't respond to every e-mail.

Don't Neglect Customers Who Aren't Online. Because Internet access isn't free, and because the Internet isn't easy to use for some people, many of your present customers don't use the Internet, and they probably won't for a long time. This means that you should provide the same services and information to non-Internet users that you provide online, where possible. As an example of what not to do, a local bookstore we know has an online directory of its inventory, but no computer in the store for customers.

B. Yellow Pages Plus

At the risk of oversimplifying things a bit, the Internet is much like the Yellow Pages of the phone book. It is a directory that can be accessed by users at their convenience and is used for seeking business information. But unlike traditional Yellow Pages, the Internet is not geographically limited; it has millions of listings covering many parts of the planet.

Because of the huge number of listings, you'll need to keep in mind two key marketing facts: First, your business listing will be part of a much larger universe than is found in the Yellow Pages. If you are one of 30 patent lawyers listed in your local printed Yellow Pages, you may find yourself among 9,000 patent lawyers listed online. The elements that distinguish you from all these other patent lawyers and might attract particular clients—years of experience, law school attended, size of firm, gender, etc.—become vitally important when you join the cyberspace business community. Potential clients need to know what makes you unique and desirable. When you're ready to compose and design your site, imagine yourself trying to make it into the Guinness Book of World Records: What feats would be appealing to prospective clients?

Second, geographical proximity may be a drawback or a bonus. If your business is geographically limited, describe those limits clearly. Even better, offer a map of your location.

For example, Jim Davis's sewer repair business is located in Seattle. On his website, a map shows that his office is in the University district about four miles from downtown. To increase the range of possible customers, he also shows the entire city of Seattle and four suburbs and color codes them as "immediate service area for emergency service." The larger area of King and Snohomish counties is marked "by appointment." The site also details that in the "immediate service area," Davis offers to give customers an exact appointment time, and if the service is late by more than one half-hour, the customer gets 20% off the bill, "except during earthquakes, snow, Super Bowl parades or other acts of God." Davis lists the names of 51 neighborhoods, suburbs and small towns in his list of service areas, just in case someone is searching the Internet for sites that contain the name of his or her own tiny local area.

Geography is not a serious limit for Lief Gunderssen, who sells accounting systems to credit unions, except that credit unions have different legal structures in different parts of the world, and his package is designed in English. Gunderssen sells his accounting system, which is part software, part paper and part files, all over the U.S. and occasionally outside the country. With the Internet, the whole world is a potential market, but Gunderssen needs to think carefully about his approach.

For prospects in the U.S. and Canada, the laws are appropriate for his accounting package so he emphasizes this fact online and lists his toll-free phone number. For eight other countries where a modified version of his package can be used, he has separate pages on his site explaining the modifications necessary for each. He also addresses the most commonly asked questions relative to that country. On his main Web page, Gunderssen has a large banner explaining that his program is based in English. The banner is there to make sure that he doesn't have to waste anyone's time answering questions about other languages. Last, he has a separate page for overseas credit unions that are part of American and Canadian corporations where he answers commonly asked questions. The use of multiple pages gives quick answers to people just glancing and detailed answers to people who need details (see Designing an Internet Site, below).

For Denise Armomot's classic sheet music reproduction business, the Internet's worldwide coverage is a bonus. She has a list of more than 2,000 titles that she provides. The list is available in seven languages, and Armomot is adding more as quickly as she can find people to help her with the translations.

The Internet Frontier

Uses of technology keep evolving long after the technology itself stabilizes. For example, the telephone was first used by businesses for short messages, inter-business orders and confirmation of meeting times. Doctors and pharmacies were also among the first to have phones, largely for emergency service. Idle chatter and personal conversations did not become common on the phone for nearly 30 years after its introduction. Widespread residential use of the phone (in two-thirds of U.S. homes) did not occur for 70 years.

Internet technology is far from stable, and we should not expect long-term patterns of usage to emerge for business or individuals for at least 15 more years. In the meantime, accept the volatility of this new medium and be innovative in your marketing. Our advice is to get online and get a feel for what others are doing—it's a challenge at first, but can be lots of fun.

C. What to Put on Your Site

Lots of businesses, big and small, have been bitten by the Internet bug. They're sure they need a site, mostly because everyone else seems to have one, but when it comes to what information to actually post on the site, they're stumped. It is important to keep in mind that a simple site full of fresh and interactive content will attract loyal customers. For the vast majority of online businesses, using lots of gimmicks is just a waste of time. As Evan I. Schwartz put it in the February, 1996 issue of *Wired* magazine, "a website that attracts just a few thousand loyal consumers will ultimately be more valuable than one in which a million new people visit each month and never return." His words are just as true now as they were five years ago: Today, an estimated 80% of people who visit a site never return.

When deciding what content to include at your site, the important questions to ask yourself are:

- what your goals are for your site, and
- what kind of investment are you willing and able to make.

Deciding what you want out of your site is a crucial first step in building it. Many businesses seem to skip this first step, thinking that the obvious answer is "to generate more business." But in order to create a truly effective website, you need to be more specific in your goals: Do you want to sell product directly from the site, or do you want to have customers call you by telephone? Do you need to explain what your cutting-edge business does? Do you want to tell potential customers where to find your product in their city? It's amazing how many websites suffer from a lack of clear purpose.

For instance, a magazine might want to create a simple website with just a couple pages as a passive marketing tool. They've decided against putting the whole magazine online, which would be too much work each week. In a hurry, the magazine decides to put the cover of the current issue on the site each week along with its table of contents so that visitors to the site can see what's in the issue, which will hopefully prompt them to go buy it. What the magazine owners fail to consider is that interested readers will want to know how to subscribe and where to buy the magazine. Without that crucial info, visitors to the site might think the magazine looks interesting but won't have any specific, simple information on how to purchase it. By posting only the cover and table of conents, the magazine also is failing to give crucial information to advertisers about ad rates and deadlines. In short, just a little planning can go a long way in making your website as effective as it can be.

Freshness is another major issue in deciding what to put at your site. Don't put anything on your website that will rapidly go out-of-date unless you have the resources to update it faithfully. While the cost of buying the computer hardware and software necessary to set up a website is usually fairly low, the cost of maintenance can be high for a small business. No ifs, ands or buts—someone has to keep the site fresh and check it often. Almost nothing makes a worse impression than out-of-date information or images. It is a clear sign of poor management, the online equivalent of a dirty place of business, and will destroy positive word of mouth recommendations.

If you decide you don't have the time to continually monitor and update your site, one option is to hire someone to keep your site fresh. This may be more complex—and more expensive—if your site provides highly specialized information and needs to be updated by an expert in the field. Oftentimes, however, the job can be done by people with good generalized knowledge such as freelance writers or editors. Of course, if you've hired someone to create your site in the first place it would make sense to have them monitor and update it as well.

If you decide to take on updating duties yourself, there are several software programs available that make the job easier than you might think. Michael uses Adobe Go Live, software that creates fairly complex websites and is easty to update without knowing Web language. Other popular and user-friendly programs include Macromedia Dreamweaver, Netscape Composer and Microsoft Frontpage.

Let's take a look at some ideas for what kinds of information might be effective at your site. Keep in mind that with the huge range of different kinds of businesses, there's no magic formula for good content. As discussed above, be sure to examine your goals for your site and choose content accordingly.

1. Your Schedule of Events

The Internet can be a great place to post your calendar of marketing events. There are two reasons for this. First, online listings can be continually updated and constantly available in a way that no other medium allows. Newspaper calendars, for example, are prepared many days in advance and customarily appear only weekly. Second, the potential for personalized sorting exists only on the Internet. That means that people interested in events, displays and meetings about overweight dogs in Duluth can have a tickler notice that tells them when anything on the subject pops up online.

Holding creative marketing events is vital to create positive recommendations for your business. (Chapter 13 is devoted to this subject.) Listing these events at your website is just as important.

2. Links to Related Sites

We assume that you understand the nature and benefits of cooperation in business, discussed in several chapters of this book. An additional advantage for a business that views itself as a constructive, cooperative member of society is that the Internet can provide automatic referrals to you from other cooperative businesses. And you can do the same for them with links to their websites. Linking sites on the Web is a great service to customers and potential customers. (Links are also commonly referred to as hot links or hyperlinks.)

Payment for links is common on the Internet, and you should consider every such potential source (see Pay for Referrals, below), but the fact that you are a cooperative business needs to be communicated to all potential sources of links. Businesses with active websites understand that offering links to other sites enhances their reputation. And just as in any marketing, you must have a well-run, trustworthy business to continue to be recommended as an interesting and informative site.

It's a good idea, when you want to link to someone else's website, to ask permission first—it's also an easy way to make people you would like to be associated with aware of your site.

Next Century, a third-world development consulting firm in Washington, D.C., reports that it is listed as a cross-referral at more than 100 Internet sites, all on the basis of mutual reciprocal benefit (cooperation). Forty of them were generated from the original list of potential referrals that Next Century developed when it launched its website. The next 60 came in at the rate of one or two a week, spontaneously,

from other businesses and nonprofits that recognized a cooperative peer.

We recommend putting your links together on a page that is easily found at your site. But don't put links on your homepage—your homepage is your business's "front door," and you don't want to usher customers out just as they're walking in. (Designing your website is discussed further in Section D.)

Putting a Community Online

Steve Killey (www.Bodeganet.com) is growing a successful business by offering a unique and cooperative service in his rural community.

Bodeganet acts like a referral for other small businesses in the Bodega, California, area. On this site you will find links to Rasberry's website, Eschenbach Construction (discussed later in this chapter) and several other small businesses. One of these is Northern Light Surf Shop which, in addition to T-shirts and surfboards, offers real-time satellite ocean data that are continually updated and show the exact heights of waves and wind speeds at nearby beaches.

Killey designed and maintains these websites at a very reasonable price. As part of his service to his community, he also maintains the sites of two candidates running for supervisor and a nonprofit land trust, all of which are listed on the primary referral page.

3. Accessibility Information

Your website is a perfect place to clearly explain how to get to your business. When you describe your location, be sure to use maps and other graphics, particularly if your business is hard to find. Be sure to mention major streets nearby, well-known points of interest and landmarks. For example, a quick print shop in Berkeley, California, marks its location on its map and also lists nearby points of interest: the Berkeley Marina, the 4th Street shopping area and the Ecology Center. For landmarks it lists some other well-known businesses nearby: the Fantasy Records company office, Orchard Supply Hardware and Takagawa Nursery. Also, remember to include information about parking.

Information about your location and directions to your business at your website will become even more important as mobile Internet service becomes more widely used. Internet access is already possible on regular cell phones, allowing users to obtain information such as addresses and phone numbers, directions, business hours and even movie times on their cell phones. As this becomes more standard, it will become essential that your site offers basic information about your business so that everyone who wants to find you can easily do so.

4. Valuable Free Information

The Internet began as a computer network linking educational and government entities; its commercial aspects are relatively new. People still go to the Internet primarily for free information, and expect to find it; if you're smart, you'll include a lot of helpful, free information on your site. In addition to satisfying users' expectations, it lets potential customers see for themselves that you are an expert.

You don't necessarily have to supply the information yourself; take advantage of the Web's capacity to link sites to each other instantly. For example, a real estate broker's website might include links to the local Chamber of Commerce site, which offers more information about the community; sites that offer good material on mortgage rates and financing; and to sites that discuss the local school system. People who are looking for a house in the community will be grateful for the leads.

Nolo.com, publisher of this book, operates a Self-Help Law Center on the Web (www.nolo.com). The site features plenty of information about Nolo books and software, but it also offers loads of free legal information on common topics such as debts, wills and trusts, small businesses and real estate.

D. Designing an Internet Site

The Internet is so new that the format of websites has not yet fully stabilized. But as it does, it is fair to guess that many of the structures of a book, which have evolved over 500 years, will be involved. These elements include a cover, with an image, title and subtitle; a back page with short reviews and recommendations; often, a jacket that contains a 300-word summary and a description of the author; and inside, standard locations for a table of contents, an introduction, a bibliography, a list of other books by the author, and an index.

In books, all of these elements help potential readers know what the contents of the book are and enable them to find what they need quickly. Similar elements will likely evolve in website structure. Already there are some standards in website design such as homepages and "return home" buttons on other Web pages at the site. The following sections describe simple ways to make your website clear and easy to navigate.

1. Your Homepage

A well-designed site starts with an uncluttered main Web page (a "homepage") that has its key message easily readable on the screen. It's also best to present any other crucial information at the homepage so that it's completely readable without using a bottom or side scroll bar.

Should You Do It Yourself?

Few small businesses have the expertise and time to design and maintain their websites. Fortunately, many individuals and companies offer this service, at a cost that ranges from minimal to expensive. As in any technology, the first questions to ask yourself are what you need and want from your website, and how much you want to spend. You absolutely do not need a lot of bells and whistles—in some businesses, such things can be inappropriate and distracting. As in all business marketing, you have to look at what others in your industry offer and what customers expect. One last warning: Don't put up your site until it's ready. It's very off-putting to visit a site that says "under construction."

Michael Eschenbach, for example, runs a construction and cabinetmaking business. His geographical business area is limited (50 miles), and for the most part, people looking for local contractors don't use the Web for this purpose. However, a few people have inquired about whether he had a website, so he had a friend help him design a simple site with a few photographs showing samples of his work: a spiral stair-case, a massage pagoda, an antique dishrack and a custom house. His site includes an e-mail link and his phone number so potential clients can just click on the link and e-mail him or pick up the phone and give him a call if they like what they see.

During the rainy season when business slacks off, he plans on adding free information about various aspects of construction. These articles will be useful over a long time period, so he won't have to update them often and can add to them when he has time. At this point, for his kind of business, a simple low-maintenance site is appropriate.

As industry norms change and more people look to the Web for contractors, he will have to change his approach. He might add a FAQ (Frequently Asked Questions) section to help educate customers while keeping his e-mail traffic down, more information about changes in his field, the latest trends in home building and tips on remodeling. He might include links to subcontractors and vendors he recommends and spend a lot more time maintaining and keeping his site fresh and informative to customers.

In the Yellow Pages, your listing must present, all at once, all the key elements your customers need: hours, credit cards, location. The Yellow Pages are also in alphabetical order by category. Neither of these things is true of the Web. Most prospective customers will find your listing by using online search engines, which search for sites that contain words a user enters. A user may search for several words at a time, assigning equal weight to each or giving some a higher priority.

In designing your homepage for your site, you need to keep in mind that a prospect delivered to your homepage may be looking for something that is on another one of your pages. The homepage should therefore clearly indicate what other material is available at the site. In essence, your homepage needs to provide a sort of Table of Contents for the site as a whole.

Also keep in mind that it's important for your site to be clear and useful to all types of visitors. Recall from Chapter 7 that customers and potential customers range from the naïve to the expert. Your introductory page should tell both the naïve user and the expert what the site offers and where to go to find specific information—without scaring a naïve prospect with the expert material, or insulting or boring an expert with the simpler material. It's often a good idea to show a sample of your primary page to a cross-section of friends and customers to make sure it appeals to a range of different people.

Since your homepage should clearly reflect what the rest of your site has to offer, you'll need to decide what else your site will offer before you can finalize your homepage. Let's take a look at some principles for designing your site as a whole.

2. Your Website's Structure

The homepage offers a central place from which users can branch out to all the other material at your site. In designing your site, you'll need to decide which pages are accessible from which—in other words, you need to establish the branching structure by linking certain pages to others. When designing your branching system, keep these guidelines in mind:

1. Always show what is ahead. Let prospects know what tables, charts, inventories and gold nuggets are still ahead of them.

2. Always allow them to go back to your homepage with one click. Each page should have an easy-to-find "home" or "main menu" button that takes the user back to your homepage. It's crucial that visitors constantly feel oriented and know how to find their way around the site. Reassure them that they can always go back to the main menu whenever they want to and provide an easy-to-understand mechanism to do so.

The overarching idea is to have the viewer feel comfortable and in control when they're at your site so they stay there, rather than getting frustrated and clicking off to a new site. To this end, be sure to design a branching structure that's clear and easy to navigate.

Encourage the visitor to bookmark your page for future reference. Web browsers such as Netscape Communicator and Microsoft's Internet Explorer allow users to create a list of their favorite pages so they can revisit them without having to enter the Web address (also called a URL, for Uniform Resource Locator).

It's very helpful in designing your website to search for businesses similar to yours online and study what works and what doesn't, using the criteria above.

E. Interactivity and Customer Screening

One of the most interesting marketing attributes of the Internet is that it allows businesses to screen their interaction with customers and prospects. Before the Internet, the voice-mail branching systems that many of us hate were the best tool for this purpose. We all recognize the voice that says, "If you want to talk to a salesperson, press 1; if you want to discuss a billing problem, press 2; ...if you want to speak to an operator, press 9." The same thing can be done on your website—without antagonizing the customer. Customers can search for their information at their own pace and with their own logic.

The interactive potential allows an online business to sort customers who visit the website, directing amateurs to pages that will educate them, and experts to pages appropriate for their knowledge level. For example, on an acupuncture clinic's online site, naïve non-users can see a short video segment of a patient being treated, as well as a graphic dictionary of terms, a brief history of this ancient medical art and testimony from successfully treated patients. Experienced patients and practitioners could be directed to pages with information about the latest studies and developments in the field, and to pages where patients could schedule appointments.

The most important and beneficial use of interactive branching is to bring new prospects exactly to the right door of your business. With the right branching system, an architect will, someday soon, answer a phone line and already know that the person on the other end wants to schedule a meeting on Thursday afternoon at 3 p.m. for a half-hour discussion of a 1,000-foot addition to her house at $120 a square foot, and that the prospect knows the architect's qualifications. When the two meet, the sale would be 90% complete.

One mechanism for weeding out browsers that is rarely used in American business is to be purposefully obtuse and obscure. In Japan, it is common to find that a master craftperson or a respected antique dealer has a storefront that is old, dilapidated and unobtrusive. Only the most sophisticated customers know where to go, so the masters don't waste time or get involved in the unpleasantness of turning the wrong people away.

The same approach can be used online. Irv Thomas, who sells books and newsletters about simple living to people who are already leading simple lives, uses it on his primary page by alerting prospects that they are facing a screening. If they get through they will probably like the product. He then lists the names of five famous and five obscure people and asks which ones have values that the prospect admires. Picking any of the right three names leads directly to Thomas's core material, and you get an explanation of why those three people are important to Thomas. Picking another three names that are close in values leads to a page that gives clues as to what is appealing about these three names and about the values that would lead the prospect to the core pages. Pick any of the four remaining names, and you are politely told that you would probably find Thomas's material inexplicable and dull.

You can separate window-shoppers from serious prospective clients based on several attributes, including taste, experience and understanding.

Taste. A tailor in Hong Kong shows a large sample of fabrics; you pick the ones you like, and he recommends the tailor whose work you are most likely to re-

spond to. He himself takes the clients who pick conservative fabrics for traditional "English gentlemen's" suits.

Experience. Sorting by experience is used by a marketing research firm seeking sophisticated clients for a technical methodology that it has perfected. Its Internet offering includes a wide range of political survey data, election results and statistical analysis programs. Users of two of its most sophisticated statistical analysis programs, a chi-square and queue-sort, are clearly the highly experienced type of people they want to offer their most sophisticated "key issues" methodology to. Users of those two programs are offered wide-open access to databases not known to others and a direct toll-free phone number for free assistance on their projects. Many of these experienced users of the secret databases have become regular customers of the key issues methodology.

Understanding. A good example of sorting by understanding is found at the online site of the University of Chicago's Committee on Social Thought. This reclusive institute holds occasional seminars for a very small number of invited cognoscenti and for the rare person who visits its Internet site and follows the branching lines all the way to the end of a Ph.D. thesis by one of the Committee's alumnae. At the end of each thesis is a flashing invitation to the next seminar, with an phone number at which people can obtain the time and location.

F. How to Help People Find You Online

People will find you on the Internet in many ways. Here are some ways to get the word out.

1. Get Covered by Search Engines

A primary method that potential customers use to locate businesses online is through search engines such as Google (http://www.google.com), Lycos (http://www.lycos.com) and Alta Vista (http://www.altavista.com), and with indexes or directories such as Yahoo! (http://www.yahoo.com). Search engine information is accessed by words or phrases; indexes use subjects and categories. To list your site with search engines, you need to submit your website address to them along with other information about your business. Dozens of businesses now exist online that submit your website address to "thousands" of search engines for a modest fee (though, since most people use one of about ten popular search engines, submitting your site to thousands of them is of questionable value).

Because search engines use key words to find you, you need to make a list of key words and keep adding to it as you think of new ones. One friend who sells a menopause product used very general words, such as "women," "health" and "fitness." These words were too vague and did not get prospects to zero in on her company. There were literally hundreds of thousands of other businesses using these words. She needed more specific words such as "workbook," "alternative medical advice" and "estrogen replacement."

Here are some ideas to stimulate your thinking:

- Location: where you are located, towns you serve, nearby landmarks.
- Skills, talents, experience, awards and degrees.
- Past and present associations and organizations you belong to that are relevant to your business.
- Trade goods, services and products.
- Employees' names, for example, if a customer might want a specific person to cut her hair or drive him to the airport. Betty Sue's Airport Van Service, for example, lists the year and model of the vans in her fleet among her key words, along with the names of her drivers, in case someone wants a specific driver whose name they remember.
- Relevant numbers: the number of years you've been in business, your birthdate, your address and zip code, your phone number with area code and your business hours if relevant.

Use a thesaurus to find synonyms to all the words you conventionally use to describe your business. Synonyms for "energy," for example, are power, force, vigor, propulsion and thrust.

2. Get Recommended on Other Sites

Other websites may link to your business. For example, publishers of vegetarian cookbooks sometimes list vegetarian retail markets by location. So Green Pastures market in Boulder, Colorado, is listed and gets automatic referrals from people who select the listing for Boulder. Green Pastures, which carries a unique line of French homeopathic remedies, also has an automatic referral from the page of the French Wholesale Company, listed under Boulder.

 The Old Ways Are Still the Good Ways. People find out about websites the same way they hear about other things—through personal recommendations. According to *Business Week magazine* (July, 19, 1996), word of mouth is what gets most people to check out a site. "With 90,000 [websites] to choose from, a lot [of people] use good old-fashioned word of mouth," concluded the magazine.

3. Distribute Your Web Address

Include your Web address on all printed, published and public material, even your outdoor sign if you have one—it's at least as important as your phone number and mailing address. Keep a list of the places your Web address is printed or posted, and if it changes, make updates quickly. We highly recommend registering a domain name in order to avoid any problems with having to change your Web address. If, instead, your address is provided to you by your Internet access provider—for example, your business called Cactus Creations has a website hosted by Mindspring, so its URL is www.mindspring.com/cactuscreations—you run the risk of having to change your Web address if you leave that access provider or if it goes out of business. Address forwarding programs are still too unreliable to be wholly effective; it's better to take care of it yourself. This is also something to keep in mind when choosing an access provider: Pick one that seems as if it will be around for a while.

4. Pay for Referrals

The Internet has many people and businesses offering to link to your site for a fee. When should you pay for referrals? Analyze it the same way you analyze your listing in the Yellow Pages: See what similar people in your business are doing, how long they use it, and what messages they present to the public. If you decide to try it, start with a limited-time arrangement so you can see what type of customers you get and whether you have the facilities to handle their inquiries.

Most important, see what company you would be keeping. To be in a referral category offered by less than desirable people can be very harmful. The early users of new technology, before government regulation is established, often include a large volume of snake oil peddlers. Extra caution is needed.

Marketing Manners on the Internet

It is a big negative to send unwanted electronic mail. Doing a mass mailing is called spamming and is the Internet version of sending junk mail. You will quickly become hugely unpopular among online folks if you do it.

Don't assume that someone who checked out your website wants to hear from you—ask before you send. When you get a person's name and e-mail address, clearly explain that you might e-mail something, or ask permission to send something such as an e-mail newsletter. When you do send something, get permission to send more. Don't treat your list like a traditional marketing mailing list, to which you might do a mailing four times a year. Never do the negative option of sending and then requiring the recipient to request that you remove his or her name.

People are very wary of having their Web use patterns followed on the Internet or their e-mail addresses given out. Anything you can say on your site to reassure them that your business does not engage in such practices is a plus. Many businesses have a policy statement on their website.

Here is an example of a good privacy policy from Book Passage in Corte Madera, California:

"We *never* sell, rent, or give away any information about our customers.

"We use the least intrusive methods possible to gather from our customers the information we need to operate our business.

(And we probably should add a third point:)

"If you show up with a subpoena looking for a customer's buying history, be prepared for a battle."

Internet Pricing

Fixed pricing, the kind we are most familiar with, where the seller has a posted price and that is the only price the seller will accept, was developed in department stores in the 1850s. It replaced haggling about price and allowed store owners to hire employees who were not family members. The owners kept their eyes on the cash register to make sure the employees weren't cheating. We now accept fixed pricing; it has been important in creating an industrial society.

Among the major industries that first deviated from fixed pricing were the airlines. Now, no one on a single airplane has necessarily paid the same price as anyone else. Early bookers and groups get low prices and late bookers get high prices. There are also frequent flyer upgrades and other perks. This deviation is called marginal pricing or dynamic pricing.

The Internet has already seen a propensity for dynamic pricing. You may be tempted to use dynamic pricing, especially for sale goods, time-sensitive goods and services for loyal customers; in these cases, dynamic pricing can make a lot of sense. But be very careful that your dynamic pricing also makes sense to your customers. The Internet is a miracle machine for spreading negative evaluations. If your low-priced product is inferior, word spreads fast. If you charge some customers higher prices based on their prior habits at your site, consumers can't be expected to understand your pricing policies. The negative word of mouth that will likely ensue can spread rapidly—as it already has for several major Internet sellers.

G. Active Internet Marketing

Actively marketing your business online can include a wide range of activities from doing an online newsletter with feedback from subscribers to participating in online discussions to running online games with thousands of simultaneous participators. The main point is that active online marketing strategy looks for opportunities and reaches out to potential customers in an endless variety of ways. Basically, this type of marketing is above and beyond simply maintaining a site (as wonderful as that site may be). Still, there are many simple ways of doing so.

Participating in discussion groups and bulletin boards online is a great way to get the word out about your business. Of course, it's essential that you participate in the spirit of the discussion group and not treat the group as purely a marketing opportunity. People participating in online discussion groups on subjects related to your business constantly ask questions and ask for recommendations about products and services. For example, a novice skier looking for equipment might ask others taking part in an online discussion for the name of a helpful ski shop in the Boston area. To get such referrals, you, a friend, a satisfied customer or an employee must be an active participant in the discussion group.

If you have an active website of your own, it's a good idea to join an online newsgroup or two and participate in ongoing discussions about topics that relate to your business. A newsgroup is an online community of people who are interested in a specific topic. They tend to have a narrow focus and can be very useful in certain fields. Your knowledgeable contributions will help you become known as an expert in your field. These newsgroups (there are thousands) are linked together; you can find ones you may be interested in through an online network known as Usenet.

When you're ready to post a message or question on a newsgroup, check out its FAQs (Frequently Asked Questions) before jumping in. It's bad form to advertise your goods or services, but if you just wrote a new program for cabinetmakers, a one-time post is fine because the other people in your cabinetmaker newsgroup would be interested.

Subscribing to a listserver, a kind of electronic newsletter dedicated to a certain topic and delivered via e-mail, is another way to let people know you are around. Subscriptions are usually free.

Tom Hargadon, who runs a multimedia newsletter and consulting business, regularly gets new subscribers and clients from people who know about him from the hundreds of cogent and valuable comments he makes in online discussion groups.

The better you are known, the more recommendations you will get. And online, recommendations travel with lightning speed across the country. For example, Paul Billings, a Palo Alto, California physician and an expert on the social problems of DNA typing, got an invitation to be an expert witness in a trial in Hawaii when the trial attorney found out about him from a colleague's referral in an online discussion group among lawyers about the Hawaii case. The attorney knew of Billings because he is a lawyer who participates in online discussions about genetic issues, including problems with DNA typing, where Billings is a highly respected contributor.

Content-Sharing as an Active Marketing Strategy

One of the active marketing strategies Nolo.com uses is to license its content to other carefully selected companies. This arrangement sometimes includes off-line content licensing as well. Obtaining content (through a license, generally) from a trusted name such as Nolo is a huge benefit to any business, whose customers will appreciate the inclusion of high-quality content, which builds trust for the entire website. Nolo has been in business for 30 years and its reputation is based on being trustworthy and offering consistently reliable content.

Nolo also has an arangement with Yahoo!. Nolo allows Yahoo! to use certain Nolo content, and Yahoo! attributes the content to Nolo and links back to the Nolo site, which enjoys increased traffic. Nolo.com has 12,000 users a day, and generates one-third of its revenue online.

Chapter 12

Designing and Implementing Your Marketing Plan

A marketing action plan for your business should include three basic elements. The first is the statement describing your business, which you completed in Chapter 7. Now it's time for you to design the next two, which we call the who and what of your marketing effort. Let's start by briefly defining the rather shorthand terms "who" and "what":

- The *who* of your action plan is simply a list of the people you already know who are in a good position to recommend your business to their friends and acquaintances.
- The *what* of your action plan is the list of marketing actions and events that will stimulate the people on your list to actually make recommendations.

Before we get into specifics, be aware that your general objective in designing a good marketing plan is to give your customers, associates and prospects a sense of participation in your business. When done well, this allows you to share your sense of excitement at the same time that you enhance trust in your business. If you can accomplish this you can significantly increase the desire and willingness of a large number of people to recommend your business to their friends.

A. Your Marketing List: The "Who" of Your Marketing Plan

One of the most important marketing tools available to the small businessperson who wants to expand is an up-to-date master list of customers, prospects, suppliers, friends and people in the community who can help spread the word. To create such a list, start by gathering all the names on your invoices, ledger cards, mailing lists, e-mail messages, personal checks you have accepted, customer sign-up sheets, Palm Pilot, etc. Some businesses add to their lists by offering a prize and holding a drawing; the entry forms include the customer's phone, e-mail and postal addresses. This technique is particularly effective at trade shows, malls and other locations where a large number of interested people are gathered. We feel it is important to make it clear when you add new people to your list, that they will from time to time receive e-mails and mailings. There is no benefit in spending postage and adding to junk e-mail by sending information to people who aren't interested.

Your marketing list should include names, e-mail and postal addresses, phone numbers, and what, if any, goods and services the customers received, along with appropriate dates. Where possible, and depending on your business, include personalized comments and notes as to who referred the people or how they heard about you. The general rule is that if you deal with a few important customers you should go out of your way to be personal, but if you sell a lot of goods and services in small units, collecting extensive personal information isn't feasible.

Whatever method you currently use for storing your list, we recommend transferring relatively small lists—fewer than 300 names—to index cards and alphabetizing them with one name per card, even if doing this duplicates a computer list. The physical presence of this box of cards is a powerful reminder to use it. However, if your list is over 300 names, then a computer database will be necessary.

Here is a sample index card that has worked for businesses we advise:

SAMPLE INDEX CARD   front

LAST NAME (OR FIRM)
FIRM (OR CONTACT)
CUSTOMER [ ]   SUPPLIER [ ]   PROSPECT [ ]
OTHER [ ]
PHONE
ADDRESS
FAX
E-MAIL
DATE CARD WAS CREATED OR UPDATED

         back

REFERRED BY
DATE AND INFORMATION ON TRANSACTIONS
PERSONAL COMMENTS

Throw a Rolodex Party. One of the most ingenious ways we've encountered to add names to a list was a "rolodex party." Developed by Joan McIntosh for Dean Sautner, who designs and builds customized shelves and desks for computers, she invited her trusted friends to a party and asked each to bring their rolodex. At the party, she provided envelopes containing brochures describing Sautner's products. Joan asked her friends to address at least six envelopes to people who might be interested in the furniture and to write a short personal note on the flyer. A good percentage of the people contacted this way responded favorably.

B. How to Evaluate Your List

The purpose of this checklist is to determine how much, if any, work is needed for your list to be usable.

Your Marketing List

Your marketing list was last updated:

☐ 6 months ago   ☐ 1 year ago   ☐ 2 years ago   ☐ 3 or more years ago

A complete list of your customers, suppliers, prospects, and business associates, relevant aquaintances and peers is available for an immediate mailing, phone invitation or e-mail contact.   ☐ YES ☐ NO

		EXCELLENT	ADEQUATE	NEEDS MORE WORK
If Yes, how current are your addresses?	customers	☐	☐	☐
	suppliers	☐	☐	☐
	prospects	☐	☐	☐
	business associates	☐	☐	☐
	acquaintances	☐	☐	☐
	peers	☐	☐	☐
How current are your phone numbers?	customers	☐	☐	☐
	suppliers	☐	☐	☐
	prospects	☐	☐	☐
	business associates	☐	☐	☐
	acquaintances	☐	☐	☐
	peers	☐	☐	☐
How current are your e-mail addresses?	customers	☐	☐	☐
	suppliers	☐	☐	☐
	prospects	☐	☐	☐
	business associates	☐	☐	☐
	acquaintances	☐	☐	☐
	peers	☐	☐	☐

If No, how long would it take you to make a list?	customers	_____ hours
	suppliers	_____ hours
	prospects	_____ hours
	business associates	_____ hours
	acquaintances	_____ hours
	peers	_____ hours

Starting now you are compiling these records from...

☐ checks
☐ customer records
☐ form letters
☐ supplier records
☐ organization membership lists
☐ your personal address book
☐ e-mail messages
☐ personal organizers (Palm Pilots, etc.)
☐ other _____

C. Marketing Actions and Events: The "What" of Your Marketing Plan

Once you generate a list of your marketing community, the next step is to plan marketing actions. These actions should generally fall into three categories:

- Direct,
- Parallel, and
- Peer-based.

Together, these make up the "what" of your marketing plan. Let's first define these terms by looking at how a small school of modern dance might use each to mount a good marketing effort designed to stimulate personal recommendations. (The next chapter gives several examples from each of these categories to show how year-long marketing plans are actually planned.)

- **Direct Marketing:** For a dance school, a good illustration of direct marketing is holding a performance by advanced students at the school. All students would be encouraged to invite their friends and family, and the school would send a notice to school alumni and friends and arrange for appropriate publicity in the dance community.

- **Parallel Marketing:** The dance school selects people from its marketing list and invites them to be guests at a local performance by a touring dance company known to do innovative work.

- **Peer-Based Marketing:** The dance school gives a reception for a visiting out-of-town artist/performer and invites the people on its list, including a wide cross-section of the local dance and arts community.

All businesses should carefully consider each of these broad community-based marketing approaches. Of course, depending on your business, there are many—often hundreds—of possibilities in each of the three categories. Often, particularly good ones become annual events that customers and friends look forward to. Christmas parties and business open houses are a popular version of this type of marketing. So are free ice cream cones for children's birthdays from the local ice cream shop. But because they are so common, and because they are not designed with intentional information content, they are not nearly as effective.

Marketing for Wholesalers Who Use Middlepersons

Many businesses have no direct contact with their final buyers. If you use representatives (reps) or sell through distributors and retailers, you will probably want to direct most of your marketing activity at the people who actually buy from you. However, if an opportunity ever comes up to deal directly with the final buyer, we advise you to take it. This doesn't mean that you should ignore your reps, just that you should try to develop alternative marketing strategies.

If your business must use reps because that system is built into the industry, try to help your distributors sell more of your product. One example is a jeweler we know who sells primarily through sales reps but still regularly sends the buyers at all her major store accounts a newsletter. The newsletter is primarily graphic; one issue showed some unusual contemporary fashions and how her jewelry is worn with them, and another highlighted interesting window and counter displays featuring her jewelry. In one issue, she included a small card with a chart that converted millimeter measurements to the 1/16-inch measurements used in the jewelry business. Because the newsletter complemented the activities of the reps and didn't threaten them, the reps were happy to have the supplier actively helping in the sales process.

You may decide, however, that you can do better without reps. For example, a woolen mill in western England faced a disastrous decline in its business, caused in part by softer, higher quality imports. Instead of closing down, as many other woolen mills have done, it reversed its decline by eliminating all of its reps and relying solely on one salesperson plus an innovative marketing strategy. Part of this strategy consisted of inviting customers to visit the factory and to stay in a local 300-year-old inn. People loved the idea and came from as far away as Japan and Canada.

The owners of the mill introduced each customer to the women on the production line, allowing time for informal interaction as well as in-depth discussion of the process of turning wool into fabric. The customers found that the factory could create a far wider range of custom fabrics than they had realized. Several customers who used the fabric in the upholstery business were able to redesign some of the material to better fit their needs. And by changing some procedures, new markets were created in the sporting goods field. This increase in business could not have happened had the mill worked exclusively through middlepersons.

We believe this lesson is valuable to almost every business. Your customers, especially since they are in business themselves, know what they need better than any rep (who is, after all, in the "rep" business), and often better than you do.

Sometimes the problem of middlepersons is difficult to avoid. Frances Peavey published a book, *Heart Politics* (New Society

Marketing for Wholesalers . . . cont'd

Press, 1985), about community organizing for social change. This is the kind of book that rarely gets widely reviewed. In other words, book reviewers—the middlepersons of the book world—weren't likely to be of much help if she simply mailed out review copies. Frances circumvented this bottleneck by doing her own publicity and direct selling to churches and peace groups. In addition, however, Frances also put some thought into how she could get the middlepersons to pay attention to her product.

During the annual American Booksellers' Association convention, which most major book reviewers from all over the country and close to 20,000 book industry people attend, Frances got a part-time job as a taxi driver. She kept her cab in front of the convention hall during the entire week of the convention, making it a point to get into conversations with passengers about her books. A few of these were reviewers, and many others knew reviewers and were so struck by the creativity of her approach that they provided introductions. Frances met more than a dozen book reviewers, representing major newspapers as well as a few key magazines. They all promised to review her book. Most of them did.

Let's now look at each of the categories in more detail to help inspire you when you create your own list of actions.

D. Direct Marketing Actions

Once you have a list of clients, suppliers, friends and prospects in front of you, you may feel the urge to pick up the phone, send a note or visit each one to tell them more about your business. For most businesses, following that impulse would be a primitive and impractical form of direct marketing. The task of this section is to get you to refine this idea so that you can contact the people on your list to tell them about an event, action, product or service that they will welcome hearing about.

Where appropriate, the most direct and effective marketing stimulus is to contact the persons on your list by telephone or in person to inform them of some new offering. If your information is genuinely useful, this approach is usually appreciated. An example is a fancy clothing boutique that calls the people on its list to tell them about a luncheon fashion show.

Many businesspeople are understandably uncomfortable phoning or otherwise directly contacting customers. They feel that if they offer a good service or product, people should appreciate them so much that they will seek them out. Often too, there is the fear of being rejected. The reality, of course, is that any business is only a small item in the busy life of its customers and can easily be overlooked.

You can test this on a small scale for yourself; call ten of your customers and tell them about something that is of benefit to them. Chances are they will be happy to hear from you and will tell you so.

1. Sampling as a Direct Marketing Technique

If you offer a quality product or service, one of the best marketing strategies consists of offering a potential customer a sample. We have all found samples of toothpaste, shampoo and soap in our mailboxes. If the sample works to our satisfaction, we may well buy the product, even if this means switching brands.

This sort of large-scale sample distribution can often be a very effective marketing tool, but it is obviously way over the budget of the ordinary small businessperson. With a little imagination, however, you can come up with smaller-scale, targeted sampling ideas to let people on your action list know what you have to offer, and do it at a very reasonable cost. For example, we have a friend, Clark Herz, who offers free foot massages at the county fair. Tired tootsies are soon rejuvenated, and a whole new group of people are introduced to Clark's massage business.

Here are a few illustrations of how to creatively use sampling techniques at a modest cost:

- If you are in the landscaping business, offer to demonstrate how your new weed-whip can spiff up a yard in short order as part of clean-up duty at a local church or community center.
- The retail food business is a natural for samples; it's wise to have small bits of food regularly available for customers to nibble. To reach large numbers of new customers, regularly contribute your special concoctions at community events. Bill's Farm Basket in Sebastopol, California, offers a wide assortment of fruit, veggies and other goodies. This popular roadside market recently added a deli, and as customers wait at the check-out counter they tempt them with hummus and crackers, salsa and bread or whatever new item they have decided to add to their selection. And you don't have to feel shy about seconds and thirds; they encourage their customers to really enjoy their products. No wonder Bill's is a favorite roadside stand of Tom Peters, author of *The Management Expert*.
- A catering business can invite its customers to drop by for a food tasting. It might offer five variations on a dessert it is contemplating serving as part of its dinner menu and take a vote as to customer preference. Presumably, if the desserts are good, a number of the people who attend will call the caterer for future events and feel confident recommending it to friends.
- In Japan, department stores generally, and cosmetic sections always, include a small sample as a gift for customers with each purchase. All sorts of small businesses can use this technique to introduce customers to new products at relatively low cost. Indeed, if you

can get the cooperation of your suppliers (who, after all, are interested in increasing sales of their products), you may even be able to provide your customers with small quantities of a new product at no cost to you.

- A tapestry weaver might send out a sample of a new "rough-knotty" yarn that he is incorporating in new designs.
- An educational game and curriculum designer could send a quiz based on one of her new products with the offer of a prize to anyone who answers it correctly.
- Welcome Wagon-type groups can be a good, relatively low-cost marketing tool to reach people new to your area. Offering a free sample or introductory discount this way is appropriate if new residents are particularly likely to need your product or service.
- America Online does mass mailings of free, easy-to-use software and offers free access time to encourage potential customers to use its service.

Unfortunately, some businesspeople tend to dismiss sampling as a marketing tool because they don't think it's sufficiently sophisticated. Consider the story of Estee Lauder, founder of the largest family-owned cosmetics company in the world. When Lauder was starting her business in the 1930s, she stopped people on New York City streets and offered to make them up then and there. She usually ended up selling them a jar of her face cream (which, incidentally, was made in a converted stable by her Uncle John).

Picking the best sample from your business is often an act of creative inspiration. It requires matching the customers' interests with something you have to offer. Think about what aspect of your business you can share with others at a reasonable cost that is likely to entice people to want more. Converse Shoes, an athletic shoe manufacturer, for example, often provides "test" shoes in popular running areas. It offers a one-hour "sample," which is a great attention-getter and a real service. What better way to see if a pair of shoes is right for you than to actually run in them? If you like the Converse shoe, you get a discount coupon redeemable at local stores.

2. Giving Customers a Little Extra

Not so many years ago, when you purchased a dozen rolls or pastries at a bakery, you got one free. In some places, smart bakeries still give their customers a baker's dozen. Similarly, See's Candy, an old-line West Coast firm that sells wonderful candy at a fair price, always gives a purchaser a free piece of candy on the spot.

In both instances, the point is the same: a good customer gets a tangible thank you. Being generous is a wonderful way to say, "We appreciate your business. Please come back."

Another form of giving a little extra is looking upon your business as part of a community. Every business has a community, but in some businesses customers are encouraged to be part of that community and feel almost part of an extended family. For example, nowadays coffee houses abound. The reason why some of these establishments have an incredibly loyal clientele is that customers trust the business for all of the reasons we have discussed in this book and they have decided to "adopt" it. Customers proudly invite their friends as if they were inviting them into their own kitchen and feel almost proprietary about the business.

A good example of business as extended family is Caffe Trieste, a flourishing business tucked away on a corner in North Beach, the old Italian neighborhood of San Francisco. One thing that sets it apart from other (often fancier) cafes in the neighborhood is its friendly, "family" atmosphere. On Saturday afternoons Caffe Trieste is jammed with customers who come to hear some of the regulars—friends and family of the owners—sing everything from Italian folk songs to Broadway hits. Audience participation is encouraged, and it's more like going to a party than to a restaurant.

Giving a little extra to good customers can build customer trust very quickly. Everyone likes a good deal, and many will pass on the good news to their friends. If you don't run a retail business, you may be saying "Sure, but this sort of technique won't work for me." Nonsense. Let's look at a few examples:

- A lawyer who specializes in helping small businesses sends a letter to her network of clients and friends saying that, in September, she plans to concentrate on incorporations because her new computer program allows her to achieve substantial efficiencies by pre-programming the standard ("boilerplate") language. As part of "incorporation month," she not only offers a free (or low-cost), one-day seminar on the pros and cons of incorporating, but also reduces her normal incorporation fee by $100 to pass along the savings a volume approach allows.

- A plumber gives every customer a bottle of liquid drain cleaner as part of house calls.

- A shoemaker includes a sample size tin of shoe polish with every major repair job.

- A one-hour film developer sells film to customers at a wholesale rate.

- A tire service sends customers a simple tool designed to measure tread wear, along with an announcement of a sale on new tires.

- An accountant sends out an inexpensive financial record-keeping book to all his clients.

This list could be nearly endless. With a little creative thinking, every small businessperson can use discounts, small gifts or extra services to make good customers feel appreciated. One good way many businesses do this is through the use of punch cards or tickets allowing customers to get one item free whenever they buy ten. We are very loyal to a video rental shop and a take-out pizza place that do this, and one of our editors brags about a children's shoe store that has the same policy, but with the nice little twist that they also keep the records of purchases for you. And we know a nice little Japanese restaurant in San Francisco that gives customers a Japanese coin good for a free order of sake at the next visit.

Osmosis, the enzyme bath and massage business mentioned in Chapter 7, gives a birthday card that you present within 30 days of your birthday for you and your guests to receive 20% off all treatments. And Pastorale, the retail store with a focus on natural fibers (also mentioned in Chapter 7) sends a card at Christmas to the approximately 13,000 people on its list inviting them to come in for a free ornament. About 600 people bring in the card each year; the ornaments are of the highest quality and have become a tradition in the community.

Of course, punch cards and coupons work better in some businesses than others, and are clearly inappropriate in a fancy restaurant where people expect to pay well for exquisite food and service. However, even in the most expensive gourmet restaurant where diners don't worry about the number of zeros on the bill, a little extra is appreciated. For example, a friend reports having a dinner at Masa's, one of San Francisco's loveliest and most expensive restaurants. This party was hosted by another friend who was treating the entire group to celebrate his big promotion. The left side of the menu contained a number of wonderful entrees as part of a complete dinner. As mouth-watering as this list was, however, the "grass is always greener" phenomenon of human nature inevitably caused some of the party to begin fantasizing about how scrumptious some of the à la carte items on the other side of the menu were sure to be.

Finally, the host beckoned the waiter and asked if substitutions were allowed, fully expecting that the answer would be no, as it usually is. Much to everyone's surprise, the waiter said it was Masa's policy to offer its customers the best eating experience possible, and that almost anything on the menu could be substituted for anything else. From then on, our friend reports the meal was a terrific success, with one of everything ordered, bites shared, and everyone getting a taste of his or her favorites. When the last bite was eaten, sip of wine drunk and the bill paid, everyone felt that they had been treated wonderfully.

One of the most ingenious of all fair price techniques we have encountered comes from Tokyo Hands, a store in Tokyo that sells hobbies, crafts, art supplies, gardening tools, auto supplies and office and bathroom goods, each on a separate floor. A customer who buys office supplies on the fifth floor is given a 20% discount coupon good for that day for any art supplies on the third floor. If he takes advantage of the offer, he is given another discount coupon good that day in a related department. In short, each department gives a discount coupon for another department that a person who patronized the first would likely be interested in.

Of course, one reason why this is such a brilliant marketing idea is that the customer is already in the store. Money spent to encourage customers to buy more when they are already on the premises is, of course, far more cost-effective than is money spent to get them there in the first place.

Incidentally, use of this sort of discount coupon technique need not be limited to stores with many departments. Any group of retail businesses located in a relatively small area which appeal to similar types of customers can use it effectively. For example, a plant nursery might give its customers a 20% discount coupon good that day at a neighboring lawn furniture store, and vice versa. And the same principle, with perhaps a little extension of the time factor, can be used by service businesses,

as would be the case if a tax accountant referred his clients to a reliable computerized bookkeeping service that offered them a slightly discounted hourly rate.

3. Product Demonstrations as a Direct Marketing Technique

Product demonstrations can make the difference between success and failure for many small businesses. For some, this marketing technique offers the only cost-effective way to make people aware of what they have to offer. Here are a few examples of successful demonstrations:

- An interior decorator, Tony Torrice, invited his list of builders, architects and developers to a house where he had just installed a specially equipped bathroom for a handicapped client. No amount of words (whether in the form of an article or even a direct conversation) could have demonstrated the unique features of this room as well as seeing it first-hand.

- A contractor had a wine-tasting event at an office where he had designed a skylight in conjunction with mirrors to bring light to a particularly dark area of the room. Actually experiencing the space allowed many of the people present to see how this kind of skylight could improve their living and working spaces.

- A rug manufacturer invited his customers to observe one of his master weavers at work on a huge loom so people could gain an insight into the rug-making process. He also displayed his finished rugs.
- The late Kaisek Wong, a woman's clothing designer, had two models wearing his stunning clothes accompany him to nearly every party, dinner and opening to which he was invited. Most people loved to invite him, especially the circle of women who bought his clothing.
- A foreign language school sent its alumni, donor and prospect list a one-page flyer of common phrases for a dozen different languages and offered a free 15-minute telephone lesson to accompany it.

4. Classes as a Direct Marketing Technique

It's often hard to remember that many products and services that are commonplace for us are complete novelties to others. The media lets us know a little about many new developments but rarely teaches us enough to make us willing to break old patterns and make new products part of our lives. For example, TV may tell you about the latest digital camcorder, but it won't teach you how to operate all the settings on one. Most people learn through classes offered free when they purchase their cameras. Stores that don't provide these instruction classes are missing an obvious marketing technique.

Because business benefits from selling all sorts of new product developments, our society leaves much of the job of educating consumers up to these businesses. Businesses that do a good job at education sell more. Here are some examples of how businesses can use classes to enhance their marketing efforts.

- A weight-lifting gym offers introductory instruction to its customers.
- A women's clothing store offers color analysis and wardrobe design classes for its clientele.
- An outdoor equipment store offers to teach people how to use the equipment it sells.
- A word processing firm teaches its techniques for high-speed mailing list input and for doing statistical tables.
- A school for children with learning disabilities teaches parents and grandparents of students about recent developments in this rapidly changing field.
- A locksmith teaches businesspersons the elements that go into creating a tight security system.
- Fireplace manufacturers have a special opportunity to teach classes to architects and decorators on the mathematical calculations necessary to design a fireplace that works.

In addition, classes are a particularly effective marketing technique for service providers such as lawyers, accountants, doctors, designers and all sorts of consultants to keep their clients up-to-date on new developments in their fields.

Should you charge for these classes? It's a tough question. Banks often offer free classes for their target clients, such as medium-size businesses. One of our favorite local banks hosts a free breakfast meeting twice a year for their business customers and invites a knowledgeable speaker to talk to the group for an hour. Free also seems to be the rule when it comes to classes and lectures taught by large accounting firms and pharmaceutical companies, where prices are comparable from company to company, and mark-ups are high. In many small business situations, however, modest fees—often below the cost of providing the class—are prevalent and accepted.

We have found that the key to classes is not how much you charge, but how much real value they provide your customers. For example, if you run a woodworking or interior decorating business and offer classes (free or not) that are little more than a sales pitch, the classes will not be well received and may even generate negative comments about your business. A far better approach is to charge a modest fee for classes that provide excellent information and training and hardly mention the services or products your business provides. If your classes are good, people will demand to know more about your business. When they do, offer them a small discount and you will have created a very satisfied customer.

This technique is followed by Bernard Kamoroff, author of the best-selling small business guidebook *Small Time Operator* (Bell Springs, 1996). Bernard (Bear to his friends) schedules classes and workshops for small businesspersons, sometimes under his own auspices and sometimes through existing educational programs such as local college extension programs. As part of the course, he distributes his book to the students so that they can refer to various charts and other information as he goes along. He asks only that the books be handled carefully and returned at the end of the lecture.

Because our friend Bear's class is so good, one or more students always inquire if they can purchase the book. When the class learns that not only can they buy the book, but that they get a 10% discount if they do, as many as 75% purchase it, and most ask to have their copies autographed.

5. Follow-Up as a Direct Marketing Technique

One of the gut responses of a businessperson with good marketing skills is to follow up with important customers to find out how things worked out. The simplest way to do this is to call and ask customers if they are happy with the product or service they received. Some people new to business are reluctant to ask either because they are afraid of the answer or feel shy. But if you don't ask you will never know—

and, as we discussed earlier, an unhappy customer probably won't tell you but will tell his or her friends. Usually a customer with a small complaint will be delighted for the opportunity to tell you and will remain a loyal customer.

You should follow up if at all possible, especially following a marketing event. The questions you want answered are:

- Did your customer like your goods or services?
- Did it meet her expectations?
- Is there anything you can do now to increase your customer's satisfaction?

There are many ways to follow up in addition or instead of calling. We suggest a few here, but you will, of course, want to use your own creativity to find an approach that is appropriate for your business:

- A friend who manufactures handmade chairs sends a letter to customers inquiring about their satisfaction with his product. He also recommends a special, hard-to-get finishing oil he uses and offers to sell it to the customers at a substantial discount.
- A knife manufacturer offers a free sharpening training session to clients.
- An illumination consultant comes by a few weeks after a lighting job is completed to see if any slight adjustments might be helpful.
- A humane society worker calls a week after a pet is adopted to see if there are any unexpected problems.

- A computer-based information retrieval service calls a day after a requested research report is sent to the client to see if additional material needs to be generated.

This is your chance to be your own business consultant and design your own direct marketing plan. These worksheets are very important. Use every creative technique you know of to write down your ideas. Eat chocolate if that will help, stand on your head if that works for you, have a brainstorming session with your associates, go running, take a vacation—whatever it takes—do it!

E. Parallel Marketing Actions

In addition to direct marketing, your marketing action plan should include parallel marketing techniques. Parallel marketing is aimed at promoting your business area in general, not just your business. Think of products and services closely related to yours or which are in some way complementary, that you wholeheartedly recommend. By telling your customers about these products or services, you provide a valuable service at the same time you give them a better perspective about your business. It is a strong form of teaching: subtle, clear and participatory. By helping your customers, you make it far more likely that they will make positive personal recommendations about your business.

Moon Travel Handbooks in Chico, California, sells state-by-state travel guides for

Designing Direct Marketing Events

SAMPLES: (items or reference guides your customers would find useful)

_____

_____

_____

_____

_____

DEMONSTRATIONS:

_____

_____

_____

_____

_____

CLASSES: (re-examine your business definition in Chapter 7 to broaden the range of topics your customers and prospects are interested in)

_____

_____

_____

_____

FOLLOW-UPS: (what related product or service delivered by mail, phone, e-mail, questionnaire or visit could make your past and present customers more satisfied with your work?)

_____

_____

_____

_____

popular tourist and camping destinations. Its marketing is largely parallel in the form of a quarterly newsletter with articles written by travel experts and a website (www.moon.com/catalog). One issue contained articles on wineries in Texas, fashions in Montana and how to avoid or treat questionable drinking water by a Ph.D. in international health. On the website are great links to travel resources and some of the best online information that we have seen about staying healthy in other countries.

A different approach to parallel marketing is provided by the Stanford University Business School, which occasionally makes available guest lecturers for alumni in major cities around the country. This is, of course, a very traditional marketing approach. Stanford is marketing itself to its alumni, to whom it will surely appeal for contributions at one time or another. But it's important to understand that there is no direct pitch at the lectures, which provide alumni with a service at the same time that Stanford's value as an educational institution is underlined.

It is helpful, in developing your list of parallel marketing actions, to make distinctions between sampling, demonstrations and classes if only to stimulate your imagination to generate more ideas.

1. Samples and Offers as Parallel Marketing

Here are some examples of parallel marketing techniques using samples and special offers:

- A Texas dentist sends out toothbrushes for patients to use without water or toothpaste while driving.
- A lawyer with a new practice sends his small business clients a copy of a booklet explaining partnership laws.
- The partners in an events organizing company alert all their clients and prospects to a wine-tasting at a local vineyard.
- A Spanish restaurant has regular drawings among customer entries for tickets to local flamenco dance performances.
- A stable that boards and rents horses sends out flyers to the people on its mailing list describing a non-toxic fly control system offered by a local company.
- A small publisher producing books for craftspeople includes materials in its mailings describing useful books and resources published by other companies.
- A florist gives a customer who buys cut flowers a sample package of a substance that extends the life of the flowers.

Each of these parallel marketing efforts provides useful information for customers that adds to their general expertise in the field. The dentist who sends out toothbrushes is clearly broadening the knowledge of his patients. They learn that using a dry toothbrush is good for the gums and can be done while driving to work, a significant departure from the "brush after every meal" advice which they probably disregard as too inconvenient.

The partnership booklet gives the lawyer's customers, in a convenient form, a better perspective on the legal issues involved in their business organization. This booklet is also a way to alert them to many issues (for example, what happens to the partnership if one partner becomes disabled) that they might never have recognized as concerns for which they might want to consult a lawyer.

Similarly, by inviting people to a wine tasting, the event's organizers are able to contact potential customers in a way that is far more effective than the standard approach of sending them a fancy brochure in the mail.

The publisher is being particularly creative by recommending books published by someone else in a related field. By doing this, the publisher is saying, "I am willing to take your interests seriously."

2. Demonstrations as Parallel Marketing

Demonstrations are among the more interesting parallel marketing events a business can offer. The color and flair they add to a business is often beneficial in itself. People, including your employees, like businesses with vitality. And of course, customers respond positively to demonstrations that provide them real value.

Depending on your particular business, it's usually worth exploring a wide range of demonstration techniques. But always remember the two key rules to a successful demonstration:

- Make your demonstrations fun, and
- Give real value.

Here are some examples of demonstrations that work as parallel marketing techniques:

- A white-water river rafting company holds a demonstration of ocean kayaking at a local beach.
- A wind generator manufacturer sponsors a one-day show displaying the most recent battery storage systems.
- A sports club invites someone who restrings racquets to demonstrate his technique in the lobby.
- A hair salon in Copenhagen offers its customers smocks to wear during their visit that are hand designed by a neighboring clothing designer.
- A community foundation in Portland, Oregon, puts on a fair to which it invites all the local accountants, lawyers and management consultants who offer special services to nonprofit organizations.

In some businesses, a demonstration is much the same as a sample or a class. The ocean kayaking business is an example. It normally takes a beginner about three hours of instruction to feel confident paddling alone. When Sea Trek of Sausalito, California, was a relatively new business in a new field, to entice potential customers into giving kayaking a try it offered one-and-a-half-hour "samplers" at a nominal fee. This demo time was credited toward the minimum three hours of instruction required before customers could rent a kayak. After the first hour, most people were eager to sign up for the remaining two hours of low-cost introductory class. Many people who completed the course became enthusiasts who rented or bought kayaks from Sea Trek. In addition, Sea Trek also invited people in the media to try out kayaking. If they liked their experience (which they all did) they would of course write an enthusiastic article or give them television coverage. Sea Trek did an excellent job of offering demonstrations as well as educating customers. It no longer offers demonstrations, as the business has become extremely popular. Sea Trek helped educate customers to the point where kayaking is now on the cover of major magazines and is often recommended as a way to relieve stress.

The concept underlying parallel marketing is especially clear in the case of classes. The benefits to the business owner are twofold. First, classes increase the level of expertise of valued customers, who in turn are better able and more confident in making personal referrals to their friends. Second, they help customers better appreciate the subtleties and nuances that make your business unique.

Here are some examples of classes as a parallel marketing technique:

- A consulting firm in the field of policy analysis sponsors a class in a specialized area of agriculture where policy analysis had been effectively used.
- A sailboat sales company sends its customers free coupons for a course in boat racing.

- A grocery store invites a produce grower to give brief talks explaining how best to determine when certain types of fruit are ripe.
- A prepaid health plan offers regular classes by outsiders to patients on dozens on health issues from "Pediatric Emergencies" to "Oh, My Aching Back."

3. Follow-Up as Parallel Marketing

Follow-up as a parallel marketing method takes a little extra thought. In direct marketing follow-up, you check on how the customer has reacted to your product or service; in parallel marketing, you keep him up-to-date on an issue that is related to your business. This allows you to demonstrate your genuine concern about your customers' needs. Parallel follow-up marketing can be as personal as a dry cleaner asking a customer, who had an elegant opera costume cleaned, how his opera performance went.

By this point, you are probably convinced that a well-planned and thought-out parallel marketing action or event can help you establish extra credibility in your field. When you play the role of an expert broker of related activities, your customers and potential customers see you as creative, competent and caring.

When you fill out the worksheet below, try to think of at least five parallel marketing events and actions for each category.

Designing Parallel Marketing Events

SAMPLES: (items or reference guides your customers would find useful)

_____

_____

_____

_____

_____

DEMONSTRATIONS:

_____

_____

_____

_____

_____

CLASSES: (re-examine your business definition in Chapter 7 to broaden
the range of topics your customers and prospects are interested in)

_____

_____

_____

_____

_____

FOLLOW-UPS: (what related product or service delivered by mail, phone, e-mail,
questionnaire or visit could make your past and present customers
more satisfied with your work?)

_____

_____

_____

_____

_____

F. Peer-Based Marketing Actions

One of the most important things propri-etors of small businesses can do is get to-gether, informally and regularly, with peers. It not only provides a great source of both moral support and tangible assis-tance, but is also a superior way to explain your business to people who can refer cus-tomers to you. Paul Terry, a small-business consultant, has a number of peers whom he takes to breakfast or lunch on a regular basis to stay in touch and to make sure that they know what direction his business is taking. Paul understands that these busi-ness friends are an important part of his re-ferral base.

If you are a graphic designer, for ex-ample, with a new business, you need to meet others working in your field, espe-cially those with established businesses, to tell them who you are and where you work. If they get overloaded, you want them to know exactly how to refer people to you. In the real estate business it is com-mon practice to visit multiple listing homes with other real estate agents. This caravanning is usually done once a week and enables agents in an area to keep in contact.

The essence of peer-based marketing is for you to understand your role as part of a group of peers in your field and to make effective use of it. All of us have unique contributions to make. Just as one doctor, say an internist, can make use of a surgeon

when the case calls for surgery, so you can help and get help from others in your field.

It is often surprising to find that friends and peers we know well through business and consider just ordinary folks are ad-mired or even held in awe by others. Think about peers whom you know well who qualify as special in your community. Don't be afraid to define the concept of community creatively. For example, if you run a motorcycle shop and are friendly with several dirt bike racing champs, these people should top your list. They may not be well known at the local Presbyterian church, but they are important in the com-munity that you care about.

The key to peer-based marketing is hav-ing these well-known people participate constructively in your business. If you can do this, you will reinforce all of the ele-ments of trust we have discussed in this book and, as a result, stimulate personal recommendations. Often your friends will be happy to help you, whether or not there is some possibility that they will ben-efit as a result of their participation. How-ever, on occasion, it is appropriate to pay an honorarium or otherwise compensate friends if their participation will involve considerable time or trouble, or if that is how they make their living. Always re-member that while you may wish to use your friendship network to help your cus-tomers, you don't want to make unfair de-mands on others.

Inviting your respected friends to recep-tions, coffee events, demonstrations, brief classes, book signings and other events can be the grounds for a whole array of marketing events which need only be tangential to the business. For example, we know of events where:

- The author of a well-known personal finance book attended a "Getting Thin" class reception.
- Several football stars attended a church bazaar to raise funds for the church's athletic programs.
- A business consultant for graphic designers invited a famous architect to an after-dinner reception for her clients.
- A lawyer who specializes in immigration law invited clients and friends to an office reception for the Governor-General of Hong Kong.
- A massage table manufacturer hosted a late afternoon reception for the factory employees, suppliers and retailers in the area, with a well-known sports doctor as the guest.
- A scuba diving store and school invited a marine biologist friend to brief its class at dive sites.
- A commercial insurance broker with a good consumer advocacy reputation had a reception for his friends and clients to meet Ralph Nader before a talk Nader gave.
- A Japanese advertising firm invited many of its client representatives to meet and hear a brief private talk by an American marketing expert on the subject of Silicon Valley electronics firms.

Profile: Fritz Maytag

It was a perfect, beautiful day in July, and we had taken a walk around the neighborhood to settle our lunch. We returned to the office full of energy. There working at the computer with our friend Wayne was an honest-to-God hero—Fritz Maytag.

Fritz is a successful entrepreneur who heads the York Creek Vineyards, which produces some of the world's finest grapes, as well as the family cheese company and the renowned Anchor Steam Brewery.

In 1969, when Fritz bought the brewery, it was near bankruptcy. He improved the product rapidly, using only the best ingredients. He created nostalgic old-fashioned bottle labels and beautiful hand-painted delivery trucks. The company, considered one of the finest beer-makers in America by gourmets and drinkers alike, does not advertise. Instead of costly ads, Maytag uses ten master distributors.

In the June 30, 1985, issue of the *San Francisco Examiner* is Jim Wood's fascinating interview with Fritz Maytag. We have excerpted, with the newspaper's kind permission, his philosophy and strategies regarding marketing.

"Like so many liberal art students, young people interested in philosophy and ideas and religion and all that stuff, I had thought that business was dumb and ugly and dishonest and just a lot of money-grubbing people running around fooling each other and talking people into buying their dumb products. That may be one reason I've never advertised very much. I always felt that if they came and bought it on its own right that I would feel better.

"I just sort of had a natural instinct for a way to market the beer, which was first to make a wonderful beer that we were sure was just superb and well made, with a true story. I used to say I wanted a beer that would please people here (pointing) on the taste buds, but also up here in the head, you know. I felt instinctively that the way to market it was slowly and gently, and let it trickle around to get some word of mouth going, tell our story to as many people as we possibly could, show them the brewery. Not to advertise.... I felt that we would stand out by not doing that....

"What we did was we opened the brewery night and day to anyone who would come and look. We had art exhibits. We had sculpture exhibits, where we turned the whole brewery over to a remarkable man, Ron Boise, who was notorious, well infamous, for having done a little thing called a 'Kama Sutra' series in copper. (Lawrence) Ferlinghetti exhibited it, and the police came down.

"Anyway, we weren't dumb. We turned the whole brewery over to him and we put this huge sculpture of a naked man and woman up on the roof where you could see it from the freeway. We made the front page of the *Chronicle* and the *Examiner*. The district attorney, or whoever it was, called up and said 'Hello, is this the Anchor Brewery?' 'Yes,' I said. They said, 'We want to

Profile: Fritz Maytag, continued

know about that sculpture on the roof.' I said, 'What do you want to know about it?' 'We want to know whether it is obscene or not.' I said 'No, it's not obscene.' He said, 'Oh. Thank you.' And he hung up.

"We had a balloon ascension on Fisherman's Wharf in 1966, before hot air balloons had even been heard of, and we made the paper again. The point being— Anchor Steam Beer was here. We were local, we were continuing and we did our packaging, labels and things, trucks, all those things, we did with as much care and sort of flair for expressing our attitude toward the beer as we possibly could. We purposely (made) them sort of naive and sincere. We put a long story on the neck label. I always said, even if people don't read it, they'll get the message there is a long story here and someday they will read it."

Before you turn to Chapter 13 and begin to design your marketing plan, we would like to tell you about Book Passage in Corte Madera, California, which is one of our favorite independent booksellers. At a time when many independents are going out of business, it appears to be thriving. Here is a sampling of some of its superb marketing, which demonstrates how one business incorporates direct, peer-based and parallel into its marketing mix. Book Passages offers excellent news and reviews in both hard copy and on its Web page (http://www.bookpassage.com). It has over 50 knowledgeable booksellers to help you, along with a "passion and exuberance for books and writers."

This commitment to writers and readers shows in the 200 or so author events the bookstore hosts every year in addition to its classes, book groups and conferences. Each Christmas, Book Passages sponsors the Giving Tree, which provides children from infancy to 18 years old with beautifully gift-wrapped books delivered by the store.

Creating Community for Your Business

Most people consider a business that they appreciate and respect as part of their community. You are part of their community; they are part of yours. Together you can help make the community vital.

Nolo.com's business is built on providing trustworthy legal information, and a major aspect of the business involves building a community. Nolo carefully develops relationships with other online businesses. For example, they license their content to CareThere.com, a company Nolo respects and whose website exudes integrity and community spirit.

Several Internet sites have been pioneers in creating communities of travelers. Lonely Planet Books, a series of guidebooks for low-budget travelers, was quick to establish a website to keep all of its lodging, dining and transportation reviews up-to-date with feedback from recent visitors. Away.com, which focuses on adventure travel, features online contributions of photographs and commentary by recent travelers to exotic travel destinations.

Mistrail restaurant in Santa Rosa California builds community in a variety of ways including online methods. Owner Michael Hirschberg teaches a class at the local junior college on food and wine pairing, hosts a special scholarship dinner called "Class in a Glass," offers a wine seminar series and manages many other special events all featuring Sonoma County products. As Michael describes it, "We are in the hospitality business and we want people to feel comfortable, accepted and part of the family. We have a mailing list of over 6,000 people and we send them a newsletter of upcoming events, which helps them feel connected to the restaurant."

BOOK PASSAGE
NEWS & REVIEWS

51 Tamal Vista Blvd., Corte Madera, CA 94925 • *www.bookpassage.com* • 2001, No. 2

800-999-7909 • 415-927-0960 • *Fax* 415-924-3838 • *E-mail* messages@bookpassage.com

March April 2001

Book Passage offers

A Strong Privacy Policy
- We never sell, rent, share, or give away any information about our customers.
- We never allow anyone to track or use any computerized data about our customers

Free U.S. Shipping
- We ship freight-free within the U.S. on any purchase of $20.00 or more.

Same-Day Local Delivery
- Our *BP2GO* service provides same-day delivery in Central Marin County

Support For Local Schools
- We donate a percentage of sales to schools participating in the Book Passage *School-Link* program. (See *www.bookpassage.com/schoollink* to see if your school is participating.)

Terry McMillan
Feb. 28, 7:30 pm

Adair Lara
March 7, 7:30 pm

Amy Tan
March 12, 7:30 pm

Chris Kraft
March 15, 7:30 pm

Jamling
Tenzing Norgay
April 29, 7:30 pm

Louise Erdrich
April 30, 7:30 pm

Late-breaking • Added Event!

Ted Koppel
Tues. March 6, 1:00 pm

Off Camera:
Private Thoughts
Made Public

A Hospital in Bangladesh

A Project for Bangladeshi Women Sponsored by *Tabra Tunoa*

An Evening Hosted by *Isabel Allende*

Book Passage is pleased to present **A Hospital in Bangladesh**, a special benefit evening on *Thursday, April 5, 7:00 pm*, to raise desperately needed funds for a rural hospital in Agarasindhur, Bangladesh.

This hospital is a project of the *Bangladeshi Woman's Organization* (called "NUK"). Through her friendship with *Mashuda Shefali*, director of NUK, *Tabra Tunoa* learned about this hospital and its need for help from the West. Tabra is the owner and founder of TABRA, makers of exquisite, unique jewelry. *(See page 30 for Tabra's story about the hospital.)*

Isabel Allende will host the evening. There will be refreshments as well as a slide show and discussion of the hospital led by Tabra, along with *Pamela Barientos* and *Suzan Goodman*, two of the medical professionals recruited by Tabra as volunteers for work at the hospital. There will be a sale and a silent auction of many unique pieces of jewelry and other items.

We are asking for a donation to the hospital of $25 (or whatever you can afford).

BOOK sense

Independent Bookstores for Independent Minds

The Last Step: Creating a Calendar of Events

*W*e have seen many good marketing plans written—but very few executed. Hardworking, sincere businesspeople need to be assured that the extra boost of energy needed to implement a marketing action plan based on the techniques discussed in this book is well worth the effort, even though:

- Each action and event takes time to plan and get going, and
- Good people with wonderful businesses often forget them when business gets busy.

Because we tend to really focus on marketing only when business slows down, it often takes a long time to get a good marketing plan activated, which doesn't do a lagging business much good. We can't emphasize this point often enough: The best time to market is when you don't need the business. If you don't heed this advice and wait until business is slow, it might be too late.

The way around this all-too-human dilemma is obviously to plan ahead and spend time and effort doing creative marketing on a regularly scheduled basis. One way to do this is to schedule events on a year's calendar, allowing ample time between events so they remain fun instead of a burden. Keep in mind your busiest seasons and schedule major events well in advance of these times.

First, fill out a worksheet, like the samples on the following pages, for each event you are planning. Then make a note of all the important deadlines on a large twelve-month calendar, with big blocks to write in important details. An oversize calendar that you can hang on the wall is a great way to remind yourself to keep at your marketing efforts.

Help People Feel Comfortable

At all of the events you schedule where members of your business community have the opportuanity to meet each other, it is important that you help them get together. Introduce people to each other, have designated hosts to help people mingle, use name tags if appropriate and do everthing else you know to create a convivial atmosphere.

The following detailed examples may help you envision a marketing plan that will work for your business.

A. Marketing Calendar for an Interior Design Firm

1. March: Open House at Greenfield home. (Direct Marketing)
2. June: Evening class on patio lighting. (Parallel Marketing)
3. October: Demonstration at office furniture store of efficient desk lamp. (Parallel Marketing)

4. December: Reception for Martha Stewart's Living's chief graphic designer. (Peer-Based Marketing)

5. May of next year: Mailing about Underwriters Lab approval of outdoor lamp design. (Parallel Marketing)

Marketing Event Worksheet

Event _____ #4: Afternoon reception for Bernard Mallen, chief graphic designer for Martha Stewart's Living magazine

Date _____ Dec. 16

Objective _____ To introduce the clients and friends on my mailing list to a college friend who has interesting ideas about design.

STEPS	DEADLINE
1. Set up exact date, time and location for reception.	Aug. 31
2. Prepare draft of invitation and description of Bernard's recent work for review by Bernard. Send to him and get response.	Sept. 30.
3. Arrange final details on event location, order catering from Nancy with approximate number and price per person.	Oct. 30
4. Print invitation, envelopes and RSVP card.	Nov. 14
5. Confirm all details with Bernard. Send out mailing.	Dec. 1
6. Estimate final number of guests for catering. Invite by phone four special guests to dinner afterward. Make dinner reservations.	Dec. 10
7. Event. Bring name cards.	
8. Follow up by calling or e-mailing people on list to see if they enjoyed.	Dec. 15

B. Marketing Calendar for Jerry and Jess's New Chiropractic Clinic

1. January: Open House for neighborhood. (Direct Marketing)

2. January: Open House for businesses within 1/4-mile radius. (Direct Marketing)

3. February: Reception at boathouse for friends of the clinic. (Direct Marketing)

4. March: Jerry give talk at Rotary Club. (Parallel Marketing)

5. April: Jerry give talk at SR Community College. (Parallel Marketing)

6. April: Jess on panel with sports experts at Women's Service Club. (Parallel Marketing)

7. May: Evening demonstration at clinic for automobile back supports. (Parallel Marketing)

8. July: Evening demonstration at clinic on posture and watching TV. (Parallel Marketing)

9. August: Participate in SR sports fair. (Parallel Marketing)

10. September: Evening demonstration and panel discussion on posture and computers. Two guest lecturers. (Peer-Based Marketing)

11. October: Jerry and Jess speak about small business marketing to Chamber of Commerce. (Parallel Marketing)

12. November: Evening demonstration and panel discussion on posture and cooking. Guest lecturer. (Peer-Based Marketing)

Marketing Event Worksheet

Event   #1: Open House for neighborhood

Date   Saturday January 20

Objective   To let all the neighbors within 1/4 mile know where the new
chiropractic clinic is located and that we are good neighbors.

STEPS		DEADLINE
1.	Design fliers and find promotional item to attach.	Nov. 30
2.	Print fliers, have banners painted.	Dec. 20
3.	Hire three students to deliver fliers to every home and attach promotional item.	Jan. 6
4.	Order 2 extra video players for display in side rooms. Order flowers and catering.	Jan. 7
5.	Get help cleaning office and putting up signs for event. Arrange for kid care.	Jan. 20

Marketing Event Worksheet

Event __#2: Open House for businesses.__

Date __Saturday January 27__

Objective __To meet the business people in the neighborhood (within 1/4 mile radius) who can make referrals. Actual event is secondary—an excuse to meet neighboring business people.__

STEPS	DEADLINE
1. Design fliers and walk neighborhood to identify key businesses to visit.	Nov. 30
2. Print fliers.	Dec. 20
3. Schedule ten two-hour segments of time for Jerry and Jess to distribute flier/invitation and talk to neighboring businesses.	Jan. 6
4. Order flowers and catering.	Jan. 7
5. Get help cleaning office and putting up signs for event.	Jan. 27

Marketing Event Worksheet

Event ___#3: Reception at boat house for friends, past clients, fellow students from chiro-___
___practic school and suppliers.___

Date ___February 19___

Objective ___To let a wide range of current supporters know that we are opening a new joint___
___practice, and let each partner's friends meet the other's friends and associates.___

STEPS	DEADLINE
1. Set up exact date, time and location for reception.	Oct. 31
2. Complete first draft of invitation. Prepare mailing list from all combined sources.	Nov. 30
3. Arrange final details on event location; order catering with approximate number and price per person.	Dec. 10
4. Print invitation, envelopes and RSVP card.	Jan. 15
5. Phone key dozen people for verbal invitation. Send out mailing.	Jan. 31
6. Estimate final number of guests for catering. Invite by phone four special guests to dinner afterward.	Feb. 10
7. Decorate room.	Feb. 18
8. Event. Bring name cards.	

Marketing Event Worksheet

Event #4: Jerry give talk to Rotary Club

Date   Sometime in March

Objective To establish Jerry as a knowledgeable health practitioner.

STEPS	DEADLINE
1. Phone chair of speaker's committee of Rotary to arrange luncheon talk.	Jan. 30
2. Prepare and send out press release to local press about Rotary talk.	Feb. 28
3. Prepare display materials for talk and hand-out flyer for audience.	Mar. 4
4. Phone friends who are members of Rotary to invite them to luncheon talk.	March, 2 weeks before talk
5. Event. Have materials to demonstrate and fliers to hand out.	

Marketing Event Worksheet

Event   5: Jerry to give talk to SR Community College

Date   April Open

Objective To establish Jerry as a knowledgeable health practitioner.

STEPS	DEADLINE
1. Phone provost for name of the organizer of guest lectures to arrange talk.	Jan. 30
2. Prepare and send out press release to local press about Community College talk.	Mar. 20
3. Prepare display materials for talk and hand-out flier for audience.	Mar. 21
4. Event. Have materials to demonstrate and fliers to hand out.	

Marketing Event Worksheet

Event   #6: Jess on panel with sports experts at Women's Service Club.

Date   April

Objective   To establish Jess as a knowledgeable health practitioner with
community ties.

STEPS	DEADLINE
1. Phone chair of speaker's committee of Women's service Club to arrange luncheon talk. Offer to get other panel members.	Jan. 30
2. Find other panel members and notify Club speaker's chair.	Feb. 15
3. Prepare display materials for talk and hand-out flier for audience.	Mar. 24
4. Phone friends who are members of the Club to invite them to talk.	April, one week before talk
5. Event. Have materials to demonstrate and fliers to hand out.	

Marketing Event Worksheet

Event   #7: Demonstration at the clinic of automobile back supports.

Date   May 25

Objective   To make potential clients conscious of spine-related issues and to associate
spine problems with the clinic.

STEPS	DEADLINE
1. Schedule time for demonstration.	Feb. 28
2. Complete final draft of flier with graphics.	Mar. 30
3. Print and mail flier.	May. 10
4. Design and print flier and reading list on subject matter. Order samples for display.	May 14
5. Clean and organize clinic.	May 24
6. Event. Have name cards. Have fliers to hand out.	

Marketing Event Worksheet

Event ___ #8: Evening demonstration at clinic on posture and watching TV; suggest relevance of issue to parents of growing children.

Date ___ July 14

Objective ___ To make potential clients conscious of spine-related issues and to associate spine problems in their minds with the clinic.

STEPS	DEADLINE
1. Schedule time for demonstration.	Mar. 30
2. Complete final draft of flier with graphics.	Apr. 15
3. Print and mail flier.	June 30
4. Design and print flier and reading list on subject matter. Order samples for display.	July 1
5. Clean and organize clinic.	July 1
6. Event. Have name cards. Have fliers to hand out.	

Marketing Event Worksheet

Event ___ #9: Participate in SR annual sports fair.

Date ___ August 8 and 9

Objective ___ To associate Jerry, Jess and the clinic with sports and health in the community.

STEPS	DEADLINE
1. Call fair organizer to make arrangements for talk and booth.	Jan. 30
2. Complete design of booth and sports fliers.	May 30
3. Print fliers, paint banners and booth display.	July 15
4. Prepare gallons of lemonade to give out at sports fair.	Aug. 8
5. Event. Make sure booth has either Jerry or Jess at all times both days.	Aug. 8-9

Marketing Event Worksheet

Event ___ #10: Evening demonstration and panel discussion on posture and computers. With two guest lecturers in computer field.

Date ___ Sept. 4

Objective ___ To let clients and prospective clients know that Jerry and Jess are current and up-to-date about health issues.

STEPS	DEADLINE
1. Schedule time for demonstration. Invite two friends to be on panel.	Jul. 20
2. Complete final draft of flier with graphics.	Aug. 15
3. Print and mail flier.	Aug. 22
4. Design and print flier and reading list on subject matter. Organize details of display. Confirm with other panelists.	Aug. 28
5. Clean clinic.	Sept. 3
6. Event. Have name cards. Have fliers to hand out.	

Marketing Event Worksheet

Event ___ #11: Jerry and Jess speak about small business marketing to the Chamber of Commerce.

Date ___ October

Objective ___ To establish Jerry and Jess as knowledgeable health practitioners.

STEPS	DEADLINE
1. Phone chair of speaker's committee of Chamber of Commerce to arrange luncheon talk.	Mar. 30
2. Prepare display materials for talk and hand-out fliers for audience.	Sept. 25
3. Phone friends who are members of the Chamber of Commerce to invite them to the luncheon talk.	Oct. one week before talk
4. Event. Have sample materials to demonstrate and fliers to hand out.	

Marketing Event Worksheet

Event #12: Evening demonstration and panel discussion on posture and cooking. Guest
　　lecturer, Ramon Giardia, well-known local chef.

Date Nov. 12

Objective To establish Jerry and Jess as knowledgeable health practitioners with
　　special knowledge about spine problems.

STEPS	DEADLINE
1. Schedule time for demonstration. Confirm with Ramon.	Sept. 30
2. Complete final draft of flier with graphics.	Oct. 30
3. Print and mail flier	Nov. 2
4. Design and print handout and reading list on subject matter. Confirm with Ramon and find out what samples he needs for display.	Nov. 10
5. Clean and organize clinic.	Nov. 11
6. Event. Have name cards. Have fliers to hand out.	

Appendix

BOOKS

1001 Ways to Market Your Services, by Rick Crandall (Editor), (NTC/Contemporary Publishing, 2000).

Getting Publicity, by T. Fletcher and Julia Rockler (Self-Counsel Press, 2000).

Small Time Operator, by Bernard Kamoroff (Bell Springs Publishing, 2000).

Financial Troubleshooting: An Action Plan for Money Management in Small and Growing Business, by Michael Pellecchia (Editor), David H. Bangs, Jr. (Editor) (Inc. Business Resources, 1999).

Mastering Guerrilla Marketing, by Jay Conrad Levinson (Houghton Mifflin, 1999).

Permission Marketing: Turning Strangers into Friends, and Friends into Customers, by Seth Godin (Simon & Schuster, 1999).

Principles of Internet Marketing, by Ward Hanson (South-Western College Publishing, 1999).

The World's Best Known Marketing Secret: Building Your Business With Word-of-Mouth Marketing, by Ivan Misner et al. (Bard Press, 1999).

Getting Business to Come to You, by Paul and Sarah Edwards and Laura Clampitt Douglas (Tarcher/Putnam Trade Paperback, 1998).

Making Money in Cyberspace, by Paul and Sarah Edwards and Linda Rohrbough (Tarcher Trade Paperback, 1998).

Guerrilla Marketing Online Weapons: 100 Low-Cost, High-Impact Weapons for Online Profits and Prosperity, by Jay Conrad Levinson and Charles Rubin (Houghton Mifflin, 1996).

How to Really Create a Successful Marketing Plan, by David Gumpert (Inc. Publishing, 1996).

Running a One-Person Business, by Claude Whitmyer and Salli Rasberry (Ten Speed Press, 1994).

Relationship Marketing, by Regis McKenna (Perseus Publishing, 1993).

Finding Your Niche: Marketing Your Professional Service, by B. Brodsky and J. Geis (Community Resource Inst., 1992).

PERIODICALS & WEBSITES

Note that several of the resources listed are published both in print and on the Web, while some are available only online. Subscription rates are for print editions; online publications are usually free.

American Demographics
$69/year (12 issues) for subscriptions entered on Website:
P.O. Box 10580
Riverton, NJ 08076-0580
(800) 529-7502
http://www.demographics.com/

Guerilla Marketing
www.gmarketing.com/

Home Office Computing
$14.97/year (12 issues)
P.O. Box 53561
Boulder, CO 80322-3561
(800) 288-7812
http://www.hocmag.net/

The Industry Standard
$49.97/year (48 issues)
http://www.thestandard.com/

Marketing Ink
$8/issue
3024 South Glencoe St.
Denver, CO 80222
(800) 749-5409
http://www.marketing-ink.com/

Quirk's Marketing Research Review
$70/year (11 issues)
P.O. Box 23536
Minneapolis, MN 55423
(612) 854-8191
http://www.quirks.com/

Web Marketing Today
http://www.wilsonweb.com/wmt/

Working Woman
$9.97/year (10 issues)
P.O. Box 3276
Harlan, IA 51593-2456
(800) 234-9675
http://www.workingwoman.com/

Working Mother Magazine
$9.97/year (10 issues)
P.O. Box 5240
Harlan, IA 51593-2740
(800) 627-0690
http://www.workingwoman.com/wwn/magazine/wm_magazine.jsp

HELP BEYOND THIS BOOK

After reading this book, filling in the worksheets, applying what you've learned to your business and thinking about the whole matter for a while, you may still have questions. Author Michael Phillips will consult with you for $180 per half hour, $360 per hour. Phone (415) 695-1591 and leave a message on the tape with the following information:

- the name and the type of business you own and operate, and

- the exact time you can be called back over the next several days.

Michael will call you collect, listen to your questions and discuss whether it makes sense to do a consulting session by phone. If the answer is yes, you'll be asked to pick a time for the phone consultation (about two weeks after the first phone call); and you'll be told the cost of the consultation. In the meantime, you'll need to send Michael:

- a copy of your answers to the worksheets in this book

- your business's most recent financial statement, including a Balance Sheet and Income/Expense, regardless of the condition they're in

- a description of your business, including number of employees, range of inventory, years in business, location or facilities and a photo of your product, where appropriate

- a brief summary of the questions you are asking, and

- a check for the amount of the consultation.

That's it. Michael Phillips has consulted with over 800 clients in a 30-year career. If he can help, he will. If he can't, he'll say so. If you are not satisfied that the consultation was worth the expense, send Michael a letter within a week of the consultation, explaining why. Half of your consulting fee will be refunded, no questions asked. If you still believe that you haven't received your money's worth, you can ask to have the matter reviewed by independent business consultants Claude Whitmyer or Paul Terry of San Francisco (or anyone else you and Michael agree on) for a $50 fee, half to be paid by you and half by Michael. If, after reviewing two-page letters submitted by you and by Michael, the consultant agrees with you, the rest of your money will be cheerfully refunded. (Incidentally, here's an example of marketing without advertising!)

Physical Appearance That Develops Trust

Evaluating Your Pricing Policy

Employee Questionnaire

Questionnaire for Suppliers

How Open Is Your Business?

What My Business Does

The Domains in Which Your Business Operates

Do People Know What You Do?

Do You "Tell Them Yourself"?

How Customers Can Evaluate Your Business

Referrals

Customer Referrals

Phone Accessibility Checklist

Mail Accessibility Checklist

Walk-In Accessibility Checklist

Listing Questionnaire

Customer Recourse Policies and Practices

Your Marketing List

Designing Direct Marketing Events

Designing Parallel Marketing Events

Marketing Event Worksheet

Physical Appearance That Develops Trust

Outside	Inside	Sales Staff	Sales Materials	Product	Mail Order/Online
signage	cleanliness	clothes	neatness	protected	answers key questions
display	clutter	breath	clutter	well marked	clear meaning
architecture	lighting	teeth	understandable	return address	exciting
cleanliness	smell	car clean	standard sizing	design	consistent style
neighborhood	spacing, general	identifiable	completeness	dated	convincing
	spacing, merchandise	prompt		labels	
	amount of stock				
	decor				

Your Business **Comments**

POOR ADEQUATE EXCELLENT

☐ ☐ ☐
☐ ☐ ☐
☐ ☐ ☐
☐ ☐ ☐
☐ ☐ ☐
☐ ☐ ☐
☐ ☐ ☐
☐ ☐ ☐
☐ ☐ ☐
☐ ☐ ☐
☐ ☐ ☐
☐ ☐ ☐
☐ ☐ ☐
☐ ☐ ☐
☐ ☐ ☐
☐ ☐ ☐
☐ ☐ ☐
☐ ☐ ☐
☐ ☐ ☐
☐ ☐ ☐
☐ ☐ ☐
☐ ☐ ☐

Evaluating Your Pricing Policy

YES NO

☐ ☐ Some customers complain about prices.

☐ ☐ Some of the trivial but necessary things I offer with my basic product or service (for example, keys, base stands, containers, refills, etc.) are priced at an amount that is more than people expect.

☐ ☐ My product or service is offered in enough different measures that by and large my customers can buy what they need.

☐ ☐ My product(s) can be bought in more than one unit of measure (bunches, pounds, bags, lugs, liters, cartons, gross, boxes).

☐ ☐ My services can be bought in time increments convenient to my customers (days, half-days, hours, minutes, etc.).

☐ ☐ My pricing practices are written down on: (flyer, price sheet, website, the wall).

☐ ☐ Any exceptions from my standard pricing practices are well explained (e.g., senior citizen discounts are stated on a sign with large type).

I estimate that approximately _____% of my customers pay for more of my product or service than they really need or want, because:

_____

_____

I estimate that approximately _____% don't buy all of my product or service that they really need because:

_____

_____

_____

My volume discounts are:

_____

_____

_____

My volume discounts are available to:

_____

_____

_____

Employee Questionnaire

	POOR	ADEQUATE	EXCELLENT
The working conditions here are generally…	☐	☐	☐
The working conditions, compared to other jobs I've had, are…	☐	☐	☐
Handling of serious employee problems that are brought to managers is…	☐	☐	☐
When most employees describe the business management they say…	☐	☐	☐

I know the established policy for handling employee problems and grievances.

☐ YES ☐ NO ☐ THERE ISN'T ONE   It is… ☐ ☐ ☐

I know the established policy for handling employee wage disputes.

☐ YES ☐ NO ☐ THERE ISN'T ONE   It is… ☐ ☐ ☐

I know the established policy for handling conflicts between employees.

☐ YES ☐ NO ☐ THERE ISN'T ONE   It is… ☐ ☐ ☐

When someone is fired most fellow workers know the circumstances
in which the employee can appeal the decision within the company.

☐ YES ☐ NO ☐ THERE ISN'T ONE   The appeal process is… ☐ ☐ ☐

	YES	NO
I am paid fairly.	☐	☐
I know what others are paid.	☐	☐
Most employees know their jobs.	☐	☐
Most employees understand the direction, policies and goals of the business.	☐	☐

Comments and suggestions for improving working conditions:

_____
_____
_____
_____
_____
_____

Questionnaire for Suppliers

I have found in my dealing with _____

that you and your key employees are generally:

	POOR	ADEQUATE	EXCELLENT
Accessible when I need you…	☐	☐	☐
Reliable in your payments and financial projections…	☐	☐	☐
Polite in your general business dealings…	☐	☐	☐
Reliable in doing what you promise on time…	☐	☐	☐
Able to handle any problems with your product and services satisfactorily…	☐	☐	☐
Careful and neat when it comes to recordkeeping…	☐	☐	☐
Generally trustworthy in all dealings…	☐	☐	☐

Comments:

_____
_____
_____
_____
_____
_____
_____
_____
_____
_____
_____
_____
_____
_____

How Open Is Your Business?

	FAMILY	FRIENDS	EMPLOYEES	ACCOUNTANT	ATTORNEY	SOME CUSTOMERS	ALL CUSTOMERS
We are willing to answer the following specific questions about our business to:							
wages...	☐	☐	☐	☐	☐	☐	☐
rent...	☐	☐	☐	☐	☐	☐	☐
cost of goods...	☐	☐	☐	☐	☐	☐	☐
source of supplies...	☐	☐	☐	☐	☐	☐	☐
financial problems...	☐	☐	☐	☐	☐	☐	☐
profits and losses...	☐	☐	☐	☐	☐	☐	☐
specific techniques...	☐	☐	☐	☐	☐	☐	☐
I personally will show or explain in detail:							
How I do what I do...	☐	☐	☐	☐	☐	☐	☐
How my equipment works...	☐	☐	☐	☐	☐	☐	☐
How I price a product or service...	☐	☐	☐	☐	☐	☐	☐
How I keep track of time...	☐	☐	☐	☐	☐	☐	☐
How I keep track of costs...	☐	☐	☐	☐	☐	☐	☐

	YES	NO
My financial statements are available to anyone who wishes to see them...	☐	☐

What My Business Does

The following is a definition of what my business does, in about 35 words:

_____

_____

_____

_____

_____

_____

_____

_____

_____

_____

_____

_____

_____

_____

_____

_____

_____

_____

_____

_____

_____

_____

_____

_____

_____

_____

_____

_____

_____

The Domains in Which Your Business Operates

The major domains in which I operate (taken from my payables) are:

_____

_____

_____

_____

_____

_____

The major domains in which I operate (from looking at checks paid to my consultants) are:

_____

_____

_____

_____

_____

_____

_____

The general functions I fulfill (the major domains in which I operate)
from a customer's perspective are:

_____

_____

_____

_____

_____

_____

_____

Do People Know What You Do?

At a party, ____% of the people who hear the name and a very brief description of my business will know a little about the details of what I really do. [For instance, 100% would know what a barber does, but only 3% would know that an oncologist studies tumors.]

At a meeting of business people generally (for example, the Chamber of Commerce), about ____% of the people who hear the name and a very brief description of my business will know a lot about it.

When a potential new customer approaches, how much does he or she really know about what I do?

☐ Doesn't know anything   ☐ Knows a little   ☐ Knows quite a bit and is very confident

Among new customers, ____% have used someone else in my field (or a similar product) before.

Are there experts in my field (or closely related fields) who have had little or no experience with my goods or services?

☐ YES   ☐ NO

List by category: _____

Are there specific categories of people who would have less than an average level of knowledge about my field who might use my business if they knew more about it, such as people who seldom travel (about the travel business), landlords, commuters, etc.? List:

_____

_____

_____

_____

_____

_____

_____

_____

Do You "Tell Them Yourself"?

Do you give verbal assurance to customers about the quality of your goods or service?

    ☐ NEVER   ☐ SELDOM   ☐ OFTEN   ☐ ALWAYS

How? What kinds of things do you tell customers?

_____

_____

_____

_____

_____

_____

_____

_____

_____

_____

_____

_____

_____

_____

Is specific evidence given to customers to back up this assessment?
[Examples: "Call me back if you don't see a result in three days."
"Measure it before and after you put it in a cold wash to make sure it doesn't shrink."]

    ☐ YES   ☐ NO

Who usually tells the customer?

    ☐ I TELL THEM   ☐ SOME EMPLOYEES TELL THEM

    ☐ MOST EMPLOYEES TELL THEM   ☐ ALL EMPLOYEES TELL THEM

Is follow-up done to check new customer satisfaction?

    ☐ NEVER   ☐ SELDOM   ☐ OFTEN   ☐ ALWAYS

Is follow-up done to check regular customer satisfaction?

    ☐ NEVER   ☐ SELDOM   ☐ OFTEN   ☐ ALWAYS

How Customers Can Evaluate Your Business

My business provides clear verbal measurements of product/service effectiveness.

☐ NEVER ☐ SELDOM ☐ OFTEN ☐ ALWAYS

My business provides training classes to new customers and prospects.

☐ NEVER ☐ SELDOM ☐ OFTEN ☐ ALWAYS

My business provides clear written measurements of product/service effectiveness.

☐ NEVER ☐ SELDOM ☐ OFTEN ☐ ALWAYS

We offer a

☐ Brochure ☐ Specification sheet
☐ Checklist ☐ Contract
☐ Informative label ☐ Questionnaire
☐ Instructions ☐ Evaluation form
☐ Worksheet ☐ Physical measurement
☐ Website ☐ Other online information (survey, newsletter, etc.)

We have:

☐ Displays/models ☐ Samples/examples
☐ Photos of successful work ☐ Other evidence of quality

Referrals

My business is: by:

KNOWN	RESPECTED	RECOMMENDED	
			Others in the same business
☐	☐	☐	Some
☐	☐	☐	Most
			Locals in the same business
☐	☐	☐	Some
☐	☐	☐	Most
			Others in closely related businesses
☐	☐	☐	Some
☐	☐	☐	Most
			Leaders in my business
☐	☐	☐	Some
☐	☐	☐	Most
			Students and former employees
☐	☐	☐	Some
☐	☐	☐	Most

Customer Referrals

I offer new customers the names and phone numbers of other customers.

☐ SOMETIMES   ☐ USUALLY

I refer customers to others for second opinions or evaluations.

☐ SOMETIMES   ☐ USUALLY

I have available:

☐ Printed lists of customer referrals

☐ Letters from satisfied customers

☐ Evidence of awards or certificates for my product

☐ Newsletter with customer comments

I display:

☐ Articles

☐ Photos of customers enjoying my product or service

☐ Certificates and awards

☐ Any other evidence of accomplishments

Phone Accessibility Checklist

WE OFFER   UPDATED YEARLY

☐ White pages listing in appropriate areas   ☐

☐ Yellow Pages listing under applicable topics and in appropriate geographical areas   ☐

☐ Answering service/system with clear instructions   ☐

☐ "800" numbers   ☐

☐ Numbers listed on cards, receipts, order forms, mailers, vehicles, repair labels   ☐
   and publications

Mail Accessibility Checklist

WE OFFER

☐ Clear, stable address

☐ Return address on everything we distribute

☐ Mail forwarding up-o-date

☐ Personal relationship with mail delivery person to avoid mistakes

☐ Clearly identifiable mailbox, with alternative places to deliver packages and
   postage-due mail

☐ If in out-of-way location, maps are included in mailings

Walk-In Accessibility Checklist

WE OFFER

- ☐ Clear, distinct signs not blocked by trees
- ☐ Neighbors given an invitation to visit so they know where we are and what our business involves
- ☐ Parking available or clearly designated
- ☐ Safe places for bicycles
- ☐ Door that opens easily, bell in working order
- ☐ Convenient hours
- ☐ Convenient parking

Listing Questionnaire

We are listed in:

☐ All appropriate professional journals and directories

_____
_____
_____
_____
_____

☐ Our alumni organizations' directories

_____
_____
_____
_____
_____

☐ Local business organizations' publications

_____
_____
_____
_____
_____

☐ Trade associations' directories

_____
_____
_____
_____

☐ Appropriate online databases

_____
_____
_____
_____

Customer Recourse Policies and Practices

We have a written customer recourse policy.

☐ YES   ☐ NO

Our written policy is:

☐ Given to all customers   ☐ Given only upon request   ☐ Displayed prominently
on the premises

☐ Our policy identifies and deals with those areas and situations where customers are
most likely to have problems with our goods or service.

☐ We have regular communication with our customers to be sure they understand our
recourse policy and know that we implement it efficiently.

A customer who complains is:

☐ Always right   ☐ Almost always right   ☐ Seldom right   ☐ Rarely or never right

The most common complaints involve: _____

_____

_____

When the customer is right, he or she gets:

☐ Full refund or replacement when: _____

_____

_____

☐ Partial refund when: _____

_____

_____

☐ We send or give questionnaires to customers to evaluate their satisfaction
with our service. _____

_____

Our liability insurance covers the following customer problems: _____

_____

When a customer deals with our insurance company, it is:

☐ Very responsive   ☐ Responsive   ☐ Slow to respond   ☐ Don't know

When the customer disagrees with our recourse offer, we have available:

☐ Appeal process   ☐ Arbitration   ☐ Industry established board of review
☐ Mediation   ☐ Nothing
☐ Other _____

Your Marketing List

Your marketing list was last updated:

☐ 6 months ago ☐ 1 year ago ☐ 2 years ago ☐ 3 or more years ago

A complete list of your customers, suppliers, prospects, and business associates, relevant aquaintances and peers is available for an immediate mailing, phone invitation or e-mail contact. ☐ YES ☐ NO

	EXCELLENT	ADEQUATE	NEEDS MORE WORK
If Yes, how current are your addresses?			
customers	☐	☐	☐
suppliers	☐	☐	☐
prospects	☐	☐	☐
business associates	☐	☐	☐
acquaintances	☐	☐	☐
peers	☐	☐	☐
How current are your phone numbers?			
customers	☐	☐	☐
suppliers	☐	☐	☐
prospects	☐	☐	☐
business associates	☐	☐	☐
acquaintances	☐	☐	☐
peers	☐	☐	☐
How current are your e-mail addresses?			
customers	☐	☐	☐
suppliers	☐	☐	☐
prospects	☐	☐	☐
business associates	☐	☐	☐
acquaintances	☐	☐	☐
peers	☐	☐	☐

If No, how long would it take you to make a list?

customers	_____ hours
suppliers	_____ hours
prospects	_____ hours
business associates	_____ hours
acquaintances	_____ hours
peers	_____ hours

Starting now you are compiling these records from…

☐ checks
☐ customer records
☐ form letters
☐ supplier records
☐ organization membership lists
☐ your personal address book
☐ e-mail messages
☐ personal organizers (Palm Pilots, etc.)
☐ other _____

Designing Direct Marketing Events

SAMPLES: (items or reference guides your customers would find useful)

_____

_____

_____

_____

_____

DEMONSTRATIONS:

_____

_____

_____

_____

_____

CLASSES: (re-examine your business definition in Chapter 7 to broaden
the range of topics your customers and prospects are interested in)

_____

_____

_____

_____

_____

FOLLOW-UPS: (what related product or service delivered by mail, phone, e-mail,
questionnaire or visit could make your past and present customers
more satisfied with your work?)

_____

_____

_____

_____

_____

Designing Parallel Marketing Events

SAMPLES: (items or reference guides your customers would find useful)

_____

_____

_____

_____

_____

DEMONSTRATIONS:

_____

_____

_____

_____

_____

CLASSES: (re-examine your business definition in Chapter 7 to broaden
the range of topics your customers and prospects are interested in)

_____

_____

_____

_____

_____

FOLLOW-UPS: (what related product or service delivered by mail, phone, e-mail,
questionnaire or visit could make your past and present customers
more satisfied with your work?)

_____

_____

_____

_____

_____

Marketing Event Worksheet

Event _____
_____

Date _____
Objective _____
_____

STEPS   DEADLINE

_____   _____

_____   _____

_____   _____

_____   _____

_____   _____

_____   _____

_____   _____

_____   _____

_____   _____

_____   _____

_____   _____

_____   _____

_____   _____

_____   _____

_____   _____

_____   _____

_____   _____

_____   _____

_____   _____

_____   _____

_____   _____

_____   _____

_____   _____

_____   _____

_____   _____

_____   _____

_____   _____

_____   _____

Index

Take 2 minutes & Give us your 2 cents

Your comments make a big difference in the development and revision of Nolo books and software. Please take a few minutes and register your Nolo product—and your comments—with us. Not only will your input make a difference, you'll receive special offers available only to registered owners of Nolo products on our newest books and software. Register now by:

PHONE
1-800-992-6656

FAX
1-800-645-0895

EMAIL
cs@nolo.com

or **MAIL** us
this registration card

REMEMBER:
Little publishers have big ears. We really listen to you.

- fold here -

NOLO REGISTRATION CARD

NAME	DATE
ADDRESS	

CITY	STATE	ZIP

PHONE	E-MAIL

WHERE DID YOU HEAR ABOUT THIS PRODUCT?

WHERE DID YOU PURCHASE THIS PRODUCT?

DID YOU CONSULT A LAWYER? (PLEASE CIRCLE ONE)   YES   NO   NOT APPLICABLE

DID YOU FIND THIS BOOK HELPFUL?   (VERY)   5   4   3   2   1   (NOT AT ALL)

COMMENTS

WAS IT EASY TO USE?   (VERY EASY)   5   4   3   2   1   (VERY DIFFICULT)

DO YOU OWN A COMPUTER? IF SO, WHICH FORMAT? (PLEASE CIRCLE ONE)   WINDOWS   DOS   MAC

We occasionally make our mailing list available to carefully selected companies whose products may be of interest to you.
❑ If you do not wish to receive mailings from these companies, please check this box.
❑ You can quote me in future Nolo promotional materials. Daytime phone number _____ .

MWAD 3.0

fold here

- -

**Place
stamp here**

nolo
950 Parker Street
Berkeley, CA 94710-9867

Attn: **MWAD 3.0**